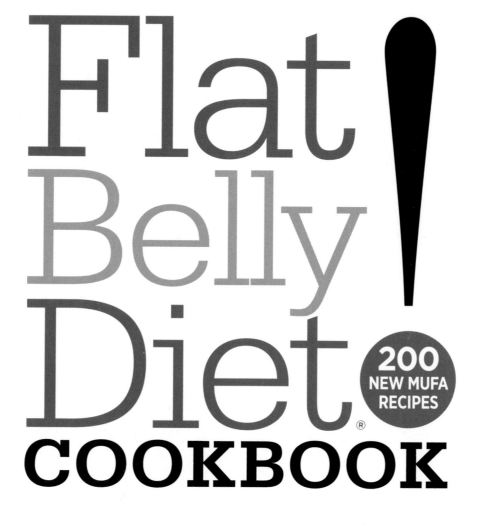

Flat Belly Diet!

200 NEW MUFA RECIPES

COOKBOOK

Flat Belly Diet!

COOKBOOK

200 NEW MUFA RECIPES

By Liz Vaccariello,
Editor-in-Chief,
with Cynthia Sass, MPH, RD

RODALE

This book is intended as a reference volume only, not as a medical manual. The information given here is designed to help you make informed decisions about your health. It is not intended as a substitute for any treatment that may have been prescribed by your doctor. If you suspect that you have a medical problem, we urge you to seek competent medical help.
Mention of specific companies, organizations, or authorities in this book does not imply endorsement by the author or publisher, nor does mention of specific companies, organizations, or authorities imply that they endorse this book, its author, or the publisher.
Internet addresses and telephone numbers given in this book were accurate at the time it went to press.

Rodale books may be purchased for business or promotional use or for special sales. For more information, please write to: Special Markets Department, Rodale Inc., 733 Third Avenue, New York, NY 10017

Prevention® is a registered trademark of Rodale Inc.
Flat Belly Diet® is a registered trademark of Rodale Inc.

Printed in the United States of America
Rodale Inc. makes every effort to use acid-free ♾, recycled paper ♻.

Photographs © Marcus Nilsson

Book design by Jill Armus

Library of Congress Cataloging-in-Publication Data

Flat belly diet! cookbook / by Liz Vaccariello, editor-in-chief with Cynthia Sass.
    p.   cm.
Includes index.
ISBN-13 978-1-60529-954-9 direct hardcover
ISBN-10 1-60529-954-5 direct hardcover
ISBN-13 978-1-60529-955-6 trade hardcover
ISBN-10 1-60529-955-3 trade hardcover
    1. Reducing diets—Recipes.   I. Vaccariello, Liz.   II. Sass, Cynthia.
RM222.2.F532   2008
641.5'63—dc22   2008025835

Distributed to the trade by Macmillan

      6 8 10 9 7   direct hardcover
2 4 6 8 10 9 7 5 3 1 trade hardcover

RODALE
LIVE YOUR WHOLE LIFE™

We inspire and enable people to improve their lives and the world around them

For more of our products visit **rodalestore.com** or call 800-848-4735

For
MUFA
LOVERS
everywhere!

{ contents }

{ plus }

{ acknowledgments }

IF IT DOESN'T LOOK GOOD, YOU'RE NOT GONNA WANT TO EAT IT. In that spirit . . . I begin by thanking the artists: The *Flat Belly Diet! Cookbook*'s simple navigation, sophisticated design, and luscious photography are the work and vision of *Prevention* creative director Jill Armus. I bow to your brilliance and am swept away by your enthusiasm for this book and the diet upon which it's based. And while we're at it? Huge hugs to *Prevention* photo director Helen Cannavale, who brought together the amazingly talented team that produced the images for this book: Marcus Nilsson, photographer; Stephana Bottom, food stylist; and Pamela Duncan Silver, prop stylist.

Very special thanks to Andrea au Levitt and Leah McLaughlin, the stewards of all things *Flat Belly Diet.* To Gregg Michaelson, Karen Rinaldi, Michael Bruno, David Kang, Janine Slaughter, and Jim Berra for their vision, enthusiasm, and support. And to Karen Mazzotta, who is tireless in her mission to spread the word.

I'd also like to extend my gratitude once again to the original members of our initial test panel, which was conducted in the summer of 2007. They first opened my eyes to how special the *Flat Belly Diet* really was. Thank you Mary Aquilar, Syndi Becker, Katherine Brechner, Donna Christiano, Evelyn Gomer, Diane Kastareck, Patty Lloyd, Kevin Martin, Nichole Michl, Colleen O'Neill-Groves, Julie Plavsic, and particularly Mary Anne Speshok, who is down 55 pounds and counting!

Thank you as always to the dedicated *Prevention* books team, including Shea Zukowski, Chris Krogermeier, Carol Angstadt, Hope Clarke, Wendy Gable, Elizabeth Krenos, Keith Biery, Donna Bellis, and Marc Sirinsky. To Katie Kackenmeister, Stephanie Breakstone, and Miriam Backes—one of the most organized and efficient writers we've ever known—we offer a round of applause.

To our recipe development team, Anne Egan, David Bonom, Miriam Rubin, and Sharon Sanders. Your imaginations have taken our MUFA ingredients to new levels. And most special thanks to JoAnn Brader, director of Rodale's test kitchen; her assistant, Stacy Petrovich; and Anita Hirsch, RD, who assisted with the menu plans and recipe analyses.

My unending gratitude to the Rodale family. For generations, through their magazines, books, and online properties, they have been committed to a special mission, that of giving people the tools and inspiration to live their whole lives. My most heartfelt thanks to Rodale CEO Steve Murphy, whose leadership means Rodale is the kind of company where creativity is nurtured and the highest standards are set—and met—daily. It all starts with the edit, Steve!

Finally, I'd like to thank my husband, Steve Vaccariello, and family (especially Olivia and Sophia Vaccariello and Martha Ludlow!) for putting up with even more late nights of writing and editing and, for this one, taste testing!!! Mom, the nutty quick bread is for you!

1

Eat for a
Flat Belly

In my job as editor-in-chief of *Prevention*, I'm amazed and inspired every day by dozens of letters and e-mails (and pictures) from readers sharing news of their weight-loss successes. But many of those same women go on to describe their frustration when it comes to losing weight around their middles. Naturally, that concerns me because at *Prevention,* we've long been aware that belly fat isn't just a bother (67 percent of our readers, in fact, say it's the body part they most want to change) but a true health concern. Belly fat is the most dangerous fat you can have on your body, and we're always evaluating the latest research to help women find better ways to fight it.

That's why in 2007 I was thrilled when Cynthia, *Prevention*'s nutrition director, brought a study published in the journal *Diabetes Care* to my attention. The study explained how scientists at Reina Sofia University Hospital in Cordoba, Spain, placed a group of overweight people on different diets for 4 weeks. Everyone ate the same number of calories every day, but they had different ratios of carbohydrate and fat. The researchers found that one type of dietary fat in particular was especially good at targeting belly fat—without additional exercise.

It sounds counterintuitive, doesn't it? Many of us have grown up with the idea that dietary fat makes us fat. It does, but only if you eat too much of it. Cynthia, who is also a registered dietitian, looked further into the research then developed the breakthrough *Flat Belly Diet*, which we put to the test on a panel of real-life dieters. And it worked! Everyone lost weight. She and I are here to say there is a delicious antidote to belly fat and it can be summed up in one simple word: MUFAs.

Known formally as monounsaturated fatty acids, MUFAs (pronounced "MOO-fahs") are plant-based fats found in some of the world's most delicious foods, including olives, avocados, chocolate, nuts, seeds, and legumes. While you're certainly already familiar with these foods and their flavors, perhaps the specific name for these good-for-you fats rings a bell, too. That's because MUFAs have recently made it big as nutritional celebrities, with study after study demonstrating their incredible disease-fighting properties. Scientists have found that MUFAs enhance heart health, protect against chronic disease, and may help promote

{ BELLY FAT ISN'T JUST A BOTHER, BUT A TRUE HEALTH CONCERN. }

weight loss. Even if you don't recall hearing about monounsaturated fatty acids, the buzz about the most famous MUFA food, olive oil, has been hard to miss—this venerable cooking staple plays a starring role in the famous Mediterranean diet.

Cut to the present, where the latest research reveals the most astonishing MUFA benefit yet: These dietary powerhouses may help transform the part of your body where fat is the hardest to lose and most hazardous to your health—that's right, your belly. And now *Prevention*, using Cynthia's expertise and experience counseling women of all walks of life, has applied this cutting-edge science to create the *Flat Belly Diet*: the only eating plan that integrates MUFAs into every meal and harnesses their newfound power to reduce belly fat. By following this carefully developed and rigorously tested plan, you will lose weight (especially in your belly), improve your physical condition, and greatly enhance your likelihood of living a longer and healthier life.

Sound like a lot of big promises? In this chapter, I'll explain the science that makes these promises absolutely realistic. Then I'll spell out how the *Flat Belly Diet* food plan works. But first, because I realize that "good-for-you fats," the most basic definition of MUFAs, may sound like a contradiction in terms, let's set the record straight regarding dietary fat.

Fat Fundamentals

If you paid attention to any of the weight-loss advice you've heard since you were a teenager, it might be hard to believe that not all fat is bad for you. After all, until fairly recently, messages from official sources like the federal government's Dietary Guidelines cautioned that all fats are high in calories and advised strict limits on intake. Healthy fats didn't always go unmentioned, but these messages helped perpetuate a "less fat is better" mind-set that led to outright fat phobia for more than a few health- and weight-conscious Americans. Cynthia tells me that, frankly, it frustrated her to no end. As a registered dietitian with a master's in both nutrition science and public health, she knew about the dangers of cutting fat too low (it can actually increase your risk of cardiovascular disease!) and had studied the benefits of plant-based fats.

SUCCESS STORY

Mary Anne Speshock

Mary Anne's husband is chasing her around the room! No wonder! She lost 55 pounds after about 6 months on the diet—and she dropped from a size 16 to a size 8! "He looks at me and says, 'Wow! I can't believe what I'm seeing!' My husband and I feel like honeymooners!"

Mary Anne's buying a lot of new clothes to fit her new body, and she's looking forward to wearing a beautiful gown that she hasn't fit into for a long time. "What a prize for reaching your goal. I feel as if the weight is melting off me. And my energy level is through the roof. The difference with this diet is you literally don't get hunger pains. It's revolutionary because you start seeing results so fast that you want to keep going."

LOST
15 LBS
AND
10 INCHES
32 DAYS!

She was delighted when the Dietary Guidelines were revised in 2005 to state not just a limit on how much total fat to consume (no more than 35 percent of the diet) but a recommended minimum intake of healthy fat: no less than 20 percent of calories, with most coming from sources of polyunsaturated and monounsaturated fatty acids (our MUFAs!).

Still sounds like a mixed message? Here's the bottom line: Getting the right mix and measure of the right kind of fats is essential. A vital energy source, dietary fat helps slow digestion, which in turn slows the release of blood sugar and helps you feel full and satisfied longer. It also helps your body absorb vitamins (such as A, D, E, and K) and manufacture cell membranes and hormonelike compounds that regulate blood pressure, heart rate, blood vessel constriction, blood clotting, and the nervous system. There's no question that eating too much of the wrong kinds of fat—saturated fat and trans fat—is hazardous to your health (see "What's So Bad about Bad Fat" on the opposite page). But it's not necessary or even healthy to try to banish all fat from your diet. As you'll soon find out, the right fats can do you a lot of good.

Understanding how to tell good fats from bad will help you strike the perfect balance in your diet (and help you conquer any lurking fears of fat). Here's a quick rundown of the basics.

{ IT'S NOT NECESSARY OR EVEN HEALTHY TO TRY TO BANISH ALL FAT FROM YOUR DIET. }

GOOD FATS

Monounsaturated fats, polyunsaturated fats, and omega-3 fatty acids are all good, heart-healthy fats. I'll cover more about MUFAs in a moment, but if you're wondering right now if any of the oils in your pantry fit the bill, here's what you need to know: MUFAs are liquid at room temperature and may thicken when refrigerated. Polyunsaturated fats are typically liquid both at room temperature and when refrigerated (that's most vegetable oils, including safflower, corn, sunflower, and soy oils). Last but certainly not least, omega-3 fatty acids are a particular kind of polyunsaturated fat found in fatty fish including salmon, albacore tuna, herring, and mackerel; other good sources are walnuts, flaxseeds, and flaxseed oil.

BAD FATS

In general, the "bad fat" label belongs to any fat that's semisolid to solid at room temperature, which is a sure sign it's saturated—picture a stick of butter or the marbling in a steak. Animal products are the main sources of saturated fat, but tropical oils—coconut oil and palm (or palm kernel) oil—and cocoa butter are also high in saturated fat.

Smaller amounts of saturated fat are present in some other plant foods, including MUFA-rich olive oil and nuts, so it's impossible to eliminate the bad fats altogether. However, you can greatly reduce the amount in your diet by substituting healthier fats, like olive oil and canola oil, for straight saturated fats like butter.

Another bad fat you've likely heard about, trans fat, is produced when hydrogen is added to liquid oils to make them solid and thereby extend their shelf life. Trans fats are found mostly in packaged products and just about every food that contains shortening.

To avoid trans fats, you have to look beyond the Nutrition Facts label because manufacturers are allowed to claim zero trans fat for any food actually containing up to half a gram per serving. Go straight to the ingredients list, where the words *hydrogenated* or *partially hydrogenated* are a clear signal that trans fats are present. If you see these terms on the label, immediately put whatever you're looking at back on the shelf and keep looking!

Now that I've covered the basics of what to avoid, let's talk about what's so good about the good guys—our MUFAs.

The Power of MUFAs

As explained above, MUFAs are unsaturated fats. They don't solidify at room temperature in your food or your body but, rather, stay soft and pliable in your arteries (whereas saturated fats harden and can clog up the works, doing grievous harm). All this is no secret. But the full benefits of MUFAs might never have come to light had researchers studying the epidemic levels of heart disease in the United States not looked to the Mediterranean for explanations and possible solutions.

WHAT'S SO BAD ABOUT BAD FAT?

Both saturated and trans fats elevate levels of waxlike LDL ("bad" cholesterol) in the blood, excessive amounts of which can build up on artery walls and boost inflammation, restricting bloodflow and increasing the risk of cardiovascular disease and stroke. But trans fat is much more harmful to heart health than saturated fat because in addition to increasing LDL, trans fat lowers levels of HDL ("good" cholesterol) that helps keep blood vessels clear. Plus, they raise the risk of clots, which can block arteries and cause strokes.

WHAT'S THE
MEDITERRANEAN
DIET?

WHAT'S THE MEDITERRANEAN DIET?

The "Mediterranean diet" is not really a single diet in the modern sense. Rather, it's the term given to the traditional approach to food in cultures that surround the Mediterranean Sea. These local cuisines share an emphasis on whole grains, seafood, and fresh, local fruits and vegetables, as well as an abundance of nuts, olives, and olive oil. Given the research citing health benefits to be gained (and pounds that can be lost), many weight-loss plans have taken a Mediterranean approach. While basic aspects of the Mediterranean diet are at the core of the *Flat Belly Diet,* this plan is unique because it goes a step better. Using the latest research, the *Flat Belly Diet* ensures you get a specific amount of a particular type of healthy fat—a MUFA—at every meal. No other diet can give you these results.

CLUES IN THE MEDITERRANEAN DIET

Cradle of more than one great civilization, the region surrounding the Mediterranean Sea is rich and varied in food traditions. It was quite literally among the olive groves that epidemiologists and nutrition researchers unearthed the first clues to the disease-fighting powers of MUFAs. Discovering that particular Mediterranean populations, most notably on the Greek island of Crete, had dramatically lower rates of disease and much greater longevity than just about anyplace else in the world—especially the United States—researchers took a closer look at the diet and lifestyles of the people who lived there. A number of long-term studies found that people live longer, healthier lives—and have lower body weights—when key features of their diets are:

O Substantial amounts of nuts, olives, and olive oil (all MUFAs!)
O An abundance of locally grown fruits, vegetables, and legumes
O Whole grains
O Lots of fish
O Very little red meat

THE ORIGINAL MUFA SUPERSTAR

Researchers investigating the benefits of a Mediterranean diet initially focused on olive oil. Described as liquid gold by Homer in ancient times and today consumed by the people of Greece at an average rate of half a liter per person weekly (that's about 6½ gallons per year), olive oil is a quintessential staple of Mediterranean cooking. As such, olive oil was the natural place to start looking for the health-giving secrets of the traditional Mediterranean diet. Sure enough, the hundreds of studies that followed showed olive oil to be amazingly heart healthy.

One report, published in the *American Journal of Clinical Nutrition* in the late 1990s, found that olive oil significantly lowered levels of harmful LDL cholesterol and triglycerides. Subsequent research at the University of Athens pinpointed olive oil as the component of the Mediterranean diet mainly responsible for lowering blood pressure.

Another study reported that adding 2 tablespoons of olive oil a day but making no other dietary changes resulted in significant reductions in LDL and marked increases in heart-protective HDL cholesterol. And more recently came the dramatic findings of yet another study, published in *Clinical Cardiology*: Use of only olive oil (rather than any other fats in cooking) cut risk of cardiovascular disease nearly in half.

In fact, seen in its entirety, the emerging evidence has been so abundant and compelling that the FDA now allows labels on olive oil and some products containing olive oil to claim that replacing saturated fats with 2 tablespoons of olive oil daily may reduce the risk of coronary heart disease.

In its announcement about the health claim, the FDA specifically cited olive oil's high MUFA content as the source of its heart-health benefits. That's exactly what the scientific community had zeroed in on and continues to explore. Further evidence of the unique heart-healthy powers of MUFAs has been piling up fast and furious ever since (see the box at right).

OLIVE OIL AND BEYOND: FIVE FANTASTIC MUFAS

Once the good news of olive oil's MUFA-rich benefits began to spread, a truly happy realization came with it. Delicious as it is, olive oil is just one of many healthfully decadent foods high in MUFAs. These plant-based fats are also plentiful in vegetable oils, nuts, olives, avocados, and even dark chocolate. In Chapter 3, I'll give you a more comprehensive list of MUFA foods, but for now our list comprises those basic broad categories. And while you're no doubt reveling in the good news about certain dietary fats, it's also worth pointing out what MUFAs offer our palates: rich flavor (as in peanut butter), lush texture (think plump, fruity olives), and lasting fullness (a salad with avocado is much more satisfying than one with lettuce and veggies alone). And being *unsaturated*, MUFAs sail through the bloodstream without causing artery-clogging buildup the way saturated fats do. That last point brings us back to the science, so let's keep going. There's a lot more good news to cover.

MUFAS PROTECT YOUR HEART

Cardiovascular disease, which includes high blood pressure, heart disease, and stroke, is the leading cause of disease-related death in the United States, so take heart in the following:

o In a study conducted at Pennsylvania State University, scientists found that a MUFA-rich diet lowered LDL ("bad" cholesterol) by an average of 14 percent in 4 weeks, with no reduction in heart-protective HDL.

o Researchers at Johns Hopkins University observed that diets low in saturated fat and high in MUFAs lowered blood pressure and improved blood fat levels.

o Canadian scientists found that a diet substituting MUFAs for some carbohydrates (but not reducing overall calorie intake) improved blood triglyceride levels and other markers for cardiovascular disease.

o Mexican researchers put a group of people with moderately high blood cholesterol levels on a high-MUFA diet and found that in 7 days, the participants had significant decreases in total cholesterol and LDL, along with an 11 percent increase in HDL.

Julie Plavsic

"I just couldn't get the scale to budge. I was eating healthy. Exercising. Nothing seemed to be working." And then the *Flat Belly Diet* came to Julie's rescue. She lost 4½ all-over inches in the first 4 days—and then went on to lose a total of 6 pounds and 6½ all-over inches! "It wasn't hard, because the food is so filling." The MUFAs, the core of the diet, amazed her. She explains, "I had to get over all those years of denying myself those high-fat foods. I'm so excited by this diet. I can't wait to get my overweight friends to try it."

LOST
6 LBS
AND
6.5 INCHES
IN
32 DAYS!

Delicious Disease-Fighters

In the world of nutritional research, the reports about MUFAs just keep getting better. In addition to the evidence that MUFAs protect against cardiovascular disease, a steady stream of research also links MUFAs to reduced rates of other serious diseases, including type 2 diabetes, metabolic syndrome, chronic inflammation, breast cancer, and Alzheimer's.

◆ **Type 2 diabetes.** Insulin is a hormone that performs a vital function in the body, allowing cells to open up and receive energy in the form of glucose. Type 2 diabetes, the most common form, occurs when the pancreas stops making enough insulin or the cells in the body ignore the insulin that's already circulating. A report published in the *American Journal of Clinical Nutrition* found a MUFA-rich diet to be highly beneficial for patients with type 2 diabetes by significantly improving their blood glucose profiles while reducing harmful triglycerides and LDL and slightly increasing healthy HDL. Subsequently, Spanish researchers examining the effects of weight-maintenance diets on overweight people found that a MUFA-rich diet improved fasting blood glucose as well as insulin sensitivity and HDL. In another study, scientists at Indiana University found that treating obese type 2 diabetes patients with a MUFA-enriched weight-reducing diet resulted not only in weight loss but also in decreases in total cholesterol and triglyceride levels—and these improvements remained even for people who eventually regained weight.

◆ **Metabolic syndrome.** Afflicting an estimated 50 million–plus Americans, this life-threatening syndrome increases risks of coronary heart disease, stroke, and type 2 diabetes. It's defined by the American Heart Association as a difficult-to-diagnose condition characterized by a group of metabolic risk factors including abdominal obesity (a.k.a. belly fat); high blood pressure; blood fat disorders such as high LDL, high triglycerides, and low HDL; insulin resistance; and glucose intolerance. MUFAs can be part of the defense against metabolic syndrome, according to a review published in the journal *Clinical Nutrition* summarizing findings that a diet rich in monounsaturated fatty acids improves insulin sensitivity and blood lipid levels. And a study at Columbia University College of Physicians and Scientists in New York concluded that treating patients with metabolic syndrome by replacing saturated fat with MUFAs in an average American diet significantly reduced the risk of coronary heart disease—even better than did replacing saturated fat with carbohydrate.

◆ **Chronic inflammation.** The body's natural defensive response to injury and illness, inflammation triggers reactions and the release of substances throughout the body. This complex biological process can run amok, becoming chronic and leading to atherosclerosis (a precursor to cardiovascular disease), rheumatoid arthritis, and asthma, among other diseases, and is a known trigger for premature aging. MUFAs work synergistically with other nutrients, such as antioxidants, to produce anti-inflammatory substances that can help reduce the severity of inflammatory symptoms in diseases like rheumatoid arthritis and asthma. There's also good reason to believe that MUFAs help reduce inflammation itself: A study in Italy linked Mediterranean diets featuring MUFA-rich foods with significantly reduced concentrations of inflammatory markers in the blood.

◆ **Breast cancer.** MUFAs are well on their way to becoming champions in the battle against breast cancer. A study in the Canary Islands found that women with the most MUFAs in their diets had 48 percent less chance of breast cancer than those whose consumption was lowest.

Meanwhile, a laboratory study published in the *Annals of Oncology* found that oleic acid (a monounsaturated fatty acid abundant in olive oil, avocado, and cashews and other nuts) enhanced the ability of cancer-fighting drugs to stop the growth of aggressive, treatment-resistant cancer cells. Dramatic results came from a Swedish study examining data on more than 61,000 mostly postmenopausal women and finding an inverse association between MUFAs and cancer risk—with a 45 percent reduction in the risk of developing breast cancer for each 10-gram increment of MUFAs consumed daily.

◆ **Brain function.** MUFAs may prove to be an important brain food as well. Italian studies have found that a high intake of MUFAs as part of a Mediterranean diet offers great protection

> { MUFAS ARE WELL ON THEIR WAY TO BECOMING CHAMPIONS IN THE BATTLE AGAINST BREAST CANCER. }

against age-related cognitive decline. And an American study published in the *Annals of Neurology* concluded that the more faithfully participants from the Washington Heights–Inwood Columbia Aging Project followed a Mediterranean diet featuring MUFAs, the lower their incidence of Alzheimer's disease. Subjects who stuck closest to the diet had 40 percent less chance of developing Alzheimer's than those who adhered to it the least.

What about the other disease affecting so many Americans—obesity? MUFAs come to the rescue on this front, too.

The Belly Fat Breakthrough

Obesity is the common risk factor among all of the health conditions discussed thus far, including heart disease, diabetes, metabolic syndrome, and chronic inflammation. It's even been linked to higher risk for breast cancer and Alzheimer's. And in an era that health experts now refer to as the age of obesity, it's time to own up to the fact that being overweight is a disease in and of itself. It's the disease behind the many other diseases that are shortening the lives of millions of Americans. The great news is that MUFAs can be an effective weapon in this battle as well.

As radical as it may seem, the idea that fat can help you slim down isn't entirely new. In 2001, researchers at Harvard-affiliated Brigham and Women's Hospital reported that a moderate-fat, MUFA-rich diet produced better long-term weight-loss results than a low-fat diet. In the study, 101 overweight men and women were randomly assigned to either a low-fat or a Mediterranean-style diet. After 18 months, the low-fat group averaged a 6-pound weight *gain*, while the Mediterranean group lost an average of 9 pounds. More evidence debunking low-fat diets came when the *Journal of the American Medical Association* published the findings of an 8-year low-fat diet trial involving nearly 49,000 women: No effect on weight was observed (nor, for that matter, was risk for heart disease, breast cancer, or colorectal cancer reduced).

Further research includes a *British Journal of Nutrition* report finding that a MUFA-rich diet that simply replaced saturated fats with unsaturated ones helped overweight people lose pounds and body fat—without reducing calorie intake or adding exercise.

What's more, according to an Australian study, MUFAs rev up metabolism: Researchers found that a breakfast high in MUFAs could boost calorie burn for as much as 5 hours.

All of this amounts to strong evidence for the fat-reducing power of MUFAs. But here's the clincher, especially for those of us whose physiques bear closer resemblance to the proverbial apple than, say, an hourglass: Carrying extra weight in the midsection is riskier for your health than being a little more amply proportioned in the hips and backside. Worse yet, the hidden fat deep in your belly (visceral fat) is not only more dangerous but, unlike superficial (subcutaneous) fat, is tough to target with diets and workouts.

Researchers are still working to identify the exact metabolic process behind the MUFA weight loss, but looking at the results, it's as if eating a MUFA-rich diet gives your body a new set of instructions: Lose belly fat! Now that you're well grounded in the science behind the *Flat Belly Diet*, that's exactly what you're ready to do. Let's start talking about what to eat!

THE TROUBLE WITH BELLY FAT

Few of us need convincing that there's a problem with belly fat. It's the area of our bodies most of us feel especially self-conscious about and would like to change. But vanity aside, extra inches at the waistline pose serious health risks, based on the type of fat that's behind the bulge.

There are two distinct types of belly fat to know about: subcutaneous and visceral. Subcutaneous fat is that inch (or so) that's just underneath your skin and easy to pinch. This visible fat becomes a health problem when too much of it puts a strain on your heart and other organs. The other type, visceral fat, resides deep in your abdomen, where it surrounds your organs. Visceral fat has been linked to a long list of adverse health conditions, including cardiovascular disease (high blood pressure, stroke, and heart disease), diabetes, breast cancer, and dementia.

Worse yet, scientists increasingly suspect that visceral belly fat is involved in inflammatory processes associated with just about every chronic disease. Researchers at Washington University School of Medicine in St. Louis, for example, have confirmed that fat cells inside the abdomen secrete molecules that increase inflammation. And an animal study at the University of Michigan Department of Internal Medicine established a direct link between visceral fat, inflammation, and the process of atherosclerosis (which in humans sets the stage for most heart attacks and strokes).

All this bad belly fat news sounds grim, but remember: MUFAs have been found to help reduce the accumulation of belly fat—specifically, visceral fat. And MUFAs are what the *Flat Belly Diet* is all about!

The Flat Belly Diet Food Plan

Belly fat is the most stubborn fat on your body, the fat that's first to appear when you gain weight and the last to disappear when you try to lose it. So in 2007, Cynthia digested all this breakthrough research and set to work devising an easy-to-follow, easy-to-maintain eating plan so people could finally eat in a way that targeted belly fat specifically. That's why the *Flat Belly Diet* is structured to help you see great results—fast—and lose all the weight you want, which means inches off your belly, hips, arms, thighs, and back.

First comes the Four-Day Anti-Bloat Jumpstart to launch the belly-flattening process. On the Jumpstart, you'll eat in a cleaner, simpler way than usual, avoiding the foods, drinks, and behaviors that ordinarily cause your body to retain unnecessary fluid or produce excess gas. You'll see results in a matter of hours—up to 7 pounds and 5 inches in just 4 days. The dramatic results will supercharge your motivation and confidence as you go forward, lighter and more svelte, with the rest of the program.

From day 5 onward, the *Flat Belly Diet* means 1,600 calories a day, a MUFA with every meal, and four meals a day, which can help you lose up to 15 pounds in 32 days. This is when you will get down to some serious belly-fat blitzing—by eating very, very well. The combination of what you eat (delicious MUFAs in just the right measure, along with other hearty and healthy foods) and when you eat (every 4 hours or so) will keep you feeling satisfied, energized, and hunger free—and will keep you burning belly fat. No willpower required.

Exercise is optional. Add it and you'll lose more weight and up your energy even further (see the box on page 14), but if you're not ready to start a fitness program, you certainly don't have to. You'll still lose weight on the *Flat Belly Diet*. How great is that?

Within a week, you'll look slimmer and feel better, and you'll be taking vital steps toward a healthier, longer life because you'll be losing the kind of body fat that most endangers your health— visceral fat that surrounds your organs and releases inflammatory substances that can trigger chronic diseases.

These are great rewards, and the *Flat Belly Diet* was designed to make it truly easy to attain them. It offers not just a diet plan but a lifestyle focusing on:

> THE *FLAT BELLY DIET* MEANS 1,600 CALORIES A DAY, A MUFA WITH EVERY MEAL, AND FOUR MEALS A DAY.

◆ **Health and energy.** Featuring wholesome, filling, MUFA-rich foods, the *Flat Belly Diet* is a healthy way to unload belly fat while maintaining energy, muscle, bone density, and your ability to enjoy life in general (all of which—especially the last part—fall by the wayside on lower-calorie diets).

◆ **Flavor and satisfaction.** If there's anything Cynthia's learned from nearly 15 years of counseling experience, it's that diets that leave you feeling hungry, bored, and deprived are hard to maintain. Having the right amount of flavorful, satisfying, wholesome fats is an easy way to stick with any reduced-calorie eating plan. Eating the *Flat Belly* way is, in fact, delicious and filling—thanks to MUFAs—and so this cookbook is filled with 200 recipes that will keep you savoring that simple truth.

◆ **Reality and flexibility.** Can anyone really subsist on cabbage soup or follow week upon week of rigid menus that dictate each and every meal? Who would want to? The good news for you is that the *Flat Belly Diet* doesn't require you to follow a prescribed day-by-day, meal-by-meal plan. Of course, you have some basic guidelines (eat four times a day, at least every 4 hours, and 400 calories each time, but I'll explain that in more detail later). Beyond that, what you eat and when is up to you.

If you do choose to use the menus at the back of the book (pages 325–331), the meals are interchangeable. If you opt to design your own plan, you'll find a huge range of easy dishes you can throw together in minutes, along with some special meals you can linger over when you're not pressed for time.

Either way, you have freedom of choice. And there's plenty of room for improvisation once you're well acquainted with your MUFAs and accustomed to getting just the right amount in the daily rhythm of the plan.

◆ **Fitness, inspiration, and motivation.** As I've already mentioned, although you don't have to exercise on this plan to lose weight, you will lose more pounds and do more to improve your health if you make exercise part of your life. Likewise, inspiration and motivation are vital fuel for successful weight loss and a lifestyle change (see "Adding Exercise" on page 14).

So there's how the *Flat Belly Diet* works. Now let's get started!

THE FLAT BELLY DIET, PART 1: FOUR-DAY ANTI-BLOAT JUMPSTART

Think of it as a spa retreat for your gastrointestinal tract. Just for these first 4 days, you will follow a 1,200 calorie-a-day eating plan (your allowance after that will be 1,600 calories a day). It's your opportunity to take a brief vacation from foods and beverages that balloon your belly with bloat, fluid retention, and GI irritation. You'll set aside not only the more obvious offenders (the salty, the fried, the carbonated, and the caffeinated) but also some wholesome foods that tend to swell your belly with bulk or gas. You'll drink Cynthia's signature Sassy Water and eat simple, tasty, gentle-on-your belly meals that you'll put together according to your taste and preference using the Jumpstart meal-building tool.

What's the payoff? Your belly will flatten dramatically as your system releases excess fluid and trapped air. You'll quickly drop pounds and inches from your midsection, and these speedy results will spark energy and motivation, as well as prime your body to shed belly fat. Here's what you'll do for 4 days.

◆ **Use the Jumpstart meal-building formula.** Daily menus dictating what you eat at every turn may make meal planning a no-brainer, but they also have the distinct disadvantage of taking away your freedom of choice, which for many of us is intrinsic to the pleasure of eating. Instead, the Jumpstart meal-building formula gives you a math-free way to stick to 1,200 calories per day that still leaves many of the choices up to you.

The formulas also provide an easy-to-use framework for adapting to one of the core principles of the *Flat Belly Diet*: eating four times a day (roughly every 4 hours). Each day you get breakfast, lunch, dinner, and a floating meal or snack. The rhythm of eating every 4 hours will help you avoid getting too hungry between meals, which can lead to overeating. Along the same lines, adjusting to this eating schedule will help recalibrate your appetite so that you enjoy smaller, more frequent meals and will get you in the habit of carefully thinking through them ahead of time so you're well prepared throughout the day. This is a key ingredient for success going forward on the *Flat Belly Diet,* which I'll talk more about in Chapter 2.

◆ **Eat slowly.** The faster you eat, the more air you gulp down with your food. This is as important as it is straightforward. Avoid drawing all that unnecessary air into your digestive system and you'll reduce bloating.

◆ **Drink Sassy Water—a full recipe each day.** This refreshing concoction will keep you hydrated *and* deflated. The ingredients give Sassy Water sparkling flavor and soothing properties: Ginger calms the GI tract; mint eases indigestion, quiets the muscles of the intestinal tract, and reduces water retention.

◆ **Follow up every meal with a 5-minute walk.** Get up and move after you eat—go around the block, or just circle the inside of your office building or the local mall. A brief leisurely stroll of at least 5 minutes (feel free to keep going!) is essential for getting things moving in your GI tract so trapped air is released and pressure and bloating don't build.

JUMPSTART MEAL-BUILDING FORMULA

Use these simple formulas below to select the building blocks for each meal.

○ **Breakfast** = 1 starch + 1 dairy + 1 fruit + ¼ cup sunflower seeds + 1 glass Sassy Water

○ **Lunch** = 1 protein + 1 dairy + 1 veggie + 1 glass Sassy Water

○ **Snack** = 1 fruit smoothie

○ **Dinner** = 1 veggie + 1 protein + 1 starch + 1 teaspoon olive oil (on veggie *or* starch)

You can shuffle the order of these meals however you like; just space them 4 hours apart. That means you can have a smoothie for breakfast if you like, dinner for lunch, or breakfast at dinnertime. Yes, smoothies make a yummy dessert, but no, you can't have one right after dinner. You could, however, have a smoothie for an evening snack; if, for instance, you had breakfast at 9:00, lunch at 1:00, and dinner at 5:00, then 9:00 p.m. would be the perfect time for a snack.

JUMPSTART BUILDING BLOCKS

Now, I'm not going to pretend that the range of choices—just for these 4 days—isn't pretty limited. That's because Cynthia designed the Jumpstart Meal-Builder to feature foods that either alleviate or minimize bloating and fluid retention. Here are the cornerstone foods:

STARCHES/GRAINS

- 1 cup unsweetened cornflakes
- 1 packet instant cream of wheat
- ½ cup red potatoes (steamed or roasted)
- ½ cup cooked brown rice

FRUITS

- ½ cup unsweetened applesauce
- 4 ounces pineapple tidbits canned in juice
- 2 tablespoons raisins
- 2 dried plums
- 1 cup fresh or frozen unsweetened blueberries
- 1 cup fresh or frozen unsweetened strawberries
- 1 cup fresh or frozen unsweetened peaches

VEGETABLES

- 1 pint fresh grape tomatoes
- 1 cup fresh or frozen green beans (steamed or microwaved)
- 1 cup baby carrots (steamed or microwaved)
- 1 cup fresh cremini mushrooms (steamed or microwaved)
- 1 cup fresh or frozen yellow squash (steamed or microwaved)

DAIRY

- 1 cup fat-free milk
- 1 piece light string cheese

PROTEIN

- 4 ounces low-sodium deli turkey
- 4 ounces grilled tilapia or other mild, lean white fish
- 3 ounces chunk light tuna in water
- 3 ounces grilled chicken breast

{ THE JUMP-START MEAL-BUILDER FEATURES FOODS THAT MINIMIZE BLOATING. }

SMOOTHIES

○ Put in blender: 1 cup fat-free milk, 1 cup fresh or frozen unsweet-ened blueberries/strawberries/peaches *or* 4 ounces canned pine-apple tidbits in juice, and a handful of ice. Whiz for 1 minute. Pour into a glass and stir in 1 tablespoon cold-pressed flaxseed oil.

SASSY WATER

Combine 2 liters water (about 8½ cups), 1 teaspoon freshly grated ginger, 1 medium cucumber (peeled and thinly sliced), 1 medium lemon (thinly sliced), and 12 small spearmint leaves in a large pitcher and let the flavors blend overnight. Drink throughout the day, and finish the pitcher by the end of each day. Sassy Water is an integral component of the Jumpstart; you don't have to keep drinking it after the fourth day, but many *Flat Belly* dieters do—it's a great way to stay hydrated. Here are a few tips to keep in mind.

○ Drink a new batch every day using fresh ingredients.

○ Feel free to omit any ingredients you just don't like.

○ Use any type of fresh mint (peppermint, pineapple mint, etc.), but don't substitute dried mint or mint extract, both of which are very unpleasant in water. The same is true for ginger: It must be fresh, not dried or powdered.

○ Strain the ingredients, or pour them into your glass along with the water (they do look pretty), and eat them if you'd like. A whole medium cucumber has just 24 calories, so you won't slow your weight loss by eating the slices.

○ If you find the flavor too strong, prepare your pitcher in the morning instead of the night before so the tastes won't intensify as much. Or use half the amounts of ginger, lemon, and mint.

HERBS, SPICES, SEASONINGS

Lay off the saltshaker completely and use the following instead.

○ Fresh or dried basil, dill, ginger, marjoram, mint, oregano, rosemary, sage, tarragon, thyme

○ Bay leaf, cinnamon, curry powder, paprika

○ Lemon or lime juice

○ Aged balsamic vinegar (use lightly: 1 tablespoon = 5 calories)

○ Salt-free seasoning blends such as Mrs. Dash

Keep in mind that this Jumpstart phase is designed to minimize bloating and fluid retention, and you will definitely notice having lost some pounds. But belly bloat is not the same as belly fat—that's what phase 2 is for. If you follow all the instructions, you can expect to lose as many as 7 pounds and up to 5¾ inches in your waist, hips, thighs, bust, and arms combined in 4 days. These are all real numbers, calculated by an expert who weighed and measured our test panelists. It can work for you, too!

DURING THE JUMPSTART, AVOID THESE FOODS

If you were to put the bad guys of bloat in a lineup, this is what it would look like.

SALT: Sodium causes water retention and bloating, so during the Jumpstart, move the saltshaker to the back of your highest cabinet and consider it off-limits, along with processed foods (the main source of excessive sodium in the average American diet). This includes sodium-laden condiments such as ketchup, mustard, relish, and barbecue sauce. The few packaged items used in the four-day meal plan are carefully screened for sodium content.

STRONG SEASONINGS: Barbecue sauce, black pepper, chile peppers, chili powder, cloves, garlic, horseradish, hot sauces, ketchup, mustard, nutmeg, onions, tomato sauce, and vinegar. Digesting foods like these can stimulate the release of stomach acid, which can cause irritation and bloating, so lay off hot stuff for a few days.

BULKY RAW FOODS: Cynthia designed the Jumpstart to meet your nutritional needs without adding extra volume to your GI tract. Space-saving cooked carrots replace raw ones, and fruit is kept to small portions of dried unsweetened fruits and fruits canned in juice.

GASSY FOODS: Beans are off the menu during the Jumpstart. Less notorious gas producers also sidelined just for these 4 days include cauliflower, broccoli, Brussels sprouts, cabbage, citrus fruits, onions, and peppers.

HIGH-CARB FOODS: Temporarily forgoing bananas, pasta, bread, and the like will prompt your body to burn off backup stores of carbohydrates. When this reserve fuel is burned off, your body releases excess fluid stored along with it.

CARBONATED DRINKS: It's a simple equation to understand: bubbles in beverages = air in belly.

CAFFEINATED/ACIDIC BEVERAGES: Coffee, tea, and fruit juices irritate and swell the GI tract.

ARTIFICIAL SWEETENERS: The sugar substitutes xylitol and maltitol are often found in low-calorie or low-carb products. Also known as sugar alcohols, these sweeteners cause gas, abdominal distention, bloating, and diarrhea.

CHEWING GUM: Studies have debunked the myth that chewing gum makes you hungry—it can actually help keep your appetite at bay. Unfortunately, it also causes you to swallow air that travels into your GI tract, so it's off-limits during the Jumpstart.

THE FLAT BELLY DIET PART II:
LOSING BELLY FAT FOR GOOD

Once you've completed the Jumpstart, you'll see a flatter belly and feel the jolt of confidence that comes with achieving such speedy results. Continued success—losing belly fat, that is—is a sure thing if you follow the three simple *Flat Belly Diet* rules.

RULE #1: EAT A MUFA AT EVERY MEAL. Make this your mantra. Unlike a Saturday-morning doughnut splurge that leaves you feeling sacked out and groggy for the rest of the day, MUFA foods, when eaten in the right amounts, have an amazing ability to provide steady, even fuel *and* quell the appetite. When enjoyed with complex carbohydrates, MUFA foods help slow digestion, which is one of the ways they help control blood sugar and insulin levels, as well as manage hunger. If you eat fruit and yogurt alone and have your MUFA a few hours later, it won't have the same satiating effect of enjoying the three foods together. That said, it's also important to get a range of MUFAs every day. I know you might have been hoping that you'd finally found the one magic diet that requires eating chocolate four times a day, but the reality here is that the easiest way to enjoy a healthy diet is to make sure it's varied. So mix up those MUFAs!

If you want to replace a MUFA in a particular recipe with another, just make sure they each have roughly the same calories. Consult the list on page 333 for suggestions.

RULE #2: STICK TO 400 CALORIES PER MEAL. The *Flat Belly Diet* is a 1,600-calorie plan. Cynthia chose this number because this daily allowance is what it takes for a 40-plus-year-old woman of average height, frame size, and activity level to achieve and maintain ideal body weight—without unnecessary and unhealthy compromises in terms of enjoyment, energy, and overall well-being, not to mention bone density and muscle mass. Dividing your 1,600 calories evenly over three meals plus a substantial snack steadily fuels your energy and metabolism. That means you keep feeling good and burning fat all day long.

Patty Lloyd

"I'd had a bad couple of years and had put on extra weight I just couldn't shake," explains 52-year-old Patty. Patty says she loved the structure of the *Flat Belly Diet* as well as the logic behind it because, as she explains, she does better when there is more to the guidelines than just food. "On most diets, the breakfast is so skimpy. You look longingly at someone else's bagel, and you think, *Oh God. Someday I'm going to let myself go and have one of those.* But on this diet, it's not like that. The food doesn't make you feel like you're being punished. It tastes so good, and there's so much of it, you feel like you're eating just like everyone else."

LOST
5 LBS
AND
3.25 INCHES
IN
32 DAYS!

GO ONLINE AND SKIP THE MATH

Members of www.flatbellydiet.com automatically receive a daily or weekly menu plan, complete with a printable shopping list. If any one of the suggested meals—or even individual foods—simply doesn't do it for you, swap it for another of equal calories and MUFA content. The system preprograms a list of choices so you don't have to do any tricky math! Plus, the interactive Food Log allows you to designate certain items as "favorites" so they'll quickly pop up when you're searching for another replacement.

RULE #3: NEVER GO MORE THAN 4 HOURS WITHOUT EATING. Timing is vital to making the most of the appetite-quelling and belly-fat-burning powers of your MUFAs. Eating smaller MUFA-rich meals more often rather than two or three larger meals spread out further keeps your blood sugar stable, which fends off cravings and prevents fluctuations in insulin that signal your body to store fat. It also keeps your energy up and hunger at bay, so you don't have bouts of fatigue and a grumbling tummy to contend with between meals—and the irritable disposition that comes with being tired and underfed.

These rules work in tandem to form the basic structure of the *Flat Belly Diet*. It is the combination of MUFAs at every meal *plus* the reduced but reasonable calorie guideline *plus* the frequency of wholesome meals that enables your body to stay energized and healthy while unloading belly fat. Read on to find out how easy and delicious it is to eat the *Flat Belly* way.

MAKING THE FLAT BELLY DIET WORK FOR YOU

All of the recipes in this book have been specially developed to fit comfortably within the framework provided by the three rules spelled out above. If you like, just follow the 14-day meal plan provided in the appendix to get started on the *Flat Belly Diet*. This maps out what to eat for breakfast, lunch, dinner, and snack for 14 days. You can follow the plan exactly or adapt it, swapping out meals to suit your taste.

Cynthia also devised these guidelines so it's easy to create your own *Flat Belly* meals. For each one, start by picking your MUFA and determining how many calories are left to work with. The basic components for any meal are MUFAs, lean proteins, whole grains or fruit, and (for lunch and dinner) vegetables. Visual cues are provided in parentheses. Here's how to build a *Flat Belly Diet* meal.

If your MUFA choice is nuts, seeds, or oil, add the following:

○ 3 ounces lean protein (about the size of a deck of cards)

○ 2 cups raw or steamed veggies (2 baseballs)

○ ½ cup cooked whole grain, such as brown or wild rice (about the size of a mini fruit cup) *or* 1 whole grain bread serving (such as half of a whole wheat pita) *or* 1 cup (baseball) fruit

Example: 2 cups baby greens topped with 3 ounces grilled chicken, 2 tablespoons almonds, and 1 cup sliced apples

If your MUFA is avocado or olives, pair it with:

○ 3 ounces lean protein *or* 2 ounces lean protein plus 1 dairy (such as 1 slice cheese or ¼ cup shredded or crumbled cheese)

○ 2 cups raw or steamed veggies

○ 1 cup starchy vegetables (beans, corn, peas, potatoes) *or* 1 cup cooked whole grain (such as brown or wild rice) *or* 2 whole grain bread servings (such as a full whole wheat pita, wrap, or English muffin)

Example: 3 ounces light water-packed tuna on top of 2 cups field greens topped with ½ cup garbanzo beans, ½ cup peas, and ¼ cup avocado

If your MUFA is dark chocolate, pair it with:

○ 1 cup fruit plus 1 cup dairy such as fat-free milk, yogurt, or cottage cheese *or* whole grain such as oatmeal or whole grain waffle

Example: ¼ cup chocolate chips mixed with 1 cup berries and 1 cup fat-free vanilla yogurt

DINING OUT FLAT BELLY STYLE

Being on the *Flat Belly Diet* doesn't mean you never get a break from cooking for yourself. Here are a few key tips for staying on track when dining out.

1. Go online to look at the restaurant menu and find meals that resemble those in the book or your meal plans. If the restaurant doesn't have a Web site, call and ask about the menu or have a copy faxed to you.

2. Rely on a safe bet. You can always order a salad made of leafy greens and raw veggies (about the size of two baseballs) topped with grilled chicken or salmon (no more than a card-deck-size portion) with balsamic or red wine vinegar, and add 2 tablespoons (two thumb tips, from where your thumb bends to its top) of seeds or chopped nuts (bring them along) or 1 tablespoon olive oil. Add a computer-mouse-size serving of one of the following: whole grain roll; baked or roasted red, white, or sweet potato; brown or wild rice or a starchy veggie such as beans, peas, or corn. This meal should keep you within your calorie budget, and it contains a MUFA!

3. Or follow the guidelines for building your own *Flat Belly* meal (see the instructions to the left of this box.)

{ WITH ALL THE DISHES TO CHOOSE FROM, YOU CAN ENJOY DIFFERENT MEAL COMBINATIONS FOR MONTHS. }

How to Use This Book

Simply select any recipe and enjoy! For recipes that fall under 400 calories, look to the "Make It a Flat Belly Diet Meal" information at the bottom of the page for suggested accompaniments. Calorie values for those foods are noted in parentheses. If those suggestions don't suit you, look for similar foods in the appropriate calorie range (see the lists on page 335). And because you can't really have two MUFA servings in the same meal (otherwise it's nearly impossible to follow rule #2—stick to 400 calories per meal), you'll also find that some recipes tell you what to omit if you want to serve one recipe alongside another. With all the dishes to choose from, you can enjoy different meal combinations for months. Then again, if you fall in love with a particular dish and want to have, say, a granola parfait for breakfast every morning and a Salmon Burger with Aioli for dinner every night—or even vice versa!—it's your call. If you prefer to see other ways to mix your meals, follow the 14-day menu plan to help you get started.

If you are a vegetarian or simply prefer to eat less meat, you'll find it's easy to tailor the *Flat Belly Diet* to your needs. (Cynthia, who has been a vegetarian for 20 years, can personally attest to this.) First off, the *Flat Belly Diet* features meat sparingly because low red-meat consumption is a key aspect of the amazingly healthful Mediterranean way of eating. So you will find plenty of meatless recipes to choose from, and those recipes that do include meat, chicken, or seafood are easy to adapt by instead using soy-based meat substitutes.

Finally, because the *Flat Belly Diet* is as much about promoting your overall health as it is about flattening your belly, Cynthia has paid close attention to the amount of sodium and saturated fat in all of the recipes in this book. *Prevention* recommends keeping total sodium below 2,300 milligrams per day and limiting saturated fat intake to 10 percent of total calories—about 17 grams per day.

So exactly how will this diet help you kick the salt habit? For starters, just by cooking from scratch and avoiding stealth salt in condiments like bottled salad dressings, you are taking a vital step toward keeping your sodium at healthy levels. According to the consumer group Center for Science in the Public Interest, salt-laden processed and prepared foods may account for up to 80 percent of daily sodium intake. In terms of the MUFA list, olives are undeniably salty, so make sure to enjoy olive dishes no more than once a day, less frequently if you're especially sodium sensitive. In the nutrition analysis for each recipe you'll find an asterisk (*) indicating when a recipe is rather high in sodium or saturated fat according to *Prevention*'s recommendations.

Finally, whatever your health status, you should first consult your physician before starting any diet, including this one. If you are allergic to any of the key MUFA foods or have a chronic condition (such as high blood pressure or type 2 diabetes) for which you are taking medication or following a special diet, the *Flat Belly Diet* might not be the right program for your needs. The only way to know for sure is to check with your doctor.

{ LOG ON FOR A FLATTER BELLY }

At **www.flatbellydiet.com,** you can find everything you need to faithfully follow the entire *Flat Belly Diet* program for life.
o Create your very own menu plans from hundreds of delicious MUFA-packed, calorie-controlled meals.
o Track your nutritional intake.
o Generate personal shopping lists.
o Read more about our success stories, whose profiles you see throughout this book—or nominate your own!
o Tap the experience, support, and motivation of hundreds of fellow *Flat Belly* dieters via message boards, blogs, and photo and video diaries.

7 Strategies for Success

2

½ cup

DATE 5.8.2008

FLAT BELLY DIET

Shopping List

ACTION

Avocados
Green beans
Strawberries
Peaches
milk
Cheese

As you now know from the previous chapter, the *Flat Belly Diet* is based on the latest and most credible science showing that foods rich in monounsaturated fatty acids may help reduce abdominal fat. This is important because belly fat isn't just difficult to shed, it's potentially deadly. And the *Flat Belly Diet* is the only plan that specifically targets belly fat by making MUFAs an essential part of every meal so that you can reap the full benefits of their belly-flattening and health-enhancing powers. Best of all, there are just three simple *Flat Belly Diet* rules to follow.

1. Eat a MUFA with every meal.
2. Stick to 400 calories per meal.
3. Never go more than 4 hours without eating.

Follow these rules and you will lose belly fat and overall body fat, gain energy, and reduce your risk of nearly every chronic disease, including cardiovascular disease, type 2 diabetes, breast cancer, and Alzheimer's disease. You'll look better, feel better, and quite possibly live a longer, healthier life.

Of course, to get these truly wonderful results, you do have to actually follow the rules. Cynthia and I have spent thousands of hours on the message boards of **www.flatbellydiet.com**, answering questions and addressing the concerns of people on this diet. To help you stay on track and avoid the pitfalls that accompany any lifestyle change, she's targeted these seven strategies. They will help you overcome any make-or-break moments that come your way.

{ THE *FLAT BELLY DIET* IS THE ONLY PLAN THAT SPECIFICALLY TARGETS BELLY FAT. }

1 **TAKE IT 1 DAY AT A TIME.** Each evening, mentally walk yourself through the coming day and picture where you'll be during meal and snack times. Start with breakfast and work your way forward (sticking, of course, to rule #3: Eat every 4 hours), and decide ahead of time what those meals will be.

Early appointment tomorrow morning? Pack a portable breakfast like the Apple and Cashew Butter Sandwich on page 75 before you go to bed, and you'll reduce the chance of rushing out the door hungry and empty-handed. Will afternoon car-pool duty interfere with the 4-hours-post-lunchtime mark? Bring along a Cherry-Almond Granola Bar (page 291) to snack on in the car, and it'll be much easier to avoid reaching for a bag of chips at the minimart or overeating when you finally sit down to dinner. Having dinner out with friends? Take a look at the restaurant menu online and plan your order in advance. (See "Dining Out Flat Belly Style" on page 21 in Chapter 1 for tips on eating out and making restaurant dishes *Flat-Belly* friendly.)

When you anticipate potential challenges, you can easily plan (and pack food!) so you don't find yourself stranded for good options. It's an indispensable way of avoiding missteps that can throw you off course.

2 MAKE GROCERY SHOPPING A PRIORITY.

Grocery shopping typically gets wedged in between life's more firmly scheduled obligations, so it can be especially challenging for some people to make thoughtful food purchases. But allowing your supplies of healthy, appealing food to dwindle (and neglecting to stock a good array of emergency backups) is the surest way to undermine your own success: If you don't have the proper food on hand, it will never find its way to your mouth. It becomes difficult if not impossible to stick to a healthy eating plan.

So put yourself at the top of the agenda and recognize that setting aside time to gather the healthy food you need is important and equally worthy of the time, energy, and effort you invest in everything else in your life. Strategy #1 in this chapter has you spending a few minutes every evening thinking about what you'll eat tomorrow. Take it a step further and map out which recipes you'd like to try in the coming week. If you join **www.flatbellydiet.com**, you can receive a customized shopping list every week based on the recipes you choose.

Once you have a list in hand, do a little legwork before you shop to figure out what time will work best for you. For example, call the store and find out when they're likely to restock (nothing like trying to navigate a shopping cart through aisles clogged with packing skids). If you would rather skip the crowds, avoid shopping right after work or at the end of the week or month, when many people get their paychecks. To make it even easier on yourself, pick the same time every week to do your shopping, and write it into your datebook.

After you've completed the Four-Day Anti-Bloat Jumpstart, consider a bulk shopping trip to a discount club to cover the next month of staple ingredients—all the MUFA foods (except avocados) have long shelf lives. You'll not only save money but find the other 3 weeks of food shopping much easier to handle, with fewer groceries to carry home and put away.

Once you upgrade grocery shopping to a high-priority item on your schedule, treat it like a doctor's appointment you must keep; after all, it's no less important to your health. Every time you do your shopping, you'll reaffirm your commitment to your own success and well-being.

3 MIND YOUR MEASUREMENTS.

Get in the habit of measuring food. It may seem tedious, especially if you're an accomplished cook who's comfortable putting together meals with a dash of this and a splash of that. But measuring your ingredients is important, especially on the *Flat Belly Diet*, because it helps ensure that this carefully calculated plan controls your hunger and gives you the health and weight-loss results you want. It will also help you be mindful of how much you're eating. And this, believe it or not, will keep you feeling satisfied.

Research shows that most people underestimate serving sizes when eyeballing them. Guesstimating measures of MUFAs and other calorie-dense foods is an especially big gamble. Take olive oil: Say you're unknowingly drizzling 2 tablespoons onto your lunchtime salad instead of the proper MUFA allowance of 1 tablespoon. At 119 calories per tablespoon, making such a mistake repeatedly, much less habitually, could seriously hinder your progress.

It seems the problem isn't linked only to serving size. Some research suggests that feeling full and satisfied, natural signals that indicate it's time to stop eating, don't necessarily kick in as quickly when people unwittingly supersize. In a study conducted at the University of Illinois at Urbana-Champaign, volunteers unknowingly eating soup from self-refilling bowls ate 73 percent more than participants eating from regular bowls, even though they did not believe they had consumed more. What's more,

{ MOST PEOPLE UNDER-ESTIMATE SERVING SIZES WHEN EYEBALLING THEM. }

they reported satiety (sense of fullness) levels no higher than participants who had eaten far less from regular bowls. In other words, overeating doesn't necessarily make you feel fuller. Many people resist measuring because they think it will make them feel deprived, but studies like this one show the opposite is actually true.

Plus, it's important to remember that on the *Flat Belly Diet,* measuring isn't merely a safeguard against accidental overindulgence. In fact, because MUFAs play a key role in controlling hunger, it's just as important to measure your MUFAs to make sure you don't skimp and miss out on their satisfying benefits.

After all, one of the things that make the *Flat Belly Diet* so easy to love is the generous portions Cynthia has devised. Take peanut butter: A 2-tablespoon mound looks like a lot, but that's the right amount to deliver this marvelous MUFA's health benefits and control your hunger. It's crucial to resist any urge to use less. If you reduce the amount, you will not only take in less MUFA overall but your hunger might return more quickly and throw off your meal timing. So measure away, and *enjoy.*

4 UNDERSTAND YOUR HUNGER.

What goes on in your head—your thoughts, attitudes, feelings—has a powerful effect on the choices you make about what you eat, how much you eat, and when you eat, not to mention how you feel about it later.

In order to switch off the mental autopilot that can steer you wrong when it comes to eating, as well as to get your mind fully engaged in keeping your weight loss on course, it's important to practice recognizing when you're *physically* hungry. Here's how.

Say you sipped your way through a creamy Mango Surprise Smoothie half an hour ago, and now you find yourself seized by a ravenous craving for french fries. Instead of agonizing over whether to make a break for the drive-thru, give yourself a quick reality check with these two questions.

1. Has this hunger come on suddenly?

2. Am I craving a specific food or type of food?

Sudden onset is a telltale sign of emotional hunger. True physical hunger, on the other hand, comes on gradually. And a specific craving for a food (such as french fries) or type of food (like sweets) is another clear sign of emotional hunger. Learning to spot hunger pangs that radiate from above the neck will help you tune them out and instead listen better to your belly (a growling stomach is a reliable sign that your body needs food).

So what should you do when you've determined that your hunger is emotional rather than physical? Try talking yourself through it. Head not for the fridge but to the nearest full-length mirror, look yourself up and down, and take stock of the visible results you've achieved thus far. Look yourself in the eye and consider the changes you've made, mental and physical, and remember the ultimate promise the *Flat Belly Diet* holds for your future: a longer, healthier life. All this is tangible proof that what you are doing is right for you. It took a leap of faith—in yourself—to get you here. Do justice to your own efforts, honor your commitment to yourself, and go the distance. You deserve nothing less than to continue to succeed.

5 **KNOW HOW TO GET YOURSELF BACK ON TRACK.** As important as it is to stick to the three cardinal rules of the *Flat Belly Diet* and as essential as it is to make the necessary changes in your life—and your attitude—that put you and your health first, it would be unrealistic to proclaim that you will never, ever break the rules. So here are a few of Cynthia's simple, tried-and-true guidelines for breaking the rules without running off the rails. I follow them whenever I need to get myself quickly back on track.

◆ **Make it a worthwhile indulgence.** For me, that means one thing: ice cream. Cakes and pies I'm not so crazy about, so birthday parties and weddings don't pose much of a problem. But I just love fresh, full-fat ice cream, and I thoroughly enjoy several huge cones every summer.

◆ **Plan your splurge. And *enjoy* it.** Maybe you're going to Chicago and deep-dish pizza is one of your great loves. Or the crème brûlée your friends serve at their New Year's party is your idea of heaven on earth. Insisting to yourself that you're going to resist and then giving in to an urge at the last minute detracts from the pleasure of the experience by adding guilt. It also increases your likelihood of really going overboard (fueling further guilt) instead of relishing your treat and moving on.

◆ **Skip the guilt.** Beating yourself up only makes it harder to get back on track. Negative self-talk ("Why, oh why, did I do that?") can trigger emotional eating, and that's the last thing you need. Remember, even if you make an unplanned misstep, one big meal or off day won't undo all the good meals and days before and yet to come, and it doesn't mean you're going to have to drag those big jeans back out of the closet.

So what should you do after an indulgence to get back on track? Compensate—with a little exercise. Absolutely do not succumb to the urge to skip a few meals—and no cutting extra calories. Remember, the *Flat Belly Diet* is not about deprivation. Instead, go straight back to your food routine, but make a firm plan for a big calorie-burning activity for the day after your splurge: a 5-mile hike or a long, hilly bike ride, whatever suits you best. Make a date with a friend or family member if that's what it takes to ensure that you follow through.

6 **FOCUS ON YOUR GOAL.** Sometimes it's harder than it should be to "just say no." A well-intentioned hostess might launch a guilt trip when she finds out you haven't sampled her famous bacon–blue cheese dip. Impatient waiters are not always kind about special orders. And let's not forget all the classic faux pas from well-meaning family members, from not getting what all this fuss is about "eating healthy" to taking your lifestyle change as a personal insult to their own ample proportions.

Whether it's insensitivity, outright peer pressure, or just the presence of a lot of food you're choosing not to eat, social situations can be especially challenging to navigate if you let them make you feel deprived. After all, it's easy to become fixated on everything you're giving up. Instead, nip negative self-talk in the bud and take a quick minute to refocus on what you're getting: a slimmer figure and a better life—not just here and now but far down the road into a future that is a lot less likely to be impaired by type 2 diabetes, high blood pressure, heart disease, and other diseases; a new relationship with food as you learn to trust your belly and recognize the triggers that lead to emotional eating; and the fun of expanding your food horizons with a lot of great new recipes to share with family and friends.

So the next time a social situation leaves you second-guessing your resolve, take a moment to look at your choices in this light. Odds are it will take on a whole different meaning.

7 **CELEBRATE ALL VICTORIES.** Maybe you've set your sights on those last stubborn 10 pounds of postpregnancy weight. Perhaps you've vowed to divest your body of the 45 pounds that somehow climbed aboard over the past several years. Or maybe your pact with yourself is less about a particular weight than it is about fitting comfortably into your favorite jeans again.

Whatever your ultimate goal, it is absolutely essential that you also define your success in small increments. Life is lived one meal at a time, so victories should be about more than just those few splendid seconds when finally crossing the finish line. You're much less likely to succumb to frustration if you give yourself full recognition where it's due, all along the way.

Pat yourself on the back for a couple of pounds lost in as many weeks, another quarter inch gone from around your waistline, or the fact that you have no more use for tentlike dresses. Reward yourself with a new outfit, a "three cheers for me" e-mail to close friends, or a night out dancing to your favorite music.

But don't stop there. To really take fair stock of your progress, it's even more important to celebrate the achievements that you can't measure in pounds and inches. Think about the scope of the changes you're making and the impact they'll add up to in your life.

If vegetables rarely passed your lips more than a couple of times a week and now you eat them twice a day, you've begun to lower your risk for a slew of chronic diseases, and that is certainly something to celebrate. If you headed into this diet thinking you'd crave junk food constantly and find you actually don't miss it much, you're probably also enjoying more balanced blood sugar, and that's a triumph in itself. What about cooking? Have you discovered a few new twists in the kitchen? Homemade meals can be very rewarding. Good for you!

Keeping a journal in which you record your thoughts and feelings, ideally along with an account of what you're eating and when, is a great way to stay aware of the progress you're making and the positive changes you're bringing about in your life.

Consider taking this one step further and creating a scrapbook, with pictures of yourself and meals you've prepared, recipes you enjoy, goals you're pursuing, milestones achieved, and plans for the new, healthier future you're creating for yourself. Studies show that journaling is one of the best predictors of sustaining weight loss.

Even the smallest ways of applauding your own success are extremely valuable. One of our test panelists got in the habit of writing something good she ate each day that she wasn't eating before and sticking it on the fridge where she'd see it over and over again. Some days she'd write down something she was glad not to be eating anymore.

Whatever form you give them, these small gestures of self-congratulation provide a vital way of keeping your motivation from flagging—and giving yourself the praise you fully deserve.

{ CELEBRATE ALL THE ACHIEVEMENTS THAT YOU CAN'T MEASURE IN POUNDS AND INCHES. }

3

Flat Belly Cooking

I've packed this chapter with details about all the MUFAs. Why? Because in order to make the diet work best, it's important to prepare your MUFAs for the most nutritional benefit (a necessary point to make, just in case you were hoping for chocolate cheesecake four times a day!).

You'll find a comprehensive guide to buying, storing, and cooking with MUFAs, along with key tips for maximizing flavor and minimizing labor. There's also advice on quick-and-easy cooking techniques to help you get great flavor without unnecessary calories and sodium; healthy preparation is essential when cooking with MUFAs, which are not low-calorie foods. And at the end of the chapter, you'll find a selection of fabulous staple recipes for flavored oils, nut toppings, and seasoning mixes that, unlike packaged products, don't contain a lot of hidden sodium, sweeteners, and other additives.

Enjoy!

Oils

FLAT
BELLY
DIET
PER SERVING
ALLOWANCE:
1 tablespoon

Oils are fundamental to good cooking. Fats in liquid form, oils conduct heat and impart flavor, richness, and texture. What's more, unlike butter (which is loaded with saturated fat) and stick margarine (which can harbor deadly trans fats), MUFA-rich plant-based oils are amazingly heart-healthy.

Running the gamut from the brash and full-bodied that hold their own at high temperatures to the exquisitely fragile whose delicate bouquets can be savored only uncooked, MUFA oils offer expert and novice cooks alike a wonderfully varied cooking palette. Rotate several in your repertoire to keep meals more interesting *and* healthier—the various oils deliver different nutritional benefits along with their MUFAs.

To help you mix it up, we've organized this section by use rather than by oil type. Note that while each oil is categorized by what we deem to be its ideal cooking use, additional suggestions are included at the end of each entry.

First, let's start off with some general guidance applying to all the MUFA oils.

◆ **Buy small and store properly.** A big jug of oil that will spoil long before you make your way through it is no bargain. All MUFA-rich oils are sensitive to heat, light, and air and will go rancid if exposed to these elements or kept too long. Rancidity robs an oil of its nutrients and gives it a decidedly unpleasant smell and taste that will ruin any dish. So don't buy more than you will use within a couple of months, and be sure to store it properly. Because they all need protection from light and temperature, you can't go wrong keeping your MUFA oils in the refrigerator. Some, like olive oil, will cloud and thicken when chilled, but this does no harm, and they resume liquid form when they return to room temperature. However, if you prefer not to house all your MUFA oils in the fridge, most will keep well in a cool, dry, dark cupboard for a few months (some that do strictly require refrigeration are noted below). For convenience, keep a small amount of the oil you use most frequently in a ceramic, stainless, or dark-tinted glass bottle somewhere near at hand, as long as it has an airtight top and is a good distance from the stove top or a windowsill (to protect it from heat and light). Refill as needed from a larger container kept in the refrigerator or a cool cupboard.

{ ALL MUFA-RICH OILS ARE SENSITIVE TO HEAT, LIGHT, AND AIR. }

◆ **Don't overheat.** What busy cook hasn't now and then set an oiled skillet on the stove to heat, turned her back to attend to something else for a moment or two, and ended up setting off the smoke alarm? Different types of oils have different threshold temperatures at which they begin to smoke. Aside from the obvious fire hazard (oil that gets too hot can ultimately burst into flame), it is important to avoid heating any oil beyond this so-called smoke point, because doing so causes its chemicals to break down, destroying flavor and degrading nutrients. If you do happen to heat any oil to the point that it starts to smoke, let it cool, discard it, carefully clean the pan, and start over. Smoke point is one of the factors taken into account in the suggested uses for the oils listed on the following pages; approximate ranges of heat tolerance in the oils are provided because specific smoke points vary among brands.

◆ **Steer clear of chemical processing.** Unrefined oil, which is often labeled "unfiltered," is simply expressed and bottled, with its natural color, flavor, and nutrients intact. In general, seek out expeller-pressed or cold-pressed oils whenever possible. These are produced using force of pressure rather than chemicals to draw the oil from seeds or nuts.

At the other end of the spectrum are refined oils, which are generally more heat tolerant and less prone to rancidity, but the steps used in processing can involve harsh solvents that sacrifice flavor and nutrients. In order to provide a range of commonly available oils suitable for high-temperature cooking, such as stir-frying, certain refined oils are recommended below.

ROAST AND SAUTÉ WITH EXTRA VIRGIN OLIVE OIL AND CANOLA OIL

These oils are perfect for cooking at moderate to high temperatures.

◆ **Extra virgin olive oil.** Two grades of olive oil are typically available in American supermarkets: extra virgin and pure. Extra virgin is most preferable because it's derived from higher-quality, more freshly picked olives through a process that does not involve chemicals, so its fruity flavor and beneficial nutrients are uncompromised. It's well suited to sautéing or roasting so long as you keep the temperature below about 375°F. Extra virgin olive oil is not appropriate for higher-temperature cooking (above medium on the stove top), as its flavor and chemical structure break down under intense heat.

Taste, color, and fragrance differ from oil to oil, depending on the variety of olives used, where they were grown, when they were picked, how soon after harvest they were pressed, and so on. When shopping for extra virgin olive oil, bear in mind that the country of origin advertised on the labels of many supermarket brands may indicate where the oil was bottled rather than the locality in which the olives were grown. It's common practice for large manufacturers to import olives from various countries for pressing, blending, bottling, and exporting.

Will a grass-green oil taste more intensely of olives than a pale chartreuse one? Is an Italian extra virgin likely to be more tongue-

> IN GENERAL, SEEK OUT EXPELLER-PRESSED OR COLD-PRESSED OILS WHENEVER POSSIBLE.

tinglingly piquant than one from Spain, Greece, or California? Such conundrums of flavor prediction are no more easily answered than is the subjective question of whether top-shelf artisanal olive oils offer an exquisite flavor experience that merits their high price tags. Connoisseurs certainly think so, but what will please your palate is a question only your own tastebuds can answer.

In essence as much a fruit juice as a cooking fat, olive oil's flavor spectrum is remarkably wide ranging, from mellow and buttery to rich and fruity to peppery and pungent. Buy little bottles to sample, and until you settle on a favorite, try a new kind each time you restock. For general cooking, you may gravitate toward an oil that lends a buttery warmth to sautés and sauces, whereas big, booming olive flavor may be just the thing for splashing across your summer tomato salad. And delicate baby greens may sing like never before when sprinkled with a demure extra virgin whose olivey essence carries hints of citrus, herbal, or even floral aromas. It's easy to see why many cooks end up with three or more that they like to have on hand, using an inexpensive all-purpose, mildly flavored oil for cooking with heat and reserving pricier ones with more complex flavor for drizzling on salads and finished dishes.

Uses: virtually unlimited, except for deep-frying

Other benefits: rich in polyphenol antioxidants, which fight cancer and heart disease

◆ Canola oil. Versatility, neutral flavor, and universal availability, combined with high MUFA content, make canola oil a must-have for the *Flat Belly* kitchen. A stable cooking medium up to about 435°F, canola is an excellent choice for cooking that requires moderately high heat. It's made from rapeseed, a plant in the mustard/cabbage family that is specially bred (but not genetically engineered) to produce canola oil. Any brand will do, although expeller-pressed organic canola oil is preferable because no chemicals are used in the growth or production processes.

Uses: baking, salad dressings

Other benefits: provides some omega-3 fatty acids, including alpha-linolenic fatty acid, which is essential for healing and other vital biological functions

STIR-FRY WITH PEANUT AND SESAME OILS

These oils can withstand intense heat.

◆ **Refined peanut oil.** Along with a high heat tolerance (up to about 450°F), refined peanut oil has a neutral flavor, so it won't compete with Asian seasonings such as ginger and chile paste. People who are allergic to tree nuts and peanuts should avoid cooking with peanut oil, too.

Uses: sautéing or roasting at high temperatures; grilling over direct heat

Other benefits: excellent source of heart-protective phytosterols that may also reduce risk of certain cancers

◆ **Sesame oil.** Select a dark sesame oil made from toasted sesame seeds to infuse simple preparations with a rich, nutty aroma. Even if you opt for a lighter type made from raw seeds, a little bit goes a long way, flavorwise, so this oil is better employed sparingly as a seasoning rather than a cooking medium. In other words, this is one MUFA oil that is not recommended in its full tablespoon allowance. The concentrated flavor is simply too overpowering in that quantity. So make your main MUFA peanut oil (if stir-frying) or any other mild-flavored oil (like safflower or canola), and add a dash of sesame oil to achieve your flavor objectives.

Uses: marinades, dipping sauces, dressings

Other benefits: rich in protective vitamin E, whose formidable disease-fighting powers may extend to various cancers and Alzheimer's disease

TOSS SALADS WITH HIGH-OLEIC SAFFLOWER AND SUNFLOWER OILS

Both safflower and sunflower oils are highly versatile. Safflower oil is pressed from the seeds of a thistlelike plant, while sunflower oil is drawn from those of the familiar flower. Being mild in taste and rich in polyunsaturated fatty acids (in addition to MUFAs) makes them especially good for salad dressings: They don't compete with delicate flavors, and they don't solidify when refrigerated—so you can dress and chill a veggie dish or pasta salad and the oil will not congeal. Both also lightly coat rather than weigh down crisp fresh veggies.

> { SAFFLOWER AND SUNFLOWER OILS DON'T COMPETE WITH DELICATE FLAVORS. }

Safflower and sunflower oils are lower in saturated fat than most other MUFA oils. Look specifically for natural, unrefined forms that specify "high-oleic" on the label; these come from plants bred to have much higher MUFA concentrations than regular safflower and sunflower oils. Refined versions of high-oleic safflower and sunflower oils are also available for high-temperature cooking. Store them in the refrigerator, where they will keep for up to 9 months.

Uses: baking; mayonnaise and dips

Other benefits: rich in omega-6 fatty acids, which in proper balance with omega-3s and as a replacement for saturated fats have been shown to reduce the risk of cardiovascular disease

MAKE SMOOTHIES AND SOUPS WITH FLAXSEED AND WALNUT OILS

Flaxseed produces a delicate oil with stellar nutritional benefits, but those properties are lost when the oil is heated. By contrast, walnut oil can be heated, but due to its high price tag, most cooks prefer to limit its use to very special dishes in which the flavor can be truly appreciated. Fortunately, there are plenty of great ways to put the rich, nutty flavor of these oils to good use. Both make a lovely addition to just about any fruity concoction, especially smoothies (try flaxseed oil with berries, walnut oil with pears and vanilla yogurt). Chilled soups offer another great opportunity to swirl in one of these MUFAs—try flaxseed in melon and berry soups or walnut in pureed vegetable soups like cucumber-dill, vichyssoise (potato-leek), and other summer classics.

When shopping, buy only cold-pressed flaxseed oil that has been kept refrigerated; store chilled, and use it within 2 months. Look for expeller-pressed walnut oil or toasted walnut oil (which will be even nuttier). It's not quite as fragile as flaxseed oil, so it may not be refrigerated in the store. Put the tin in the fridge and the oil should keep for 6 months.

Uses: especially nice on salads made with tender greens and fruit such as raspberries and mandarin oranges

Other benefits: high in particular omega-3 fatty acids that promote bone health and brain function

MIST ON YOUR OIL

When preparing recipes that feature non-oil MUFA ingredients, a mister is a great tool to help you control the amount of cooking oil (and thus calories) you add to a dish. Put your favorite fruity extra virgin olive oil in a mister and keep it at the ready for misting salad greens. Better yet, fill it up with an herb-infused oil (see recipes, page 63) and spritz onto grilled fish or chicken, veggies, even popcorn. Another good use for a mister: Fill it with your preferred all-purpose cooking oil and skip packaged cooking sprays—and the aerosols and additives that come with them.

Misters are available at most stores that sell kitchen gadgets. Before making a purchase, it's a good idea to consult a knowledgeable salesperson or read a few online consumer reviews. Not all misters are made alike, and some deliver a much better mist than others.

FLAT
BELLY
DIET
SERVING
ALLOWANCE:
2 tablespoons

Nuts, Legumes, and Seeds

The foods in this category epitomize healthy decadence: They're extraordinarily rich not just in MUFAs but also in protein and flavor—all this in a diverse array of remarkably compact packages, from the chunky Brazil nut to the shapely edamame to the tiny sesame seed. For anyone in search of quick and easy ways to put a fresh spin on everyday dishes, cooking with these foods is nothing short of delightful. Run-of-the-mill steamed vegetables and pureed soups take on new interest—not to mention higher nutritional value—with a mere sprinkling of toasted pistachios, almonds, or walnuts. Roll tofu cubes with sesame seeds next time you stir-fry or sauté, or pat pumpkin seeds onto chicken breasts before cooking and discover a healthfully crispy crust—and a new weeknight favorite.

Portability makes nuts and seeds the go-to MUFA for food on the go—most of them make great take-along snacks in and of themselves, and they do double-duty as BYO ingredients that turn your lunchtime trip to the salad bar into a perfect *Flat Belly* meal.

An altogether different way of enjoying nuts and seeds is in ground form—as butters and pastes. From the all-time American classic, peanut butter, to the Middle Eastern staple, tahini, these make great spreads and dips. They're also terrific for flavoring and thickening sauces and soups. Long available in health food stores, a wider variety of nut and seed butters is commonly stocked in super-markets nowadays. While developing the recipes for this book, we even took to whizzing nuts into flour mixes using a food processor; used this way, nuts add remarkable body to many baked goods, including our Cranberry-Pecan Scones (page 88) and Chocolate-Almond Macaroons (page 295).

General storage and shopping information is provided for each subcategory—nuts, legumes, and seeds—along with flavor descriptions and recommended uses for each individual food, plus any particular selection, storage, or preparation requirements.

NUTS

◆ **Whole versus shelled.** The high oil content in nuts makes them vulnerable to rancidity. Buying nuts whole, with their natural protective covering intact, is the best way to ensure freshness and thus better taste and longer shelf life. It's also much more economical than buying shelled nuts.

Whenever possible, buy whole nuts from a good produce or bulk-foods department (with frequent turnover) where you can see the nuts in a bin up close instead of hidden in a bag. Depending on where you live, farmers' markets can be a great source for fresh nuts in season. Select nuts that are clean, avoiding any with cracks or holes in the shells or that rattle freely (indicating they're old and dry). Whole nuts can be stored in a cool, dark place for 2 to 3 months.

If you prefer not to crack your own nuts, the baking and snack aisles of the average supermarket offer a limited range of options, but stores that specialize in natural foods or have a good organic section will reward you with far greater variety and quality of shelled nuts, so it's worth making regular trips to such stores. Wherever you buy your shelled nuts, take care to select unsalted ones. Those that are roasted are sometimes salted or even oiled in the process, so read packages carefully.

Fresh shelled nutmeats should look plump; pass over any that appear darkened, mottled, crumbly, or shriveled, all of which are signs of age and poor storage. To best preserve shelled nuts, store them in airtight containers in the refrigerator, where most will keep for 3 to 4 months. Alternatively, if well wrapped, shelled nuts can be kept in the freezer for up to a year.

◆ **Toasted is tastier.** Raw nuts are healthy as is, but it's safe to say that all nuts are improved by toasting, which brings out a rich butteriness in many varieties and is especially important for those that tend to be a little bitter (such as walnuts and pecans) or flat-tasting (like pine nuts, almonds, and hazelnuts) in their uncooked state. Toasting takes only a few minutes, requires no oil, and is easily done in a bare skillet over medium heat or on a bare baking sheet in a 250°F oven. Shake the pan frequently to prevent the nuts from scorching, and remove it from the heat when the nuts give off a mild, toasty aroma. Use toasted nuts within a few days because they quickly go rancid.

Note: For hazelnuts, walnuts, peanuts, and pistachios, toasting makes the skins (which contain bitter-flavored tannins) easier to remove. Transfer the toasted nuts to a clean, dry towel and rub to remove the skins. Or transfer the nuts to a rack set over a baking sheet; rub the nuts against the wire grid, and the skins will come loose and fall onto the baking sheet.

◆ **Almonds.** An elegant and versatile nut with a smooth flavor and impressive nutritional profile, the almond is well known to most Americans yet underused in the typical home kitchen. Supermarkets commonly sell shelled almonds in several forms. As long as they are unsalted, you can choose from whole, with the brown skin intact (sometimes called natural) or removed (blanched); sliced; slivered; and chopped. Unsalted dry-roasted may be available, but they don't keep as long as raw nuts. Tinned almonds typically have added salt and oil and are best avoided. Look for vacuum-sealed bags of all-natural, unsalted nuts or nuts packed in plastic containers that are clearly marked with a sell-by date. (Dry-roasted is okay, but oil-roasted is not.)

Uses: sliced or slivered on soups, salads, fruit-and-yogurt parfaits; chopped to top or encrust fish fillets or chicken breasts; pureed with herbs for a pesto alternative; whole pressed into the tops of cookies or muffins

Other benefits: decent source of protein and fiber, offering 6 grams and 3 grams, respectively, for each 1-ounce serving of whole nuts (about 23 almonds)

◆ **Brazil nuts.** The largest of the tree nuts, Brazil nuts are grown in the Amazon and have a mild flavor and rich, coconut-like texture. Because they're generally more expensive than other nuts and therefore less likely to turn over as quickly in a store, they're best purchased whole to ensure freshness.

Uses: coarsely chopped in rice pilaf or grain-based salad (such as quinoa, bulgur, or brown rice)

Other benefits: among the most concentrated sources of selenium, a mineral that protects cells from free radical damage, boosts infection-fighting elements of the immune system, and activates substances that protect the eye from cataracts and the heart from muscle damage

◆ **Cashews.** These unctuous, kidney-shaped nuts are sold only shelled and roasted because heat is necessary to destroy a caustic resin in its husk. Familiar to many people as a salty snack, cashews are also a versatile cooking ingredient with a deep flavor and creamy texture well suited to savory main dishes and sweet desserts.

Uses: whole or pieces in fruit salads (especially with tropical fruits like mango and papaya), stir-fries (especially with lean beef, chicken, shrimp, asparagus, broccoli), and curried dishes

Other benefits: high in copper, which helps the body absorb iron and maintain healthy bones and connective tissues

◆ **Hazelnuts (filberts).** Perhaps best known for their role in French pastries and confections, hazelnuts impart a sweet flavor and lush texture that make them an especially delightful baking ingredient but qualify them for inclusion in a wider range of dishes as well.

Uses: whole or chopped in granolas and mueslis, fruit salads, pilafs and grain-based salads, and spinach salads; divine in sweet baked goods, especially chocolate ones

Other benefits: good source of folate, a B vitamin that helps keep your brain young

◆ **Macadamia nuts.** These lusciously buttery nuggets are the most decadent of nuts, with the highest fat content and highest price tag; thus, they're to be enjoyed only occasionally and in carefully measured portions. They are perhaps the only nut with raw flavor that's so full, toasting is truly unnecessary.

Uses: whole in sumptuous fruit salads along with tropical fruits such as pineapple, kiwifruit, and mango; chopped atop grilled fish; as a garnish for thick slices of grilled fresh pineapple for a special dessert

Other benefits: rich in potassium, a mineral that helps regulate muscle and nerve function

PEOPLE WHO EAT NUTS ARE SLIMMER
A study published in the journal *Obesity* debunks the once-prevalent fear that eating nuts causes weight gain. Researchers found quite the opposite: People who ate nuts at least twice a week were much less likely to gain weight than those who almost never ate nuts.

◆ **Pecans.** Best known for their starring role in the well-loved classic Southern dessert, pecans have a sweetly rich flavor and tender crunch worthy of attention outside a piecrust as well (and they really do not need to be suspended in a blend of butter and sugar to be enjoyed!).

Uses: in pieces atop salads (especially good with spinach and entrée salads featuring sliced chicken breast), rich pureed soups, roasted squash, and baked apples; tossed with green beans or other crisp-tender vegetables; stirred into waffle, pancake, or muffin batter or cookie dough

Other benefits: with higher concentrations of oleic acid than olive oil, may be an even stronger nutritional weapon against breast cancer

◆ **Pine nuts.** Just as their name suggests, these sweet, buttery, nutlike seeds are borne in the cones of certain varieties of pine trees. Pine nuts are typically sold hulled, without their protective shells, and are highly vulnerable to rancidity, especially from humidity. So be selective to avoid buying already spoiled nuts, store them in the freezer or refrigerator, and consume them within a few weeks of purchase.

Uses: pureed in pesto; whole, toasted in salads (especially with greens and pears or apples and dried fruit such as raisins or cranberries) and pasta dishes (featuring fresh tomatoes or roasted red pepper), tossed with sautéed greens (spinach, kale, or chard), stirred into grain dishes, or rolled onto classic Italian pignoli cookies

Other benefits: rich source of the trace mineral manganese, an essential component of biochemical reactions that affect bone, cartilage, brain function, and energy supply

◆ **Pistachios.** As much as you may have enjoyed them pried from the shell and munched as a snack—or as the crunchy component in that inexplicably green ice cream of childhood— these MUFAs are a revelation in savory dishes, where they pair as beautifully with garlic and herbs as they do with dried fruits and tangy cheeses.

Uses: toasted, atop pasta (try combining with Parmesan and wild mushrooms), sautéed chicken, salads (with fresh or dried figs and baby greens, or with cranberries and goat cheese), vegetables (especially sautéed or roasted cauliflower or Brussels sprouts), or any cooked whole grain; folded into cookies (especially with cranberries, currants, or other rich dried fruit)

Other benefits: source of dietary fiber

◆ **Walnuts.** Along with almonds, pistachios, and peanuts, walnuts are among the relatively few nuts readily recognizable to most Americans in their whole unshelled form. Perhaps this is because they're native to much of North America and therefore easy to come by when in season. In any case, eating them from the shell is a singularly satisfying experience—with just enough work required to crack the hard, wrinkly shell and free the lobed kernel from the woody membrane within that the sizable nutmeat seems a rich reward. Shelled walnuts have their advantages, too: With a longer shelf life (9 to 12 months in the refrigerator) than many other nuts, they make a good staple nut to stock in the fridge (or freezer); and the tender kernels are easily broken by hand so a few can be crumbled into several dishes weekly—no knives and chopping required. Whether you buy walnuts whole or shelled, their sweetly earthy flavor and toothsome, almost velvety texture make them an appealing snack and a versatile cooking ingredient.

Uses: toasted and broken atop almost any salad (especially good with pears); in slaws along with dried fruit; crumbled onto pastas and soups; pureed into a hummuslike dip; tossed with rolled oats, cinnamon, and a little brown sugar or maple syrup and spread atop apples or berries or a combination of fruits and baked as a crisp

Other benefits: high in omega-3 fatty acids and heart-protective antioxidants; good source of melatonin, which aids sleep

{ WALNUTS ARE NATIVE TO MUCH OF NORTH AMERICA AND THEREFORE EASY TO COME BY WHEN IN SEASON. }

LEGUMES

Edamame and peanuts are two popular foods that make the MUFA list. Unlike nuts, which are all generally good MUFA sources, not all legumes offer beneficial amounts of healthy fats. Here's what you need to know about these two superstars.

FLAT
BELLY
DIET
SERVING
ALLOWANCE:
1 cup shelled

SOY POWER

A 2007 study links soy to the prevention of fat gain around the belly in postmenopausal women. Researchers at the University of Alabama at Birmingham found that among a group of 15 postmenopausal women, those who drank a soy-based shake every day for 3 months gained less belly fat than those who had a milk-based shake.

FLAT
BELLY
DIET
SERVING
ALLOWANCE:
2 tablespoons
shelled nuts or
peanut butter

◆ **Edamame (soybeans).** If you come across fresh soybeans at a local farmers' market and the fuzzy pods are deep green, firm, and unbruised, by all means buy them! Boil them in salted water for a few minutes and you'll be in for a tender, protein-rich treat. Happily, frozen edamame are almost as good, and most large supermarkets carry them in one or more of the following forms: shelled and cooked, whole and cooked, or whole and uncooked (follow package instructions for specific cooking times). The slightly hirsute pods aren't edible, but don't shuck them all at once unless you're going to add them to a dish. Straight from pod to mouth is a delightful (and authentically Japanese) way to enjoy edamame: Hold the pod lengthwise near your lips and pinch its outer edge to press the beans against the inner seam, which will split so that the sweet and tender beans pop into your mouth.

Uses: warm or cold in pods as a snack; shelled and added to salads (try with thinly sliced celery and water chestnuts over a nutty green like watercress) or Asian-seasoned vinaigrette along with flaked salmon, blanched vegetables, and whole wheat noodles

Other benefits: a broad spectrum of protection against heart disease, various cancers, and osteoporosis; see "Soy Power" (left).

◆ **Peanuts.** Housed in its corrugated woody shell, clad in slippery red skin, stripped to a curvy bare kernel, or pulverized to a paste, the peanut is an American icon. This humble fixture of ballpark, circus tent, and country fair has lately proven worthy of its privileged position in the American diet—that is, when significant adjustments are made to added salt and, in the case of peanut butter, when sweeteners, hydrogenated oils, and other additives are left by the wayside. The peanut is rich enough in protein, fiber, and phytonutrients that before long it may be declared the newest superfood. Peanuts are also a handy and healthful cooking ingredient. As long as you are careful to avoid peanuts that have been oil-roasted and/or salted, you can choose as you like from whole, skin-on, or blanched; raw, dry-roasted, or boiled.

Uses: whole or halves, pan-roasted and added to stir-fries (especially with crisp vegetables and spicy Asian chile sauce);

chopped and sprinkled over whole wheat noodle salads and other whole grain dishes; minced and added to a marinade or sauce for sautéed chicken; as peanut butter (see below) in dressings for Asian-style noodle dishes, sauces for curried vegetables and spicy stir-fries, and dips for grilled skewered chicken, shrimp, lean meat, or vegetables, as well as in baked treats

Other benefits: rich in antioxidant vitamin E, bone-building magnesium, muscle-friendly potassium, and immunity-boosting vitamin B_6; especially with skins on, a good source of the cancer-fighting and artery-protecting antioxidant resveratrol

THE PLEASURE OF PEANUT BUTTER

Peanut butter is indigenous to culinary traditions all over the globe, but nowhere is it loved so passionately as in the United States. Even if your favorite means of delivery will always be between two slices of bread or straight up aboard a spoon, if you are a peanut butter lover, you owe it to yourself to explore its culinary versatility.

In general, it's best to buy all-natural peanut butter to avoid emulsifiers and other unhealthy additives. With even the most conventional brands introducing "naturals" into their product lines, there's a profusion of choices nowadays. Whether or not you rove through the natural foods section to explore the full range of options, check the ingredients carefully to make sure you are getting a straight MUFA, with no palm oils or soy lecithins added. A little salt, peanut oil, and even a touch of sugar (often masquerading as molasses or evaporated cane juice) or honey is okay.

In both homemade and prepared all-natural peanut butter, the oil is not hydrogenated, so it separates and sits on top of the spread. Resist any urge to pour off the oil—it's full of MUFAs, and dispensing with it will leave you with a stiff, dry, unspreadable paste. Before you open a new jar, put it in the refrigerator *upside down*. (You can also do this with an opened jar; just be sure to screw the lid on tightly first.) Kept upside down and chilled, much of the oil will integrate itself into the peanut butter, and most excess will be at the bottom of the jar, out of your way, next time you go to use it. Alternatively, you can pour or scoop the entire contents of the jar into a wide, fairly shallow, plastic, sealable container and stir to incorporate the oil, then keep it in the refrigerator, where it will reward you for your trouble by remaining blended.

Making your own peanut butter is easy. Process 2 cups roasted shelled peanuts, 1 tablespoon peanut oil, and 1 teaspoon salt (optional) in a food processor or blender on the liquefy setting until smooth, pausing to scrape down the sides with a rubber spatula. For a crunchy butter, stir a handful of coarsely chopped peanuts into the smooth puree. Transfer to a jar and keep refrigerated.

FLAT
BELLY
DIET
SERVING
ALLOWANCE:
2 tablespoons

SEEDS

As with nuts, seeds are generally best purchased from a good natural foods store or specialty department within a supermarket, where they're typically available in prepackaged containers and sometimes also in bulk bins (though these are becoming increasingly rare). Whether purchasing seeds packaged or loose, be on the lookout for discoloration, holes, shriveling, and other signs of age, moisture, or insect damage. If possible, smell the seeds before you buy them, as old ones tend to give off a telltale rancid or musty aroma.

So long as they are left whole, seeds are generally less susceptible to spoilage than nuts are. Still, they should be kept in airtight containers in the refrigerator and taste best if consumed within a couple of months. Once ground, seeds go bad quickly, sometimes within a few days.

The three MUFA-rich seeds spotlighted here all benefit from toasting, which brings out their oils and unlocks their sweet and nutty flavors. To toast hulled seeds, place them in a dry skillet and cook over low heat, tossing frequently, until fragrant. Transfer to a cool plate to prevent excessive toasting and a bitter flavor.

◆ **Pumpkin seeds (pepitas).** Within the whitish fibrous hull of the pumpkin seed lies a deliciously chewy dark-green kernel. Whether you buy pumpkin seeds whole or just the tender inner kernel is a matter of taste and, perhaps, availability. Unhulled pumpkin seeds keep longer, and some people enjoy eating them whole, with the hulls on, or shelling as they go, which has the advantage of keeping you from snacking away too quickly. But unless you've harvested them from the pumpkin yourself (see below), the hulls may prove too tough to eat, and splitting and removing them is a more tedious job than the pleasant cracking and nibbling ritual associated with whole sunflower seeds. A key cooking ingredient and favorite snack in traditional Mexican cuisine, pumpkin seeds have become much more widely available stateside and are often labeled only with their Spanish name, pepitas, especially when sold hulled and roasted. However you buy them—hulled or shells intact, raw or dry-roasted—take care to avoid any that have been salted or oil-roasted.

Whether or not jack-o'-lanterns are part of your fall routine, it can be great fun to enjoy pepitas the old-fashioned way: straight from the pumpkin. Use a sharp paring knife to cut a "lid" away from the top of the pumpkin, around the stem. Reach in and scoop out the seeds with your hands or a large serving spoon. Deposit them in a bowl or on a baking sheet and remove any stringy pulp by wiping them with a paper towel. Spread the seeds evenly on a brown paper bag or sheet of parchment and leave to dry overnight. The next day, transfer the seeds to a rimmed baking sheet and lightly roast on the lowest temperature in the oven for 15 to 20 minutes, until slightly golden. Eat whole or remove the shells. If your seeds come from pie pumpkins (a.k.a. sugar pumpkins) rather than jack-o'-lantern pumpkins (their stringy flesh isn't worth cooking), cut the pumpkins into quarters and roast, flesh side down, in $\frac{1}{4}$ inch of water, in a baking pan in a 400°F oven for about 45 minutes or until very tender. Puree and use for pumpkin soup—topped with toasted pepitas, of course!

Uses: raw kernels, sprinkled atop breads and muffins before baking; toasted kernels, scattered across hot or cold cereal, leafy green salads, grain salads, sautéed vegetables; toasted and ground, folded into veggie or turkey burger mix; ground, as a base for sauce (mole) with aromatic spices for chicken, turkey, lean pork; whole, for snacking (season with lime juice, a few drops of chile sauce, and a pinch of kosher salt)

Other benefits: excellent source of magnesium, a vital mineral for healthy bones and nerve and metabolic function

{ ENJOY PEPITAS THE OLD-FASHIONED WAY: STRAIGHT FROM THE PUMPKIN. }

◆ **Sesame seeds.** Nutty and slightly sweet, these crunchy seeds are too small to snack on, but their cooking uses are endless. Sesame seeds are typically sold in small, overpriced jars stocked in the dried spices aisle of the average grocery store, but if your supermarket has an extensive selection of shelled nuts or, better yet, a rack of bulk, lower-priced spices packaged in plastic containers, you may be in luck. Generous packets of ivory-colored sesame seeds are often stocked among the peppercorns and other spices cooks like to buy in quantity. You may even find other colors—snow-white and jet-black ones are increasingly common (and make a delicious and dramatic crispy crust for baked or pan-roasted salmon fillets).

Tahini, a creamy, subtly sweet paste made from ground raw sesame seeds, is a Middle Eastern pantry staple and primary ingredient in hummus and baba ghannouj. It's generally available in tins or jars and should contain only sesame seeds, with no additives. Asian sesame paste is made from toasted seeds and consequently darker and stronger in nutty flavor.

Uses: toasted, sprinkled on Asian-inspired noodle dishes or steamed vegetables dressed with lemon juice (especially broccoli, green beans, and asparagus); toasted whole or ground, as a flavorful component for dressings and marinades; as tahini, spread on toast or pita and topped with cucumber and tomato slices, combined with bean purees to make dip for crudités, added to vinaigrette for creamy and nutty salad dressing, or tossed with rice or noodles and vegetables and a little reduced-sodium vegetable stock

Other benefits: high in calcium, which is essential to healthy bones, nerve and muscle function, and blood clotting

◆ **Sunflower seeds.** Fruit of the sunflower, these are deliciously oily seeds with a nutty flavor and tender crunch. Hulled sunflower seeds are useful for cooking, but cracking the shells open with your teeth is so satisfying a part of eating them out of hand that people who favor sunflower seeds as a MUFA snack would do well to keep both hulled and whole in the pantry. Select shell-on seeds that are not broken or dirty and do not look at all soft. Shelled seeds should be grayish-brown; yellowish ones have probably gone rancid. As with other seeds and nuts, smelling them is a good way to determine if they are fresh.

Uses: whole, toasted, sprinkled on cereal, yogurt and fruit, or any tossed salad; stirred into tuna, chicken, or turkey salad (especially with dried cranberries or diced apple or sliced grapes); added to savory baked goods

Other benefits: high in cholesterol-lowering phytosterols (plant compounds)

> TAHINI IS A MIDDLE EASTERN PANTRY STAPLE AND PRIMARY INGREDIENT IN HUMMUS.

Avocados

An incomparably buttery fruit, the avocado is commonly available in two varieties. The type known as Hass or California has pebbled green skin that turns dark brown as the fruit ripens, while the considerably larger Florida variety has smooth green skin. Both have creamy yellow-green flesh around an inedible brown pit. Hass is preferable for its creamier, more flavorful flesh. For either variety, buying unripe or just barely ripe ensures the best flavor and texture: Purchase fruits that are quite firm or give only ever so slightly to a gentle squeeze—despite what their labels might say, avocados that are soft are overripe, which means off flavor and brown-spotted flesh. Don't be afraid to buy downright hard avocados; ripening typically takes just a day or two (no more than three or four at most) and is as easy as leaving them out on a flat surface at room temperature. Putting the fruit in a brown bag can speed the ripening process by about a day.

FLAT
BELLY
DIET
SERVING
ALLOWANCE:
¼ cup

CUTTING AN AVOCADO

With their thick skins encasing such slippery, squishy flesh, avocados can be tricky to work with. Follow these simple steps to easily and neatly produce pretty slices or tidy chunks or just mash your avocado without a lot of mess.

1. Use a small serrated knife or steak knife to cut through the skin and around the pit lengthwise.

2. Gently grasp the two halves and twist in opposite directions to separate. If you are using the whole avocado, proceed to step 4.

3. If you are using only part of the avocado, leave the skin and pit in place in the half you're not using, brush lemon juice on the exposed flesh, cover tightly with plastic wrap, and refrigerate for up to 2 days. Place the remaining half flesh side down on a cutting board and cut in half lengthwise, through the skin. Then proceed to step 5.

4. If you are using the whole avocado, cut each half in two lengthwise; twist the two quarters still holding the pit, and it should release. (If the pit remains attached to one quarter, the best way to remove it without mangling the fruit is to hold the wedge skin side down in the palm of one hand and carefully press the blade of your steak knife into the pit. The serrated edge will bite into the pit so that you can lift it away from the flesh. Remove the pit from the knife by tapping it on the edge of the sink or trash can.)

5. To peel, start at the narrow, pointed end of each wedge and lift the skin away from the flesh. Mash with a fork then and there, on the cutting board or after transferring to a bowl. To slice or chop, proceed to step 6.

6. To slice, place each avocado wedge flat side down on a cutting board and cut lengthwise into arcs of your desired thickness. To cut into chunks, hold the slices together and cut again, crosswise.

Refrigerate whole avocados as soon as they become ripe because they will progress to overripe surprisingly quickly. Cover cut avocados tightly in plastic wrap. As with an apple, exposure to air will darken the flesh; to prevent this, leave on as much skin as possible, leave the pit in place (see "Cutting an Avocado," page 53), and rub a little lemon juice on any exposed flesh. Keep cut avocado refrigerated, and use it within a day or two.

Uses: sliced or chopped in salad along with any citrus (ruby grapefruit, clementines, or drained mandarin oranges from a can) or tropical fruit (like mango) over tender salad greens, such as butter lettuce, all dressed with a light vinaigrette; as uncut quarters to hold a scoop of chicken or turkey salad or black bean salad

Other benefits: high in cancer-fighting carotenoids; shown to improve the body's ability to absorb carotenoids from other vegetables, such as carrots, lettuce, spinach, and tomatoes (another reason to include avocado in salads and salsas!)

Olives

FLAT
BELLY
DIET
SERVING
ALLOWANCE:
10 olives

Along with the surge in popularity of Mediterranean foods has come an expanded selection of olives in most local supermarkets. You may no longer have to journey to a gourmet shop or ethnic grocery to find variety, but some traveling within the supermarket might be necessary, as olives tend to be distributed all over—the condiment/pickle aisle, natural foods section, deli, international department. Look for jars from California, Greece, France, Spain, and Israel. Better yet, check the deli or prepared foods area for prepacked plastic containers of fresh olives or, best of all, self-service barrels.

Try to get unpasteurized olives, which have superior flavor and texture: Green ones are zestier and crisper when pasteurized; black are richer and meatier. Tasting is the surest way to gauge freshness, but if you have to judge by sight alone, whether jarred or straight from the barrel, olives should have uniform color (no spots) and firm flesh (no shriveling—except for oil-cured, which are supposed to look a little wizened).

Here's a selection of the types of olives commonly found in supermarket olive bars, with basic information about taste and texture. An asterisk (*) indicates types that are particularly good for cooking. Olives from the barrel are sold by weight, so buy just a few of each type that interests you, and get to know which ones you like.

- **Arbequina**: small, round, brown Spanish olives with mild smoky taste
- **Cerignola** (Bella di Cerignola): large Italian olives with a fresh, mild taste; colors include pale green, bright purple, light red, and deep black (which are softer)
- ***Gaeta**: small Italian olives, dark purple when brine-cured, with a salty strong flavor
- ***Kalamata**: pointed almond-shaped black olives from Greece, with a briny, winey flavor and firm texture
- **Manzanilla**: pungent, firm green olive from Spain; classic martini olive
- **Mission** (or California): bland, firm; sold mainly in cans or jars
- ***Nicoise**: very small French olives with mellow, nutty rich flavor and meaty texture
- **Morrocan oil-cured:** black, wrinkled, often rather bitter, with a prunelike meaty texture
- **Nyon**: small black French olive, usually dry-cured and with a salty, slightly bitter taste
- ***Picholine**: tiny, green, torpedo-shaped French olives with a tart, bright buttery flavor and slightly crisp texture
- **Sevillano**: large green Spanish olives with mild taste and crisp texture

Three main factors determine olives' color and flavor: plant variety, ripeness of the fruit at harvest, and how it was fermented and cured. The resulting hues range from bright green to dusky purple, rosy taupe to ruddy plum, nut brown to deepest ebony. The flavor spectrum is no less extensive, from sharply piquant to winey pungent, fruity sweet to richly meaty.

Unpasteurized olives have more complex flavor and firmer texture than pasteurized ones. When olives are pasteurized for bottling, they undergo high-temperature processing that basically cooks them, sometimes leaving musty flavor and mushy texture. If you have a choice, pass up jarred olives and go with unpasteurized

TO PIT OR NOT TO PIT

Whole olives are generally superior to pitted in terms of quality. Especially when eating olives on their own (rather than as part of a dish), gnawing the rich flesh from the pit is part of savoring the luscious fruit. It also slows you down, maximizing satisfaction and helping to prevent overeating.

To pit an olive for use in a recipe, press the whole fruit firmly with the flat of a large kitchen knife or chef's knife and use a slight side-to-side motion. This will loosen the flesh from the pit so you can cut or squeeze it free. Some people swear by olive pitters, nifty gadgets that extract the pit for you. As with all kitchen equipment, it pays to research before buying to ensure you get an effective implement rather than another tool whose only function is to take up space in your kitchen drawer!

ones that have been kept immersed in brine, which keeps them fresh indefinitely (they deteriorate rapidly when exposed to air, so don't buy olives displayed this way). Some olive bars try to pass off pasteurized olives for fresh, so be on the lookout for telltale drab color and soft texture—especially in pitted olives and highly seasoned mixes (two ways of masking inferior quality). Try to shop at a store that has quick turnover, so you know that the supply is often replenished. And don't be afraid to ask if the olives are pasteurized or where they come from—a reputable seller will know.

Olives can be kept in airtight containers at room temperature, but they'll last longer stored in the refrigerator. Their oils and brine may congeal when chilled, which will make them look a little waxy when cold, but this will dissolve again when returned to room temperature.

Uses: whole, pitted, or sliced in salads with sturdy crisp vegetables, stewed chicken dishes, and robust pasta sauces

Other benefits: good source of vitamin E, an antioxidant that protects cell membranes and reduces inflammation

TAPENADE

In the regional cooking of Provence, France, where tapenade is a traditional condiment, its essential ingredients are black olives as well as capers, anchovies, and olive oil. Additional seasonings may include lemon juice, garlic, basil or other herbs, liquor such as brandy, mustard, and sometimes bits of tuna. Stateside, the term *tapenade* has been adopted to advertise spread or dips made of "Mediterranean" ingredients, so packaged tapenades you find in the condiments aisle or deli case may contain green olives rather than the traditional black—or no olives at all, much less the other classic Provencal ingredients. Some instead feature artichokes, sun-dried tomatoes, roasted red peppers, even figs. To count as a MUFA, a packaged tapenade must list olives as the main ingredient. Be on the lookout for additional, nontraditional ingredients that add unnecessary fat or calories. Check the ingredients and nutritional information on the package; each tablespoon should be about 40 calories.

Making your own tapenade is incredibly easy, gives you control over the ingredients, and is sure to yield a spread that better pleases your palate. You can adjust the proportions of the basic components to your liking and experiment with your own personal touches (a dash of lemon juice here, perhaps, or a pinch of oregano there). Plus, you save money—packaged tapenades can be pricey! See page 181 for the recipe for Tapenade.

Dark Chocolate

Is any food loved more ardently than chocolate? A heavenly marriage of heady flavor and melt-in-the-mouth texture, plus some potent mood-altering properties, chocolate inspires passion, even obsession. For many people, the pleasure of eating chocolate simply has no comparison—or competition. So much the better, then, that guilt-free chocolate consumption (in limited quantities, of course) is one of the singular joys of the *Flat Belly Diet*!

Dark chocolate, specifically, is a MUFA. This excludes milk chocolate, so if that's always been your chocolate of choice, your tastebuds have a bit of adjustment to make—but what a pleasant one. Get this: Dark chocolate includes semisweet, bittersweet, and extra bittersweet, all of which have more of the stuff that makes chocolate chocolatey—the cacao, or cocoa butter and cocoa solids. Translation: richer, deeper chocolate flavor.

So what should you buy? A wonderful variety of dark chocolate is widely available, so you don't have to venture beyond your local supermarket (or pay boutique prices) to begin tasting your way through a number of different brands to see what you like. Between the secretiveness of chocolate makers and the endless variables involved in transforming bitter cacao beans into the voluptuous substance we so dearly love, labels mean very little. Just because one brand's 60 percent cacao bar hits your palate with too much intensity doesn't mean that another maker's 73 percent block won't transport you straight to nirvana with perfectly intoxicating deep chocolate flavor. Start at 60 percent (many cooks find a good multipurpose chocolate in this range), sampling a variety to see how they suit you for different purposes. Heat affects flavor and consistency, so your favorite eating chocolate may not be the best performer as a baking chocolate or the basis for Decadent Dark Chocolate Sauce. Note that bar form is generally best (see "Making the Most of Chocolate," page 58), and steer clear of liquid chocolate, which contains vegetable oil in place of some of the cocoa butter.

Chocolate should be stored in its original wrapping in a cool, dry, airy place (but not in the refrigerator, which is too cold and moist) and away from odiferous items (chocolate absorbs odors). Stored properly, most dark chocolate has a shelf life of upward of a

FLAT BELLY DIET SERVING ALLOWANCE: 1 ounce (¼ cup semisweet chocolate chips)

UNEXPECTED PAIRINGS

Chocolate is the Fred Astaire of foods: The delectable flavor seems perfection on its own, but pair it with a worthy partner and you'll enjoy it in a whole new way. You're likely well acquainted with the pleasures of chocolate in the company of sweet fruits and savory nuts, but consider coupling it with foods from other, more highly contrasting points on the flavor spectrum—salty and spicy, for example, offers surprising delight. The stronger and closer to bitter your chocolate, the more profoundly the contrasting combination will pique your palate. Try adding a dab of jalapeño jelly on a square of superdark chocolate to see what we mean.

MAKING THE MOST OF CHOCOLATE

Many good-quality dark chocolates come in large bars, which are usually scored with grooves so you can break them apart by bearing down firmly and evenly with a heavy chef's knife. To make smaller chunks, about ¼ inch to ½ inch each, work diagonally from the corners of the bar to break off shards. For finer, more evenly broken pieces (essential for melting), pulse the chunks in a food processor or place in a ziplock bag and pound with a rolling pin or the flat side of a meat tenderizer.

When melting chocolate, remember that it scorches easily, so *low* and *slow* are the operative words for making a smooth transition from chunks or chips to silky molten liquid. Direct heat on the stove top is too intense, even on the lowest setting. Melting in a double boiler works well enough, but even a drop of water or a moist spoon will make warm melted chocolate stiffen into dry lumps (this is called seizing and can be fixed only by adding oil and remelting). Micro-waving can sap moisture from chocolate and will not melt it all the way into a smooth liquid. So what's the best way to get silken warm chocolate? The oven!

Use small pieces of uniform size for quick and even melting. Place the chocolate in a bone-dry heatproof bowl and set it in the oven on the lowest heat. *Leave the door of the oven ajar.* Check after 3 minutes: Wearing oven mitts, remove the bowl from the oven and swirl it in a circular motion to see if the chocolate has melted and to incorporate any remaining solid bits. If most of the chocolate has melted, continue to swirl, or stir it with a dry wooden spoon or rubber spatula until completely smooth (the heat from the liquid chocolate will melt the remaining bits). If large unmelted pieces remain, put the bowl back in the oven and check again within 3 minutes, repeating the swirling method. Continue this way until the chocolate is smooth. Only large amounts should take more than 6 to 9 minutes.

year. If not stored properly, chocolate will develop whitish "blooms," which indicate that the cocoa butter crystals within the bar have melted and migrated to the surface. This may mar the texture, but it won't ruin the taste.

Use: chips, small nuggets, or curls in fruit-and-whole-grain granola, sprinkled atop whole grain waffles or pancakes or mixed into the batter, or swirled into oatmeal with bananas or peaches; melted (or as chocolate sauce) in yogurt smoothies; in squares atop or sandwiched between dried apricots; finely chopped and stirred into aromatic spicy sauce for chicken (mole)

Other benefits: high in antioxidant, heart-healthy flavonols

Flat Belly Diet Cooking

You know by now that the healthy fats and other nutrients that make MUFA foods heavyweight champs nutritionally and gastronomically also make them dense in calories. By their very definition, MUFA foods are high in fat—albeit the good-for-you variety. So when it comes to following the *Flat Belly* food plan and staying within the daily calorie and sodium guidelines, it's especially important to have a full arsenal of cooking techniques that don't add unnecessary fat and calories.

Here are our favorite quick-and-easy, low-fat and low-sodium cooking methods. They're well suited to bringing out the full flavor of MUFA foods, and we've provided a few key tried-and-true test-kitchen tips for each one.

◆ **Roasting transforms vegetables.** Virtually any vegetable benefits from being tossed with a little canola oil, a pinch of kosher salt, and some freshly ground black pepper and then roasted at fairly high heat (400°F+) for 30 to 45 minutes or until nicely browned, with crisped edges and tender middles (poke with a fork, skewer, or small knife).

Make sure to roast in a shallow baking dish—the bottom of a broiler pan or even a rimmed cookie sheet is fine—so the hot air surrounds the veggies and browns them nicely. Avoid deep casseroles and don't cover the dish, or you won't get the desirable color or crispiness.

If you're new to roasting, here are some of our favorite transformations: Pale, bland cauliflower caramelizes to golden brown and takes on rich nutty flavor. Brussels sprouts lose the bitterness that turns so many of us against them in childhood; gone, too, is the mushiness that often results from stove-top steaming—roasted sprouts are sweet and pleasingly crisp-tender. Carrots go from run-of-the-mill to savory-rich. Sliced first into thin circles, potatoes emerge from the oven with a crispy chiplike crust surrounding a tender center and prove a worthy rival of french fries; combine with similarly slivered yams for a more colorful, flavorful, and nutrient-rich side dish.

◆ **Poaching is perfect for fish.** Poaching is a superbly simple way to quickly and gently infuse flavor without adding fat. Immerse fillets of any mild-flavored, firm-fleshed fish in barely simmering liquid and cook until just opaque all the way through—typically, 20 to 30 minutes, depending on thickness. Our favorite poaching fishes include salmon, sea bass, cod, and halibut.

For a quick poaching liquid: Roughly chop a carrot or two, a stalk of celery, and an onion; add to a pan of water with a splash of vinegar or lemon juice; and toss in a few whole black peppercorns, a bay leaf, a sprinkling of kosher salt, and fresh herbs (like dill) you happen to have around. Remove the fish and vegetables when done and turn up the heat to reduce the poaching liquid to a sauce.

{ POACHING IS A SIMPLE WAY TO QUICKLY AND GENTLY INFUSE FLAVOR WITHOUT ADDING FAT. }

◆ **Slow-cooking makes the whole meal for you—ahead of time.** Slow cookers have earned a permanent position on many a kitchen countertop because they offer a combination of convenience, taste, and versatility that no other appliance can match. They're veritable miracle workers for cooks looking to maximize flavor and minimize fat—low-fat proteins, lean cuts of meat, and dried beans alike slow cook to succulent perfection.

There are a few basic rules to consider: For example, cut raw meat into pieces and place them at the bottom of the slow cooker so that it heats up relatively quickly, and make sure cooking times are specific to your appliance (they're different for 3-quart versus 6-quart). It's most important to acquaint yourself with the instructions that come with your slow cooker, especially those concerning food safety, before using.

◆ **Grilling can't be beat for fast, low-fat, flavorful meat.** Cooking over a flame drains off fat while imparting delicious smoky flavor to meat, chicken, and seafood. For speed and simplicity, select proteins that cook within about 25 minutes over direct heat, such as steaks and chops, chicken pieces, fish steaks, tofu, and burgers—or skewer variations of these in cubed or meatball form.

Keep foods moist and flavors full by searing on all sides to lock in juices and marinating proteins before grilling. If you like, baste with marinade a few times while cooking. Cook seafood just until opaque at the center, but don't rely on visual appearance to judge doneness of meat or chicken. Instead, invest in an instant-read thermometer, which is much more reliable. Remove meat from the grill when it's within 10 degrees of doneness. Set it aside for several minutes while the temperature continues to rise. It's ready to serve when the thermometer reaches the temperature for doneness.

◆ **Stir-frying is a swift means to a one-dish meal.** A little oil and a lot of heat add up to a superfast low-fat cooking method. Stir-frying requires some slicing and dicing up front but pays off big with meals that cook up in as little as 10 minutes. It's the ideal route for cooks who like to prep ingredients in advance and then throw a delicious dinner together at top speed when mealtime comes. No time to chop veggies? Buy them prewashed and pre-cut—consider raiding the supermarket salad bar for a wide variety of ready-to-cook veggies in whatever proportion and quantity you fancy. Another advantage of stir-frying: It allows you to experiment with infinite combinations of proteins and vegetables. Thin strips

STOCKING THE FLAT BELLY PANTRY

One trip to the grocery store is all it takes to give your pantry a quick makeover á la *Flat Belly.* Here are a few key switches to keep in mind next time you load your shopping cart.

BYPASS	BUY INSTEAD
Low-fiber cereals and breads	Whole grain varieties
Processed/packaged snack foods	Dry-roasted or raw MUFA-rich nuts, unsweetened dried fruits
Pure or light olive oil	Extra virgin olive oil
Butter/stick margarine	Any MUFA oil
Corn oil or blended vegetable oil	Canola, sunflower, or safflower oil
Regular peanut butter	Peanut butter clearly labeled "all natural"
Salted or oil-roasted nuts	Unsalted raw or dry-roasted nuts
Bottled dressings and marinades	MUFA oils and flavored vinegars
Milk-chocolate baking chips	Semisweet or bittersweet dark chocolate

or slices cook quickly and evenly over high heat—vegetables retain flavor and crisp-tenderness, while proteins stay tender.

Here are our favorite stir-fry secrets: Roll tofu cubes or strips of chicken in sesame seeds for a delicious crunch. Use baby vegetables, which are sweet (to look at and to taste) and require little to no prep. Stir in a cup of frozen chopped spinach (slightly thawed) for 1 minute before your stir-fry is done to add color, iron, and flavor.

The Flat Belly Pantry Staples

Now that you have all the details about the MUFA foods and how to cook the *Flat Belly* way, it might help to have on hand a few key ingredients and staples you can make ahead. Use the following recipes interchangeably with other dishes in this book. Just make sure to stick to the usual MUFA serving size: 1 tablespoon oil or 2 tablespoons nuts per serving.

DAIRY

Many recipes in this book call for Greek-style yogurt, a dairy product that's essentially yogurt that's been strained to be distinctly thick, about the same consistency as sour cream. However, Greek-style yogurt is a better nutritional bargain. Ounce for ounce, fat-free Greek yogurt has about $\frac{1}{3}$ fewer calories compared to fat-free sour cream.

If you can't find Greek yogurt in your grocery or health food store, make your own. Here's how: Place 1 quart yogurt in a large colander lined with a double thickness of cheesecloth or paper towels. Place the colander in a larger bowl and let stand in the refrigerator to drain to the desired thickness, up to 8 hours or overnight. Makes $1\frac{1}{2}$ to 2 cups.

INFUSED OILS

There are plenty of great-tasting MUFA-rich oils to choose from, but loading up on all of them at once can get pricey. Instead, use the following recipes to add a twist to your basic olive oil or approximate the flavor of a nut oil. Remember that olive oil becomes cloudy when refrigerated but quickly returns to its clear hue when brought to room temperature.

Garlic-Infused Oil
MAKES 2 CUPS

4–6 cloves garlic, thinly sliced
6 large green olives, coarsely chopped
A sprig or 2 of your favorite herb, such as basil or oregano
2 cups extra virgin olive oil, divided
1/2 teaspoon black peppercorns

1. Combine the garlic, olives, herbs, and 1/2 cup of the oil in a small saucepan.

2. Heat gently over medium heat for about 5 to 7 minutes or until the garlic turns golden.

3. Remove the pan from heat and let cool. Strain the oil through a fine cheesecloth and discard the garlic, olives, and herbs. Add the strained oil to the remaining 1 1/2 cups of oil. Add the peppercorns and place in a sterilized jar or bottle. Refrigerate for up to 2 weeks.

Nut-Flavored Oil
MAKES 2 CUPS

1 cup walnuts, hazelnuts, or almonds
2 cups extra virgin olive oil

1. Place the nuts and 1/2 cup of the oil in a blender or food processor. Process until the nuts are finely chopped. Add to the remaining 1 1/2 cups oil and place in a sterilized jar or bottle.

2. Cover and refrigerate for 10 days. Strain the nuts from the oil and return the oil to the refrigerator. Use within 1 month.

NUT TOPPINGS

Use these mixed-nut toppings to complement your favorite salads, fruit crisps, or coffee cakes—any dish suited to a sweet, nutty flavor.

Basic Sweet Nuts

■ MAKES ¾ CUP

¼ cup chopped walnuts
¼ cup chopped pecans
¼ cup chopped Brazil nuts
½ teaspoon cinnamon
1 tablespoon agave nectar

1. Preheat the heat to 350°F. Line a small baking sheet with foil and coat the foil with nonstick spray.

2. Combine the walnuts, pecans, Brazil nuts, and cinnamon in a medium bowl. Add the agave nectar and toss to coat.

3. Spread the nut mixture evenly on the prepared pan and bake for 8 to 10 minutes.

4. Cool completely and store in a ziplock bag.

Chocolate Dessert Nuts

■ MAKES 1 CUP

1½ tablespoons brown sugar
1 tablespoon Dutch process cocoa or 2 tablespoons semisweet chocolate chips, chopped fine
¼ teaspoon cinnamon
½ cup chopped pecans
½ cup chopped hazelnuts
2 teaspoons canola oil

1. Preheat the oven to 350°F. Line a small baking sheet with foil and coat the foil with nonstick spray.

2. Combine the sugar, cocoa, and cinnamon in a small bowl. Add the pecans, hazelnuts, and oil and toss to coat.

3. Spread the nut mixture evenly on the prepared pan and bake for 8 to 10 minutes.

4. Cool completely and store in a ziplock bag.

HOMEMADE SEASONING MIXES

The spice aisle is teeming with dozens of seasoning mixes that are quick, convenient—and a good deal more costly than the sum of their parts. If you keep a good supply of basic herbs and spices on hand, though, you can whip up your own mixes for a fraction of the cost. Store each blend tightly covered in a cool, dry place.

Curry Powder

■ MAKES ½ CUP

¼ cup ground coriander
1½ tablespoons ground turmeric
1 tablespoon ground fenugreek

1 tablespoon ground cumin
1 teaspoon ground cardamom
1 teaspoon ground ginger
1 teaspoon cinnamon

1 teaspoon allspice
⅛ teaspoon ground red pepper (or more to taste)

Cajun Spice Mix

■ MAKES ⅔ CUP

2 tablespoons paprika
2 tablespoons freshly ground black pepper
1 tablespoon garlic powder

2 teaspoons red pepper flakes
2 teaspoons dried thyme
2 teaspoons dried oregano

2 teaspoons onion powder
2 teaspoons dry mustard

Middle-Eastern Spice Mix

■ MAKES ⅔ CUP

2 tablespoons freshly ground black pepper
1½ tablespoons ground cumin

1 tablespoon ground coriander
1 tablespoon salt

1½ teaspoons ground cardamom
¾ teaspoon ground cloves

Breakfast

4

Granola Parfait

■ **5 MINUTES** ■ **2 SERVINGS** ■ *420 CALORIES* ■ **MUFA: WALNUTS**

This elegant parfait is the perfect way to start any morning, and it's so easy to put together! Raspberries offer nearly 50 percent more antioxidant activity than strawberries do, according to research conducted in the Netherlands.

1 banana, sliced
1 cup raspberries
1 container (5.3 ounces) fat-free Greek-style yogurt
1½ cups Granola (page 70) or store-bought granola

Layer the banana, raspberries, yogurt, and granola in 2 tall glasses. Serve immediately.

NUTRITION PER SERVING

420 calories
14 g protein
67 g carbohydrates
13 g fat
1 g saturated fat
0 mg cholesterol
140 mg sodium
14 g fiber

{ **Make It a FLAT BELLY DIET MEAL** } A single serving of this recipe counts as a *Flat Belly Diet* Meal without any add-ons!

Granola

45 MINUTES ▪ **10 SERVINGS (¾ CUP EACH)** ▪ **294 CALORIES** ▪ **MUFA: WALNUTS**

This maple-kissed granola is a cinch to make—try it once and you'll never return to store-bought. Feel free to customize it to your tastes, but don't forget the MUFA! Store it in a tightly covered container for up to 3 weeks.

  2 cups oatmeal
1¼ cups walnuts, chopped
  ½ cup unprocessed bran
  ⅓ cup ground flaxseed
  ⅓ cup apple juice
  ½ cup maple syrup
  1 teaspoon minced
      crystallized ginger
  1 cup dried apples,
      chopped
  ⅓ cup dried sweetened
      cranberries

1. Preheat the oven to 300°F. Coat a rimmed baking sheet with cooking spray. Combine the oats, walnuts, bran, and flaxseed in a large bowl.

2. Combine the juice, syrup, and ginger in a small saucepan. Cook over medium heat until the mixture simmers. Pour over the oats, stirring to coat.

3. Spread onto the prepared baking sheet. Bake for 25 to 35 minutes or until lightly browned, stirring twice. Place in a bowl and stir in the apples and cranberries.

NUTRITION PER SERVING

294 calories
7 g protein
43 g carbohydrates
12 g fat
1 g saturated fat
0 mg cholesterol
112 mg sodium
8 g fiber

{ Make It a **FLAT BELLY DIET MEAL** } Serve with 1 cup 1% milk (118).
TOTAL MEAL: 412 calories

Maple-Walnut Oatmeal

■ 5 HOURS ■ 4 SERVINGS (¾ CUP EACH) ■ 321 CALORIES ■ MUFA: WALNUTS

No need for added cream (and calories) with your oatmeal when you cook it in a slow cooker. The cereal takes on a very thick, smooth consistency. If you're short on time or prefer a more traditional approach, see the note below.

2 cups 1% milk
1 cup oatmeal
½ cup chopped dried pears or apples
3 tablespoons maple syrup
½ teaspoon salt
2 cups water
½ cup chopped walnuts, toasted

1. Combine the milk, oats, dried pears, syrup, salt, and water in a 2½- to 4-quart slow cooker. Cover and cook on low for 5 hours or overnight (or cook on high for 2 to 3 hours).

2. Toast the walnuts in a large nonstick skillet over medium heat, stirring often, for 3 to 4 minutes or until lightly browned and fragrant. Tip onto a plate and let cool.

3. Divide the oatmeal among 4 bowls and sprinkle with the walnuts.

Note: To cook on the stove top, combine the milk, oats, pears, maple syrup, and salt in a medium pot. Bring to a simmer and cook, stirring occasionally, for 5 minutes or until the oats are tender. Sprinkle with the walnuts.

NUTRITION
PER SERVING

321 calories
10 g protein
45 g carbohydrates
12 g fat
2 g saturated fat
6 mg cholesterol
481 mg sodium
4 g fiber

{ Make It a FLAT BELLY DIET MEAL } Serve with the Mom's Turkey Breakfast Sausage on page 82 (100). **TOTAL MEAL:** 421 calories

Mango Surprise Smoothie

■ **5 MINUTES** ■ **1 SERVING** ■ **268 CALORIES** ■ **MUFA: AVOCADO**

Avocado goes undercover and lends this breakfast drink a silky smoothness. Mango juice—loaded with cancer-fighting beta-carotene—can be found in most supermarkets.

¼ cup mango cubes
¼ cup mashed ripe avocado
½ cup mango juice
¼ cup fat-free vanilla yogurt
1 tablespoon freshly squeezed lime juice
1 tablespoon sugar
6 ice cubes

Combine the mango, avocado, mango juice, yogurt, lime juice, sugar, and ice cubes in a blender. Process until smooth. Pour into a tall glass. Garnish with sliced mango or strawberry, if desired, and serve.

NUTRITION PER SERVING

268 calories
5 g protein
53 g carbohydrates
6 g fat
1 g saturated fat
1 mg cholesterol
84 mg sodium
4 g fiber

{ **Make It a FLAT BELLY DIET MEAL** }
Serve with 2 slices reduced-sodium turkey bacon (140).
TOTAL MEAL: 408 calories ■ To serve as part of another *Flat Belly Diet* Meal, omit the avocado (210).

Blueberry Breakfast Sandwich

▨ 5 MINUTES ▨ 1 SERVING ▨ 360 CALORIES ▨ MUFA: PUMPKIN SEEDS

If you can't find Pepperidge Farm Breakfast Bread, choose any other type of bread that contains at least 3 grams of fiber and 90 calories per slice.

¼ cup fat-free Greek-style yogurt

2 tablespoons pumpkin seeds

1 teaspoon honey or maple syrup

2 slices whole grain bread with blueberries, toasted (we used Pepperidge Farm)

½ banana, thinly sliced

Combine the yogurt, pumpkin seeds, and syrup. Spread evenly over the toast. Top 1 slice with the banana and place the other slice, spread side down, on top. Cut in half before serving.

NUTRITION PER SERVING

360 calories
17 g protein
73 g carbohydrates
6 g fat
0 g saturated fat
0 mg cholesterol
340 mg sodium
8 g fiber

{ Make It a FLAT BELLY DIET MEAL } A single serving of this recipe counts as a *Flat Belly Diet* Meal without any add-ons!

Apple and Cashew Butter Sandwich

■ **5 MINUTES** ■ **1 SERVING** ■ **345 CALORIES** ■ **MUFA: CASHEW BUTTER**

If you haven't tried cashew butter, it's time to see what you've been missing. (You may not go back to plain old PB & J again!) Look for it next to the peanut butter. See the note below if you'd prefer to make your own.

1 whole wheat English
   muffin, toasted

2 tablespoons cashew
   butter

2 teaspoons orange
   marmalade

4 thin apple slices

Spread both sides of the muffin with the cashew butter and marmalade. Arrange the apple slices in the center and serve open-faced.

Note: To make cashew butter, place $\frac{1}{2}$ cup of unsalted roasted cashews in a food processor fitted with a metal blade or a blender. Process, scraping down the sides of the bowl as needed, until a paste forms. If a thinner butter is desired, add a few drops of canola oil and process to blend. Store leftover cashew butter in a tightly sealed container in the refrigerator. Makes $\frac{1}{2}$ cup.

NUTRITION PER SERVING

345 calories
12 g protein
50 g carbohydrates
14 g fat
2 g saturated fat
0 mg cholesterol
319 mg sodium
7 g fiber

{ Make It a
**FLAT
BELLY
DIET
MEAL** }
Serve with $\frac{1}{4}$ cup fat-free ricotta cheese (50) drizzled with 1 teaspoon honey (30).
TOTAL MEAL: 425 calories

Huevos Rancheros

30 MINUTES ▪ **4 SERVINGS** ▪ **331 CALORIES** ▪ **MUFA: AVOCADO**

A recent study found that eating eggs for breakfast at least 5 days a week can help you lose more weight—especially around your middle. Study participants also reported having more energy. Like your eggs spicy? Add a dash of hot-pepper sauce for more kick.

1 teaspoon ground cumin

1 can (15 ounces) no-salt-added pink beans, rinsed and drained

4 scallions, sliced

1 small red bell pepper, cut into thin strips

½ cup reduced-sodium chicken broth

2 cloves garlic, minced

4 eggs

1 cup sliced avocado

4 tablespoons fat-free Greek-style yogurt

4 tablespoons salsa

8 (6") corn tortillas, toasted
Dash of hot-pepper sauce (optional)

1. Heat a 10" nonstick skillet over medium-high heat. Add the cumin and cook, stirring occasionally, for about 30 seconds or until fragrant. Add the beans, scallions, bell pepper, broth, and garlic. Bring to a boil, then reduce the heat so the mixture simmers. Cook for 8 minutes or until the vegetables are tender and most of the broth is evaporated. With the back of a large silicone or wooden spoon, smash the beans until they are lumpy.

2. Use the back of the spoon to make 4 indentations in the beans. Working one at a time, break each egg into a custard cup and pour in each indentation. Cover and cook for about 8 minutes or until the eggs are cooked to the desired doneness.

3. Scoop each portion of egg-topped bean mixture onto a plate. Scatter the avocado slices over and around the beans. Top each serving with 1 tablespoon of the yogurt and 1 tablespoon of the salsa. Serve with the tortillas and hot-pepper sauce, if desired.

NUTRITION PER SERVING

331 calories
16 g protein
42 g carbohydrates
12 g fat
3 g saturated fat
213 mg cholesterol
245 mg sodium
10 g fiber

{ **Make It a FLAT BELLY DIET MEAL** } Serve with 1 cup reduced-sodium tomato juice (53). **TOTAL MEAL:** 384 calories

breakfast

Asparagus Frittata

■ **25 MINUTES** ■ **4 SERVINGS** ■ **218 CALORIES** ■ **MUFA: OLIVE OIL**

Just a hint of orange zest adds the perfect touch to this Italian spin on an asparagus omelet. Use a fruity olive oil if you have one.

¼ cup olive oil
½ pound asparagus, cut into 1" pieces
¼ onion, finely chopped
4 eggs
2 egg whites
2 tablespoons cold water
2 teaspoons freshly grated orange zest
¼ teaspoon salt
Freshly ground black pepper

1. Preheat the oven to 350°F. Heat a 10" nonstick ovenproof skillet over medium heat for 1 minute. Add the oil and heat for 30 seconds. Add the asparagus and onion. Cook, stirring, for about 2 minutes or until the asparagus is bright green.

2. Meanwhile, whisk the eggs, egg whites, water, orange zest, and salt. Pour into the pan and cook for 2 minutes or until starting to set on the bottom. Use a silicone spatula to lift up the set edges and allow the uncooked mixture to run underneath. Season well with the pepper.

3. Transfer to the oven and bake for 6 minutes. Use the spatula to lift the edge of the egg mixture, and tip the pan to allow any uncooked egg and oil to run underneath. Bake for about 6 minutes longer or until puffed and golden.

NUTRITION PER SERVING

218 calories
9 g protein
4 g carbohydrates
19 g fat
3 g saturated fat
212 mg cholesterol
245 mg sodium
1 g fiber

{ Make It a **FLAT BELLY DIET MEAL** }
Serve with 1 whole wheat English muffin (120) and 2 teaspoons trans-free margarine (56).
TOTAL MEAL: 394 calories

Ham and Avocado Omelet

■ 15 MINUTES ■ 2 SERVINGS ■ 313 CALORIES ■ MUFA: AVOCADO

If you can't find organic deli meats, look for products labeled nitrate-free. Boar's Head brand is one option.

3 eggs

3 egg whites

4 scallions, chopped

1/8 teaspoon hot-pepper sauce

1/2 cup shredded reduced-fat Cheddar cheese

2 ounces sliced lower-sodium natural ham, chopped

1/2 avocado, chopped

1. Coat a nonstick skillet with cooking spray and place over medium heat.

2. Whisk together the eggs, egg whites, scallions, and hot-pepper sauce in a medium bowl. Pour into the prepared skillet.

3. Cook for about 3 minutes or until the eggs are just set in the center, using a silicone spatula to lift up the set edges and allow the uncooked mixture to run underneath.

4. Scatter the cheese over half of the omelet. Cover and cook for 2 minutes or until just set.

5. Top half of the omelet with the ham and avocado. Carefully loosen the omelet with the spatula and fold in half.

6. Let rest for 1 minute or until the cheese melts. Cut in half to serve.

NUTRITION PER SERVING

313 calories
29 g protein
7 g carbohydrates
19 g fat
7 g saturated fat*
347 mg cholesterol
600 mg sodium
3 g fiber

*Limit saturated fat to 10% of total calories—about 17 grams per day for most women—and sodium intake to less than 2,300 milligrams.

{ Make It a **FLAT BELLY DIET MEAL** } Serve with 1 cup fresh pineapple slices (100).
TOTAL MEAL: 413 calories

Eggs Florentine with Sun-Dried Tomato Pesto

20 MINUTES ▪ 4 SERVINGS ▪ 175 CALORIES ▪ MUFA: PESTO

If you're a brunch fan, invite some friends over next weekend and impress them with this belly-busting creation. Don't worry if you've never poached an egg before—the dash of vinegar in the water helps the egg white hold its shape.

1 teaspoon olive oil
1 package (9 ounces) prewashed spinach
⅓ cup fat-free Greek-style yogurt
¼ cup sun-dried tomato pesto
1 teaspoon vinegar
Pinch of salt
4 large eggs
2 whole grain English muffins, split and toasted
Freshly ground black pepper

1. Heat the oil in a large nonstick skillet over medium-high heat. Add the spinach and cook (in batches, if necessary) until wilted.

2. Combine the yogurt and pesto. Stir ¼ cup into the spinach and remove from the heat. Cover to keep warm.

3. Meanwhile, heat a medium saucepan containing 1" of water to a boil over high heat. Add the vinegar and salt and reduce the heat to low. Break an egg into a custard cup and gently tip the egg into the water. Repeat with the remaining 3 eggs. Cover and simmer, shaking the pan 2 or 3 times, for 3 to 5 minutes for a soft-cooked yolk or until the whites are completely set and the yolks begin to thicken.

4. Place an English muffin half on each of 4 warm plates. Spoon ¼ of the spinach onto each muffin. Remove the eggs with a slotted spoon, and drain over paper towels (still in the spoon), before placing on the spinach.

5. Stir 1 tablespoon of the poaching liquid into the yogurt mixture to make it smoother. Spoon evenly over each egg and grind some pepper over the top.

NUTRITION PER SERVING

175 calories
12 g protein
21 g carbohydrates
6 g fat
2 g saturated fat
212 mg cholesterol
462 mg sodium
5 g fiber

{ Make It a FLAT BELLY DIET MEAL } Serve with the Mom's Turkey Breakfast Sausage on page 82 (100) and 1 pear, sliced (104).
TOTAL MEAL: 391 calories

Mom's Turkey Breakfast Sausage

■ **20 MINUTES** ■ **8 SERVINGS (ABOUT 2 PATTIES EACH)** ■ **100 CALORIES**

These tasty sausages don't boast beneficial amounts of MUFA ingredients, but they will help you control your sodium intake. Compared to prepared links that can have close to 400 milligrams of sodium per serving and almost 6 times the fat, these homemade sausages are a better nutritional value. Make up a batch on the weekend and reheat in the microwave during the week.

2 tablespoons maple syrup

1½ teaspoons freshly ground black pepper

1½ teaspoons ground sage

½ teaspoon salt

½ teaspoon onion powder

1¼ pounds extra lean ground turkey

2 teaspoons olive oil, divided

1. Combine the syrup, pepper, sage, salt, and onion powder in a large bowl and mix with a fork until smooth.

2. Add the turkey and mix gently until the seasonings are evenly distributed. Roll into small balls about 1" each.

3. Heat 1 teaspoon of the oil in a skillet over medium-high heat. Place half of the balls in the skillet. Cook for 2 to 3 minutes per side, flattening with a spatula when flipped, until cooked through. Add the remaining 1 teaspoon oil and repeat with the remaining patties.

Tip: Instead of rolling the balls, use a small cookie scoop to transfer the turkey mixture directly to the hot skillet.

NUTRITION PER SERVING

100 calories
18 g protein
4 g carbohydrates
2 g fat
0 g saturated fat
30 mg cholesterol
190 mg sodium
0 g fiber

{ Make It a **FLAT BELLY DIET MEAL** } Serve as part of a sandwich with 2 slices of toasted whole grain bread (150); 1 egg, scrambled (75); and ¼ cup avocado, mashed (96).

TOTAL MEAL: 421 calories

Easy Pancake Mix

■ **5 MINUTES** ■ **12 SERVINGS (⅓ CUP PER SERVING)** ■ **130 CALORIES**

If you like using store-bought, trans-free pancake mixes, by all means go ahead and add 2 table-spoons of nuts per serving to enjoy a *Flat Belly Diet* breakfast. But if you want to try something new, this handy make-ahead mix contains more fiber and can serve double duty for waffles (page 86) and fruit crepes (page 302).

1½ cups all-purpose flour

1½ cups whole wheat
    pastry flour

 6 tablespoons yellow
    cornmeal

 6 tablespoons sugar

 1 tablespoon baking
    powder

 1 teaspoon baking soda

½ teaspoon salt

Combine the all-purpose flour, pastry flour, cornmeal, sugar, baking powder, baking soda, and salt in a bowl and mix well. Store in a cool, dry place.

**NUTRITION
PER SERVING**

130 calories
3 g protein
29 g carbohydrates
0.5 g fat
0 g saturated fat
0 mg cholesterol
303 mg sodium
2 g fiber

Banana Pancakes with Walnut Honey

■ 20 MINUTES ■ 4 SERVINGS (3 PANCAKES EACH) ■ 425 CALORIES ■ MUFA: WALNUTS

Who needs syrup? Honey and walnuts make the perfect sweet and crunchy topping for these sensational pancakes.

PANCAKES

1⅓ cups Easy Pancake Mix (page 83)
¼ teaspoon ground cinnamon
1 cup low-fat buttermilk
¼ cup water
1 egg
1 tablespoon canola oil
1 teaspoon vanilla extract
1 large banana, halved lengthwise and cut into thin slices
½ cup fresh raspberries

WALNUT HONEY

½ cup walnuts, chopped
⅓ cup honey
1 tablespoon water

1. To prepare the pancakes: Combine the pancake mix and cinnamon in a large bowl. Combine the buttermilk, water, egg, oil, and vanilla extract in a separate bowl. Whisk into the pancake mix and stir until smooth. Fold in the banana. Set aside.

2. To prepare the walnut honey: Combine the walnuts, honey, and water in a small bowl.

3. Coat a large nonstick skillet with cooking spray and set over medium heat. Add the pancake batter in scant ¼ cupfuls and cook, in batches, for about 2 minutes or until the pancakes have puffed and the undersides are lightly browned. Turn the pancakes and cook for about 2 minutes longer or until lightly browned. Serve with the walnut honey and raspberries.

NUTRITION PER SERVING

425 calories
10 g protein
67 g carbohydrates
15 g fat
2 g saturated fat
55 mg cholesterol
387 mg sodium
5 g fiber

{ Make It a FLAT BELLY DIET MEAL } A single serving of this recipe counts as a *Flat Belly Diet* Meal without any add-ons!

breakfast

Cinnamon-Pecan Waffles

■ **25 MINUTES** ■ **4 SERVINGS (1 WAFFLE PER SERVING)** ■ **395 CALORIES** ■ **MUFA: PECANS**

Belgian waffles are the ultimate breakfast treat. But loaded with MUFA-rich pecans and fresh fruit, they're *Flat Belly Diet*–friendly, which makes them even better.

1⅓ cups Easy Pancake Mix (page 83)

¾ teaspoon ground cinnamon

½ cup pecans, finely chopped

1¼ cups low-fat buttermilk

1 tablespoon canola oil

2 eggs

1 teaspoon vanilla extract

2 cups strawberries, stemmed and sliced

1 large banana, sliced

1 teaspoon sugar

1. Combine the pancake mix, cinnamon, and pecans in a large bowl. Combine the buttermilk, oil, eggs, and vanilla extract in a separate bowl. Whisk into the pancake mix and stir until smooth. Set aside.

2. Toss the strawberries and banana with the sugar in a medium bowl. Set aside.

3. Preheat a Belgian waffle maker coated with cooking spray. Pour a generous ½ cup batter per waffle onto the waffle maker and cook per the manufacturer's directions. Repeat with the remaining batter. Arrange the waffles on 4 serving plates and top each with an equal amount of the fruit mixture.

NUTRITION PER SERVING

395 calories
11 g protein
50 g carbohydrates
18 g fat
2 g saturated fat
109 mg cholesterol
420 mg sodium
6 g fiber

Make It a FLAT BELLY DIET MEAL

A single serving of this recipe counts as a *Flat Belly Diet* Meal without any add-ons!

Peanut Butter–Stuffed French Toast

■ **40 MINUTES** ■ **4 SERVINGS** ■ **418 CALORIES** ■ **MUFA: PEANUT BUTTER**

What's not to love about French toast? This delightful version, inspired by a classic PB&J combination, is the ultimate decadence for peanut butter lovers everywhere. (Try it another morning with cashew butter—you'll swoon.)

¼ cup maple syrup

2 cups sliced strawberries

½ cup creamy natural
  unsalted peanut butter

8 slices light whole wheat
  bread

3 eggs

2 tablespoons 1% milk

1 teaspoon vanilla extract

1. Preheat the oven to 350°F. Coat a baking sheet with butter-flavored cooking spray.

2. Place the syrup in a medium glass bowl and microwave on high for 30 seconds or until simmering. Add the strawberries and set aside.

3. Spread 2 tablespoons of the peanut butter on each of 4 bread slices and cover with the remaining 4 slices, making sandwiches.

4. Beat the eggs, milk, and vanilla extract in a 13″ × 9″ baking dish. Soak the sandwiches in the egg mixture, turning once. Place on the prepared baking sheet.

5. Bake for 25 minutes or until browned, turning once. Top with the reserved strawberry mixture.

NUTRITION PER SERVING

418 calories
17 g protein
46 g carbohydrates
21 g fat
3 g saturated fat*
159 mg cholesterol
299 mg sodium
11 g fiber

*Limit saturated fat to 10% of total calories—about 17 grams per day for most women—and sodium intake to less than 2,300 milligrams.

{ Make It a
FLAT
BELLY
DIET
MEAL }
A single serving of this recipe counts as a *Flat Belly Diet* Meal without any add-ons!

Cranberry-Pecan Scones

■ **40 MINUTES** ■ **8 SCONES** ■ **308 CALORIES** ■ **MUFA: PECANS**

Whip up a batch of these nutty, fruity scones on the weekend and wrap the leftovers individually in plastic wrap before storing in the freezer. Pull one out to thaw before you head to bed and you'll have the perfect grab-and-go breakfast.

2 cups whole wheat pastry flour
1 cup pecans, chopped
2 teaspoons baking powder
½ teaspoon baking soda
½ teaspoon salt
1¼ cups low-fat vanilla yogurt
2 tablespoons canola oil
1 teaspoon freshly grated orange zest
⅔ cup dried sweetened cranberries

1. Preheat the oven to 400°F. Lightly coat a 9" round baking pan with cooking spray.

2. Whisk together the flour, pecans, baking powder, baking soda, and salt in a large bowl.

3. Whisk together the yogurt, oil, and orange zest in a small bowl.

4. Make a well in the center of the flour mixture and add the yogurt mixture and cranberries. Stir just until blended.

5. Press into the prepared pan. Score the dough with a knife to form 8 triangles. Bake for 20 to 25 minutes or until lightly browned and a wooden toothpick inserted in the center comes out clean.

NUTRITION PER SERVING

308 calories
6 g protein
38 g carbohydrates
15 g fat
1.5 g saturated fat
2 mg cholesterol
350 mg sodium
5 g fiber

{ Make It a **FLAT BELLY DIET MEAL** }

Serve with 1 cup fat-free milk (80).
TOTAL MEAL: 388 calories

Pumpkin-Raisin Muffins

■ 40 MINUTES   ■ 12 SERVINGS   ■ 274 CALORIES   ■ MUFA: PUMPKIN SEEDS

Layers of pumpkin seeds, both within the muffins and toasted on top, lend an especially pleasant crunch to these amazing breakfast treats.

1½ cups pumpkin seeds,
   divided
¼ cup raisins
 1 cup whole wheat
   pastry flour
¾ cup all-purpose flour
1½ teaspoons baking powder
½ teaspoon baking soda
¾ teaspoon ground
   cinnamon
½ teaspoon salt
¾ cup canned pumpkin
   puree
¼ cup maple syrup
 2 eggs
¼ cup canola oil

1. Preheat the oven to 375°F. Coat 12 (2½") muffin cups with cooking spray.

2. Place ½ cup of the pumpkin seeds in the bowl of a food processor fitted with a metal blade or in a blender. Process until ground into powder. Add the raisins. Pulse several times until the raisins are chopped. Transfer to a large bowl.

3. Add the pastry flour, all-purpose flour, baking powder, baking soda, cinnamon, and salt. Mix with a fork. In another bowl, combine the pumpkin puree, syrup, eggs, and oil. Beat with a fork until smooth.

4. Add the pumpkin mixture to the dry ingredients and stir just until blended. Stir in ¾ cup of the pumpkin seeds. Divide the batter among the prepared muffin cups and scatter the remaining ¼ cup seeds on top. Press lightly to adhere.

5. Bake for 20 minutes or until the muffins spring back when pressed with a finger.

6. Set on a rack to cool for 5 minutes. Serve warm.

NUTRITION PER SERVING

274 calories
8 g protein
24 g carbohydrates
16 g fat
2 g saturated fat
35 mg cholesterol
216 mg sodium
2 g fiber

{ Make It a FLAT BELLY DIET MEAL } Serve with 2 eggs scrambled in a nonstick pan coated with cooking spray (150). **TOTAL MEAL:** 424 calories

Nutty Quick Bread

45 MINUTES + COOLING TIME ■ **12 SERVINGS** ■ **340 CALORIES** ■ **MUFA: WALNUTS**

Loaded with walnuts and just a hint of chocolate, this quick bread is destined to become a family favorite. Make sure to cool completely before slicing.

1 cup whole wheat
   pastry flour
1 cup unbleached
   white flour
2 teaspoons baking powder
½ teaspoon baking soda
1½ teaspoons ground
   cinnamon
¼ teaspoon salt
2 eggs
½ cup packed dark brown
   sugar
½ cup canola oil
1 cup fat-free plain yogurt
1 teaspoon vanilla extract
1½ cups chopped walnuts,
   toasted, divided
½ cup mini chocolate chips

1. Preheat the oven to 375°F. Coat a 9" × 5" loaf pan with cooking spray. Line the pan with wax paper and spray the paper.

2. Combine the pastry flour, white flour, baking powder, baking soda, cinnamon, and salt in a large bowl. Whisk the eggs, brown sugar, and oil in a medium bowl until well blended and free of lumps. Stir in the yogurt, vanilla extract, 1¼ cups of the walnuts, and the chocolate chips.

3. Pour the wet ingredients over the dry and stir to mix. Pour into the prepared pan. Top with the remaining ¼ cup walnuts. Bake for 30 to 35 minutes or until lightly browned, springy to the touch, and a wooden toothpick inserted into the center comes out clean.

4. Transfer to a rack and cool for 30 minutes. Turn out of the pan onto the rack, peel off the wax paper, and let cool completely.

NUTRITION PER SERVING

340 calories
6 g protein
32 g carbohydrates
22 g fat
3 g saturated fat
35 mg cholesterol
200 mg sodium
3 g fiber

{ Make It a **FLAT BELLY DIET MEAL** } Serve with ¼ cup fat-free ricotta cheese (50) and 1 tablespoon apple butter (29).
TOTAL MEAL: 419 calories

5

Soups & Sandwiches

Old-Fashioned Peanut Soup

1 HOUR ■ **4 SERVINGS (1¼ CUPS EACH)** ■ **300 CALORIES** ■ **MUFA: PEANUT BUTTER**

A Southern classic, this rich and creamy vegetarian soup is surprisingly satisfying. The peanut butter melts into the broth, creating a bisquelike consistency, without the cream.

1 tablespoon canola oil
1 onion, chopped
2 ribs celery, chopped
2 carrots, chopped
1 clove garlic, minced
3 cups reduced-sodium vegetable broth, divided
½ cup creamy natural unsalted peanut butter
2 tablespoons freshly squeezed lemon juice
2 tablespoons chopped unsalted peanuts

1. Heat the oil in a large pot or Dutch oven over medium-high heat. Add the onion, celery, and carrots. Cook, stirring occasionally, for 5 minutes or until the onion softens.

2. Add the garlic and 2 cups of the broth. Reduce the heat to low, cover, and simmer for 30 minutes or until the vegetables are very tender.

3. Transfer the soup to a food processor fitted with a metal blade or a blender (in batches, if necessary). Process until smooth.

4. Return the soup to the pot and stir in the peanut butter, lemon juice, and remaining 1 cup broth. Cook for 5 minutes or until the peanut butter melts and the flavors blend.

5. Ladle into 4 bowls and sprinkle with the chopped nuts.

NUTRITION PER SERVING

300 calories
9 g protein
18 g carbohydrates
22 g fat
3 g saturated fat
0 mg cholesterol
156 mg sodium
5 g fiber

{ Make It a **FLAT BELLY DIET MEAL** }
Serve with a baked sweet potato (103) and ½ cup cooked greens (25).
TOTAL MEAL: 428 calories

Pumpkin Bisque

■ **40 MINUTES** ■ **4 SERVINGS (2 CUPS EACH)** ■ **210 CALORIES** ■ **MUFA: PUMPKIN SEEDS**

This elegant soup packs almost half a day's worth of fiber into 1 serving. A finishing drizzle of balsamic vinegar lends the perfect touch.

2 teaspoons olive oil

2 onions, chopped

1 large red bell pepper, chopped

1 potato, peeled and diced

1 tablespoon minced garlic

1 tablespoon oregano

4 cups reduced-sodium vegetable broth

1 can (15 ounces) pumpkin

½ teaspoon salt

½ teaspoon freshly ground black pepper

½ cup chopped roasted unsalted pumpkin seeds

2 teaspoons balsamic vinegar

1. Heat the oil in a large pot or Dutch oven over medium-high heat. Add the onions, bell pepper, potato, garlic, and oregano. Cook, stirring occasionally, for 5 minutes or until the onion is softened. Add the broth, pumpkin, salt, and pepper. Simmer for 10 minutes or until the potato is very tender.

2. Transfer the soup to a food processor fitted with a metal blade or a blender (in batches, if necessary). Process until smooth.

3. Return the soup to the pot. If necessary, add water to thin to desired consistency. Reheat if needed.

4. Ladle into 4 bowls and top each with 2 tablespoons of pumpkin seeds. Drizzle lightly with the balsamic vinegar.

NUTRITION PER SERVING

210 calories
6 g protein
36 g carbohydrates
5 g fat
1 g saturated fat
0 mg cholesterol
451 mg sodium
10 g fiber

{ Make It a **FLAT BELLY DIET MEAL** } Serve with the Chicken Piccata on page 196, but use only 1 tablespoon oil (210). **TOTAL MEAL:** 420 calories ■ To serve as part of another *Flat Belly Diet* Meal, omit the pumpkin seeds (170).

Curried Apple and Pear Soup

■ **45 MINUTES** ■ **4 SERVINGS (1½ CUPS EACH)** ■ **226 CALORIES** ■ **MUFA: ALMONDS**

Almonds provide a pleasant crunch to an otherwise velvety soup, while calcium-rich yogurt balances the delicate heat of the curry powder.

2 tablespoons olive oil
1 large onion, chopped
2 medium carrots, chopped
1 rib celery, chopped
2 teaspoons sugar
2 teaspoons mild or
   hot curry powder
½ teaspoon ground cumin
½ teaspoon salt
2 pears, peeled, cored, and
   coarsely chopped
2 Granny Smith apples,
   peeled, cored, and
   coarsely chopped
2 cups low-sodium
   vegetable broth
2 cups water
½ cup fat-free Greek-style
   yogurt
½ cup sliced almonds,
   toasted

1. Heat the oil in a large pot or Dutch oven over medium heat. Add the onion, carrots, and celery and sprinkle with the sugar. Cook, stirring often, for 8 to 10 minutes or until tender and the onion is lightly golden and caramelized.

2. Add the curry powder, cumin, and salt. Cook and stir for 30 seconds or until fragrant.

3. Add the pears and apples and stir to coat. Add the broth and water, cover, and bring to a boil. Reduce the heat to low and simmer for 15 minutes or until the fruit is very tender.

4. Transfer the soup to a food processor fitted with a metal blade or a blender (in batches, if necessary). Process until smooth.

5. Return the soup to the pot and warm through.

6. Ladle into 4 bowls and top each with 2 tablespoons of the yogurt and 2 tablespoons of the almonds.

NUTRITION
PER SERVING

226 calories
6 g protein
23 g carbohydrates
13 g fat
1 g saturated fat
0 mg cholesterol
411 mg sodium
5 g fiber

{ **Make It a FLAT BELLY DIET MEAL** } Serve with the Spinach Steak Roulade on page 246, but omit the pine nuts (206). **TOTAL MEAL:** 432 calories ■ To serve as part of another *Flat Belly Diet* Meal, omit the almonds (155).

soups & sandwiches

Smoky Tomato Soup

■ 1 HOUR 15 MINUTES ■ 4 SERVINGS (1¼ CUPS EACH) ■ 180 CALORIES ■ MUFA: AVOCADO

Layered with three distinct smoky flavors, this updated version of a classic tomato soup will draw rave reviews. If you enjoy spicy food, turn up the heat with a little extra chipotle chili powder (easy to find in the spice section of the supermarket). The yogurt and avocado will help tame the flames.

1 can (28 ounces)
   fire-roasted tomatoes
½ sweet onion, sliced
1 cup reduced-sodium
   vegetable broth
1 cup water
1 tablespoon smoked
   paprika
¼ teaspoon chipotle chili
   powder
1 cup buttermilk
¼ cup fat-free Greek-style
   yogurt
1 avocado, sliced

1. Preheat the oven to 350°F.

2. Pour the tomatoes (with juice) into an 11" × 17" baking dish. Scatter the onions on top and bake for 1 hour or until the mixture is thick and the onions begin to brown.

3. Transfer the mixture to a blender. Add the broth, water, paprika, and chili powder and puree until smooth.

4. Heat the soup mixture in a pot over medium-low heat for 5 minutes or until heated through. Add the buttermilk and stir to combine.

5. Ladle into 4 soup bowls and garnish each with 1 tablespoon of the yogurt and the avocado slices.

NUTRITION
PER SERVING

180 calories
6 g protein
22 g carbohydrates
7 g fat
1.5 g saturated fat
0 mg cholesterol
550 mg sodium
6 g fiber

{ Make It a FLAT BELLY DIET MEAL } Serve with a grilled cheese sandwich made from 2 slices of whole grain bread (150) and a slice of reduced-fat provolone (77). **TOTAL MEAL:** 407 calories ■ To serve as part of another *Flat Belly Diet* Meal, omit the avocado (100).

Creamy Broccoli Soup

35 MINUTES ▪ **4 SERVINGS (1½ CUPS EACH)** ▪ **200 CALORIES** ▪ **MUFA: OLIVE OIL**

This garden-fresh soup owes its velvety texture to a flour-and-oil combination added at the end of the cooking process—no dairy here! Don't pass it up—broccoli is one of the most powerful cancer-fighting foods you can eat.

¼ cup olive oil, divided
1 onion, chopped
4 cups low-sodium
   vegetable broth
1 pound broccoli crowns,
   chopped
2 cups fresh spinach
3 tablespoons all-purpose
   flour
½ teaspoon salt
¼ teaspoon freshly
   grated nutmeg
   Freshly ground black
   pepper

1. Heat 1 tablespoon of the oil in a large pot over medium-high heat. Add the onion and cook, stirring occasionally, for 8 minutes or until golden brown.

2. Add the broth and broccoli. Cover, reduce the heat to low, and simmer for 15 minutes or until the broccoli is tender. Turn off the heat, add the spinach, and stir until the spinach is wilted. Transfer the mixture to a blender or leave it in the pot if using an immersion blender. Puree until smooth.

3. Meanwhile, heat the remaining 3 tablespoons oil in a small pan over medium heat. Add the flour and stir until smooth. Cook, stirring occasionally, for 2 to 3 minutes or until light brown. Set aside.

4. Heat the soup in a pot over medium-high heat just until it begins to boil. Reduce the heat to low to maintain a simmer. Add the reserved flour mixture and stir until the soup thickens.

5. Add the salt, nutmeg, and pepper to taste.

NUTRITION PER SERVING

200 calories
6 g protein
17 g carbohydrates
14 g fat
2 g saturated fat
0 mg cholesterol
480 mg sodium
6 g fiber

{ Make It a **FLAT BELLY DIET MEAL** } Serve with the Layered Nut-and-Cheese Spread on page 257, but omit the almonds (90), and 4 whole wheat crackers (80).
TOTAL MEAL: 412 calories

Beefy Onion Soup

■ 1 HOUR 20 MINUTES ■ 4 SERVINGS (ABOUT 1¼ CUPS EACH) ■ 310 CALORIES ■ MUFA: SAFFLOWER OIL

Every bit as tantalizing as a classic French onion soup, this updated version lowers the sodium considerably by offering tender strips of succulent beef tenderloin in place of cheese.

4 tablespoons safflower oil, divided
8 ounces beef tenderloin, trimmed
3 large onions, thinly sliced
2 teaspoons sugar
2 cloves garlic, minced
2 tablespoons balsamic vinegar
4 cups reduced-sodium beef broth
1 teaspoon Worcestershire sauce
½ cup fresh whole wheat bread crumbs (see note)
Chives (optional)

1. Heat 1 tablespoon of the oil in a large pot over medium-high heat. Add the beef and cook for about 2 to 3 minutes per side for medium rare. Transfer to a cutting board and let stand for 5 minutes. Slice across the grain into thin strips.

2. Add the remaining 3 tablespoons oil to the pot and reduce the heat to medium. Add the onions and sugar and cook, stirring occasionally, for 24 to 25 minutes or until golden.

3. Add the garlic and cook for 2 minutes.

4. Increase heat to medium-high, pour in the vinegar, and bring to a boil. Cook, stirring constantly, for about 1 minute or until the vinegar is almost completely evaporated.

5. Add the broth and Worcestershire sauce. Bring to a boil, reduce to a simmer, and cook, covered, for 15 minutes.

6. Stir in the bread crumbs and cook for 2 to 3 minutes or until slightly thickened.

7. Ladle the soup into 4 bowls. Garnish each with the reserved beef slices and chives, if desired.

Note: To make your own whole wheat bread crumbs, whirl day-old bread in the food processor. One slice makes ½ cup.

NUTRITION
PER SERVING

310 calories
18 g protein
20 g carbohydrates
18 g fat
2 g saturated fat
33 mg cholesterol
528 mg sodium
2 g fiber

{ Make It a FLAT BELLY DIET MEAL }

Serve with 1 slice whole grain French bread, toasted and rubbed with garlic (90).

TOTAL MEAL: 400 calories

Squash Soup with Pecans and Greens

50 MINUTES ▦ **4 SERVINGS (1½ CUPS EACH)** ▦ **187 CALORIES** ▦ **MUFA: PECANS**

Squash and greens are a natural pairing, but the addition of toasted pecans raises this delicious soup to new levels. Any winter squash can be substituted for the butternut squash called for here.

1 butternut squash
    (about 2 pounds)
2 tablespoons water
1 teaspoon canola oil
1 small onion, chopped
3 cloves garlic, minced
1 tablespoon freshly
    grated ginger
½ teaspoon salt
2 cups coarsely chopped
    collard greens
4 cups reduced-sodium
    vegetable broth
½ cup chopped pecans,
    toasted
    Hot-pepper sauce
    (optional)

1. Cut the squash in half lengthwise. Scoop out and discard the seeds and pulp. Pierce the squash several times all over with a small sharp knife. Arrange on a microwave-safe dish and sprinkle with the water. Cover with plastic wrap and microwave, rotating often, for about 10 minutes or until the squash yields slightly when pressed. Remove and cover with foil.

2. Peel the squash when cool enough to handle and cut the flesh into 1" chunks.

3. Heat the oil in a large pot or Dutch oven over medium-high heat. Add the onion, garlic, ginger, and salt. Stir. Cover and cook, stirring frequently, for about 3 minutes or until softened.

4. Add the greens, broth, and squash. Bring almost to a boil, then reduce the heat so the mixture simmers. Simmer for 10 minutes or until the squash is tender. If desired, smash some pieces of the squash against the side of the pot to thicken the broth.

5. Ladle into 4 bowls and top each with 2 tablespoons of pecans. Pass hot-pepper sauce, if using, at the table.

NUTRITION PER SERVING

187 calories
3 g protein
20 g carbohydrates
12 g fat
1 g saturated fat
0 mg cholesterol
439 mg sodium
6 g fiber

{ **Make It a FLAT BELLY DIET MEAL** } Serve with 3 ounces roasted center-cut pork loin (199).
TOTAL MEAL: 386 calories ▦ To serve as part of another *Flat Belly Diet* Meal, omit the pecans (80).

Tuscan Bean Soup with Bitter Greens

3 HOURS + SOAKING TIME ▪ **8 SERVINGS (1 CUP EACH)** ▪ **290 CALORIES** ▪ **MUFA: OLIVE OIL**

Pull out your slow cooker and let this delicious soup come together while you attend to other things. Just before serving, use your favorite olive oil to add a luxurious MUFA twist to this wholesome soup.

1½ cups dry great Northern beans

7 cups cold water, divided

1 can (14½ ounces) diced tomatoes with roasted garlic

2 cans (14½ ounces each) reduced-sodium chicken broth

1 large onion, chopped

4 carrots, chopped

1 tablespoon chopped dried rosemary

½ pound escarole, coarsely chopped

½ teaspoon salt

½ cup grated Romano cheese

½ cup extra virgin olive oil

1. Rinse the beans, place in a large bowl, and cover with 4 cups of the water. Soak overnight.

2. Drain the beans and rinse. Place in a 3- to 6-quart slow cooker with the tomatoes, broth, onion, carrots, rosemary, and remaining 3 cups water.

3. Cover and cook on high for 2 to 3 hours, or until the beans are tender. Add the escarole and salt during the last 15 minutes of cooking. Stir in the cheese.

4. Ladle into 8 bowls and drizzle each with 1 tablespoon of the oil.

NUTRITION PER SERVING

290 calories
11 g protein
24 g carbohydrates
17 g fat
4 g saturated fat*
5 mg cholesterol
440 mg sodium
8 g fiber

*Limit saturated fat to 10% of total calories—about 17 grams per day for most women—and sodium intake to less than 2,300 milligrams.

{ **Make It a FLAT BELLY DIET MEAL** } Serve with 2 ounces lean Italian turkey sausage (95).
TOTAL MEAL: 401 calories ▪ To serve as part of another *Flat Belly Diet* Meal, omit the olive oil (180).

Thai Corn and Crab Soup

■ **30 MINUTES** ■ **4 SERVINGS (1¾ CUPS EACH)** ■ **355 CALORIES** ■ **MUFA: CANOLA OIL**

Fish sauce, a popular ingredient in Thai cooking, adds savory, salty, and sour notes to this lusty soup. Its strong flavor is so assertive, you only need to use a little, which helps keep the sodium count down. Look for it next to the soy sauce in the international section of your grocery store. If you can't find it, there isn't really an appropriate substitute, unfortunately.

1 bag (16 ounces) frozen corn kernels, thawed

3 cups reduced-sodium vegetable broth, divided

¼ cup canola oil

1 red bell pepper, cut into very thin strips

1 small jalapeño chile pepper, seeded and finely chopped

8 scallions, sliced

1 tablespoon reduced-sodium fish sauce

¾ pound fresh crabmeat, picked over to remove any cartilage or shells

¼ cup chopped fresh cilantro

¼ teaspoon ground red pepper (optional)

1. Place 1½ cups of the corn and 1½ cups of the broth in a food processor fitted with a metal blade or a blender. Process until smooth. Set aside.

2. Heat the oil in a large pot or Dutch oven over medium-high heat. Add the bell pepper and chile pepper and cook, stirring occasionally, for 3 minutes. Add the scallions and cook for 3 minutes or until the vegetables are tender.

3. Add the fish sauce, reserved corn-broth mixture, remaining corn kernels, and remaining 1½ cups broth. Bring to a simmer and reduce the heat. Cover and cook for 10 minutes or until thickened.

4. Stir in the crab, cilantro, and red pepper, if using. Serve immediately.

NUTRITION PER SERVING

355 calories
24 g protein
30 g carbohydrates
16 g fat
1 g saturated fat
90 mg cholesterol
657 mg sodium*
5 g fiber

*Limit saturated fat to 10% of total calories—about 17 grams per day for most women—and sodium intake to less than 2,300 milligrams.

{ Make It a **FLAT BELLY DIET MEAL** } Serve with ¼ cup shelled edamame (50). **TOTAL MEAL:** 405 calories ■ To serve as part of another *Flat Belly Diet* Meal, prepare with 1 tablespoon oil and reduce the serving size to ¾ cup (134).

Chicken-Barley Soup with Vegetables and Pesto

1 HOUR 15 MINUTES ▨ **6 SERVINGS (1¾ CUPS EACH)** ▨ **260 CALORIES** ▨ **MUFA: PESTO**

For best results, make sure all of the chopped vegetables are about the same size. Your antioxidant-packed soup will cook more evenly, and the flavor will be more balanced.

4 cups low-sodium chicken broth

2 cups water

½ cup pearled barley

12 ounces boneless, skinless chicken breast halves

1 can (14½ ounces) no-salt-added stewed tomatoes

1 large leek (white and tender portion of green), halved lengthwise, rinsed well, and cut into ½" slices

1 large onion, chopped

2 large carrots, chopped

2 ribs celery, chopped

½ cup frozen corn kernels

6 tablespoons Pesto (page 122) or store-bought pesto

1. Bring the broth and water to a boil in a large pot or Dutch oven over high heat. Add the barley and chicken, reduce the heat to low, cover, and cook for about 30 minutes or until the barley is tender, stirring several times. Remove the chicken to a cutting board. Shred when cool enough to handle. Set aside.

2. Add the tomatoes (with juice), leek, onion, carrots, and celery and raise the heat to high. Reduce the heat to low when the mixture comes to a boil, cover, and simmer for 20 minutes or until the vegetables are tender.

3. Add the corn and reserved chicken. Simmer, uncovered, for 5 minutes or until warmed through.

4. Ladle into 6 bowls and top each with 1 tablespoon of the pesto.

NUTRITION PER SERVING

260 calories
21 g protein
31 g carbohydrates
7 g fat
2 g saturated fat
35 mg cholesterol
250 mg sodium
6 g fiber

{ Make It a FLAT BELLY DIET MEAL } Serve with ½ White Pita Pizza on page 276 (129).
TOTAL MEAL: 389 calories ▨ To serve as part of another *Flat Belly Diet* Meal, omit the pesto (210).

Chicken Avocado Sandwich

■ 10 MINUTES ■ 1 SERVING ■ 260 CALORIES ■ MUFA: AVOCADO

This is a super-quick sandwich to put together after a long day at work because it can be made with leftover chicken. An ounce of chicken is about the size of a shot glass.

1 teaspoon canola oil

2 corn tortillas
(6" diameter)

¼ avocado, sliced

1 ounce thinly sliced
cooked skinless
chicken breast

1 leaf lettuce, cut
into shreds

2 teaspoons store-bought
salsa

2 teaspoons minced
fresh cilantro

1. Heat the oil in a nonstick skillet over medium-high heat. Cook the tortillas for about 1 minute on each side or until lightly browned (they will become crisp as they cool).

2. Transfer the tortillas to a work surface. Place the avocado on 1 tortilla. Top with the chicken, lettuce, salsa, cilantro, and remaining tortilla. With a serrated knife, cut into 2 half-moons.

**NUTRITION
PER SERVING**

260 calories
13 g protein
27 g carbohydrates
13 g fat
2 g saturated fat
25 mg cholesterol
112 mg sodium
6 g fiber

{ Make It a
FLAT
BELLY
DIET
MEAL }
Serve with the Smoky Tomato Soup, page 98, but omit the avocado (100).
TOTAL MEAL: 360 calories

Olive Bread

■ **50 MINUTES + RISING TIME** ■ **9 SERVINGS** ■ **290 CALORIES** ■ **MUFA: OLIVES**

Cutting slits in this loaf before baking is hardly just for decoration—it's an essential step so that steam escapes properly and bubbles don't ruin the shape of the loaf. Make sure to cut all the way through the top layer for best results.

1 loaf (1 pound) frozen whole wheat bread dough
2 teaspoons olive oil
1 onion, chopped
2 cloves garlic, minced
90 Niçoise olives, pitted and coarsely chopped (about 3 cups)
1/2 teaspoon red-pepper flakes (optional)
1 egg
1 tablespoon water
1 cup shredded reduced-fat mozzarella cheese

1. Thaw the dough per the package directions. Let rise until doubled.

2. Preheat the oven to 350°F. Coat a baking sheet with cooking spray.

3. Heat the olive oil in a large skillet over medium-high heat. Cook the onion and garlic for 4 minutes or until tender. Remove from the heat and stir in the olives and red-pepper flakes, if desired.

4. Whisk together the egg and water in a small bowl. Set aside.

5. On a lightly floured surface, roll the dough into a 14" × 10" rectangle. Spread the olive mixture to within 1/2" of the short edges and 1" of the long edges. Sprinkle with the cheese.

6. Roll up jelly-roll style, starting with a long side. Pinch the seam to seal and arrange seam side down on the prepared baking sheet. Tuck the ends under the loaf.

7. Brush the top with the egg wash and make 8 evenly spaced slits into the top layer of bread.

8. Bake for 25 to 30 minutes or until golden brown. Cool for 5 minutes on the pan. Remove to a rack. Let stand for at least 10 minutes. Cut along the slits to make 9 slices.

NUTRITION PER SERVING

290 calories
11 g protein
30 g carbohydrates
15 g fat
3 g saturated fat
30 mg cholesterol
991 mg sodium*
3 g fiber

*Limit saturated fat to 10% of total calories—about 17 grams per day for most women—and sodium intake to less than 2,300 milligrams.

{ Make It a **FLAT BELLY DIET MEAL** } Serve with the Summer Salad with Green Goddess Dressing, page 120 (145).

TOTAL MEAL: 435 calories

Tapenade and Tomato Wrap

■ 5 MINUTES ■ 1 SERVING ■ 189 CALORIES ■ MUFA: TAPENADE

Creamy ricotta cheese sets the stage for the complementary flavors of tapenade and tomato in this quick and easy wrap.

1 whole grain tortilla
(8″ diameter)

2 tablespoons part-skim
ricotta cheese

1 tablespoon Tapenade
(page 181) or store-
bought tapenade

¼ teaspoon dried oregano

1 small tomato, thinly sliced

¼ cup slivered baby spinach
leaves

1. Warm the tortilla in a dry skillet over medium-high heat for about 1 minute (it should still be flexible enough to roll).

2. Transfer the tortilla to a work surface. Spread with the ricotta and swirl with the tapenade. Sprinkle with the oregano. Arrange the tomato slices evenly and top with the spinach.

3. Fold the right and left sides of the tortilla so that they cover the very edges of the filling, then fold the bottom over and roll up burrito-style.

NUTRITION PER SERVING

189 calories
7 g protein
25 g carbohydrates
7 g fat
2 g saturated fat
10 mg cholesterol
386 mg sodium
5 g fiber

{ Make It a
FLAT
BELLY
DIET
MEAL }
Serve with 1 cup red or green grapes (60) and 1 cup sliced mango (110).
TOTAL MEAL: 359 calories

Spicy Olive and Turkey Pita Sandwich

■ **10 MINUTES** ■ **2 SERVINGS** ■ **242 CALORIES** ■ **MUFA: OLIVES**

Taste how an ordinary turkey sandwich becomes instantly extraordinary with a hearty topping of spicy olive salad. When using olives, it's important to watch the sodium content of your other ingredients. Boar's Head and Applegate Farms are two good sources for lower-sodium turkey breast.

10 pitted green pimiento-stuffed olives, chopped

10 pitted black olives, chopped

1 teaspoon balsamic vinegar

1 teaspoon extra virgin olive oil

1/8 teaspoon red-pepper flakes

1 whole wheat (6" diameter) pita, halved crosswise

4 ounces deli-sliced lower-sodium turkey breast

1/2 cup mixed greens

1. Combine the green and black olives, vinegar, oil, and red-pepper flakes in a small bowl.

2. Fill each pita half with 2 ounces turkey breast, 1/4 cup greens, and half of the olive mixture.

NUTRITION PER SERVING

242 calories
15 g protein
17 g carbohydrates
12 g fat
1 g saturated fat
20 mg cholesterol
1,177 mg sodium*
2 g fiber

*Limit saturated fat to 10% of total calories—about 17 grams per day for most women—and sodium intake to less than 2,300 milligrams.

{ Make It a FLAT BELLY DIET MEAL } Serve with 1 cup pitted cherries (100) and a salad made from 1/2 cucumber, sliced (12), tossed with 1 cup grape tomatoes (30) and 2 tablespoons minced red onion (12).
TOTAL MEAL: 396 calories

Mediterranean Pizza Wrap

■ **10 MINUTES** ■ **1 SERVING** ■ **300 CALORIES** ■ **MUFA: TAPENADE**

Tomatoes, cheese, and onion—all the pizza ingredients are here in the ideal Mediterranean combination. Be sure to keep the feta cheeses to just a tablespoon—that flavorful little ingredient is very high in sodium, which can be bloating.

1 whole wheat wrap
(10" diameter)

2 tablespoons Hummus
(opposite page) or
store-bought hummus

1 plum tomato, seeded
and chopped

¼ cucumber, peeled
and chopped

1 tablespoon chopped
red onion

1 tablespoon crumbled
feta cheese

1 tablespoon Tapenade
(page 181) or store-
bought tapenade

1. Place the wrap on a work surface. Spread the hummus in a line across the center of the wrap, leaving a 1½" border at each end. Top the hummus with the tomato, cucumber, onion, cheese, and tapenade.

2. Fold the right and left sides of the wrap so that they cover the very edges of the filling, then fold the bottom over and roll up burrito-style.

**NUTRITION
PER SERVING**

300 calories
9 g protein
38 g carbohydrates
12 g fat
3 g saturated fat
10 mg cholesterol
590 mg sodium
6 g fiber

{ **Make It a
FLAT
BELLY
DIET
MEAL** }
Serve with 2 cups chopped watermelon (90).
TOTAL MEAL: 390 calories ■ To serve as part of another *Flat Belly Diet* Meal, omit the tapenade (268).

Hummus

■ **10 MINUTES** ■ **8 SERVINGS (¼ CUP EACH)** ■ **126 CALORIES** ■ **MUFA: TAHINI**

Loaded with 4 cloves of heart-healthy garlic and a generous amount of lemon juice, this hummus sings with bright flavor. Naturally, use fewer cloves if you're not a big garlic fan.

1 can (15½–19 ounces) garbanzo beans, rinsed and drained
½ cup tahini
4 cloves garlic
¼ cup freshly squeezed lemon juice
¼–½ cup water
¼ teaspoon salt

Place the beans, tahini, garlic, lemon juice, ¼ cup of the water, and salt in a food processor fitted with a metal blade. Process until smooth. Add more water, if needed, until the hummus reaches the desired consistency.

NUTRITION PER SERVING

126 calories
5 g protein
10 g carbohydrates
9 g fat
2 g saturated fat
0 mg cholesterol
121 mg sodium
2 g fiber

{ Make It a FLAT BELLY DIET MEAL }

Serve with 4 whole wheat crackers (80) and the Curried Apple and Pear Soup on page 97, but omit the almonds (155).
TOTAL MEAL: 361 calories

Greek Salad Wrap

■ 10 MINUTES ■ 1 SERVING ■ 230 CALORIES ■ MUFA: TAPENADE

This wrap is for serious olive lovers only. A hint of orange provides just the right contrast to the olives.

1 whole grain tortilla
(10" diameter)

2 tablespoons fat-free
Greek-style yogurt

1 tablespoon Tapenade
(page 181) or store-
bought tapenade

1½ teaspoons freshly
squeezed orange juice

¼ teaspoon freshly grated
orange zest

1½ cups loosely packed
baby spinach

¼ cup grape tomatoes,
halved

¼ small cucumber, peeled,
halved, seeded, and sliced

1 tablespoon crumbled feta
cheese

1. Warm the tortilla in a dry skillet over medium-high heat for about 1 minute (it should still be flexible enough to roll).

2. Meanwhile, whisk together the yogurt, tapenade, orange juice, and orange zest in a large bowl. Add the spinach, tomatoes, and cucumber and toss to coat well.

3. Transfer the tortilla to a work surface. Arrange the spinach mixture on top and sprinkle with the cheese.

4. Fold the right and left sides of the tortilla so that they cover the very edges of the filling, then fold the bottom over and roll up burrito-style.

NUTRITION PER SERVING

230 calories
8 g protein
29 g carbohydrates
10 g fat
2 g saturated fat
10 mg cholesterol
680 mg sodium*
7 g fiber

*Limit saturated fat to 10% of total calories—about 17 grams per day for most women—and sodium intake to less than 2,300 milligrams.

{ Make It a FLAT BELLY DIET MEAL } Serve with 3 ounces
light tuna packed in water (120).
TOTAL MEAL: 380 calories

Roasted Bell Pepper and Avocado Sandwich

■ 10 MINUTES ■ 1 SERVING ■ 330 CALORIES ■ MUFA: AVOCADO

This vegetarian sandwich verges on Dagwood proportions! Sweet roasted peppers are easy to make yourself (see note below).

1 teaspoon Dijon mustard
½ teaspoon honey
2 slices multigrain bread
1 leaf Boston lettuce
½ red bell pepper, roasted
¼ avocado, sliced
¼ cup alfalfa sprouts
1 slice Cheddar cheese
   (about ½ ounce)

1. Combine the mustard and honey in a small bowl. Spread half onto 1 slice of the bread.

2. Top with the lettuce, pepper, avocado, sprouts, and cheese.

3. Spread the remaining bread slice with the remaining honey mustard and set, mustard side down, on top of the cheese. Serve.

Note: To roast peppers, preheat the broiler. Cut each bell pepper into 4 panels and toss with 1 teaspoon olive oil. Place skin side up on a baking pan that has been coated with cooking spray. Broil 4 inches from the heat source for about 3 to 5 minutes or until the skin is blackened. Remove the baking sheet from the oven and let the peppers cool on the pan. When the peppers have cooled, remove the skins, wiping off any blackened pieces with a paper towel.

NUTRITION PER SERVING

330 calories
13 g protein
40 g carbohydrates
14 g fat
4 g saturated fat*
15 mg cholesterol
650 mg sodium*
13 g fiber

*Limit saturated fat to 10% of total calories—about 17 grams per day for most women—and sodium intake to less than 2,300 milligrams.

{ Make It a FLAT BELLY DIET MEAL }

Serve with 2 medium plums (60).

TOTAL MEAL: 380 calories ■ To serve as part of another *Flat Belly Diet* Meal, omit the avocado (260).

Roast Beef Panini with Avocado, Tomato, and Dijon

■ **10 MINUTES** ■ **1 SERVING** ■ **249 CALORIES** ■ **MUFA: AVOCADO**

Forget grilled cheese! Pressed sandwiches like this panini taste great in part because there are so many delicious flavors that meld during cooking.

2 slices reduced-calorie multigrain bread

2 ounces store-roasted, deli-sliced lean roast beef

2 beefsteak tomato slices

¼ avocado, sliced

⅛ cup baby arugula

1 teaspoon Dijon mustard

¼ teaspoon extra virgin olive oil

1. Place 1 slice of the bread on a work surface. Top with the roast beef, tomato slices, avocado slices, and arugula. Spread the remaining bread with mustard and set, mustard side down, on the arugula.

2. Heat a ridged nonstick grill pan over medium heat until hot. Lightly brush the outsides of the sandwich with the oil and place on the pan. Set a heavy-bottomed skillet on top of the sandwich and cook for 1 to 2 minutes per side or until toasted and warm in the center.

NUTRITION PER SERVING

249 calories
17 g protein
24 g carbohydrates
10 g fat
2 g saturated fat
32 mg cholesterol
634 mg sodium*
4 g fiber

*Limit saturated fat to 10% of total calories—about 17 grams per day for most women—and sodium intake to less than 2,300 milligrams.

{ **Make It a FLAT BELLY DIET MEAL** }

Serve with Caponata on page 258, but omit the pine nuts (86), and 1 large carrot cut into sticks (41). **TOTAL MEAL:** 376 calories ■ To serve as part of another *Flat Belly Diet* Meal, omit the avocado (190).

6

Salads & Sides

Summer Salad with Green Goddess Dressing

15 MINUTES ▪ **4 SERVINGS** ▪ **145 CALORIES** ▪ **MUFA: CANOLA MAYONNAISE**

This dressing, invented in the 1920s, is a California classic. Here, canola-based mayonnaise stands in as a MUFA in place of cholesterol-rich regular mayonnaise.

½ cup low-fat plain yogurt

¼ cup canola mayonnaise

¼ cup fresh Italian parsley, chopped

2 scallions, coarsely chopped

1 clove garlic

1 tablespoon white wine vinegar

1 tablespoon chopped fresh tarragon

⅛ teaspoon salt

1 package (7 ounces) mixed salad greens

1 cup grape tomatoes, halved

1 cucumber, peeled, halved, seeded, and sliced

1. Combine the yogurt, mayonnaise, parsley, scallions, garlic, vinegar, tarragon, and salt in a blender or a food processor fitted with a metal blade. Process until smooth.

2. Combine the greens, tomato, and cucumber in a large bowl. Toss with the dressing.

NUTRITION PER SERVING

145 calories
3 g protein
7 g carbohydrates
12 g fat
1 g saturated fat
7 mg cholesterol
203 mg sodium
2 g fiber

{ Make It a FLAT BELLY DIET MEAL }

Serve with the Chicken-Barley Soup with Vegetables and Pesto on page 106, but omit the pesto (210).
TOTAL MEAL: 355 calories

Pesto Caesar Salad

▪ **15 MINUTES** ▪ **4 SERVINGS** ▪ **260 CALORIES** ▪ **MUFA: OLIVE OIL**

It's time to rethink the traditional Caesar salad. This version still delivers great flavor but replaces the standard crouton component with a broiler-crisped tortilla for a lighter crunch.

1 flour tortilla
(10" diameter)
¼ cup olive oil
2 teaspoons grated
Romano cheese
2 hard-boiled eggs
2 tablespoons freshly
squeezed lemon juice
1½ tablespoons Pesto
(page 122) or
store-bought pesto
½ teaspoon anchovy paste
or Thai fish sauce
6 cups torn romaine lettuce
Freshly ground black
pepper

1. Preheat the broiler.

2. Brush the tortilla with a small amount of the oil. Sprinkle with the cheese. Place on a sheet of foil. Broil 6" from the heat source for about 1 minute or until golden and crisp. Remove from the oven and use a pizza cutter to slice into small squares. Set aside.

3. Peel the eggs and halve lengthwise. Remove the yolks and discard 1 or save it for another recipe. Coarsely chop the whites. Set aside.

4. Use a fork to smash the yolk against the side of a large bowl. Add the remaining oil, the lemon juice, pesto, and anchovy paste. Whisk until smooth. Add the romaine and reserved egg whites. Toss to coat. Season generously with the pepper.

5. Scatter the tortilla pieces over the salad before serving.

**NUTRITION
PER SERVING**

260 calories
7 g protein
13 g carbohydrates
21 g fat
4 g saturated fat*
109 mg cholesterol
225 mg sodium
3 g fiber

*Limit saturated fat to 10% of total calories—about 17 grams per day for most women—and sodium intake to less than 2,300 milligrams.

{ Make It a FLAT BELLY DIET MEAL } Serve with ½ cup Tuscan Bean Soup with Bitter Greens on page 103, but omit the olive oil (90), and a slice of whole grain bread (75). **TOTAL MEAL:** 425 calories

Pesto

■ **10 MINUTES** ■ **24 SERVINGS (2 TABLESPOONS EACH)** ■ **71 CALORIES**

This sauce alone is a great reason to grow fresh basil. Originally associated with the city of Genoa in the Liguria region of northern Italy, pesto's international popularity is well deserved. It's also a *Flat Belly Diet* must-have. Our advice: Make several batches when basil is in season—and freeze what you don't need.

½ cup pine nuts

6 cups packed fresh basil

1 clove garlic

½ cup grated Parmesan cheese

1 teaspoon salt

¼ teaspoon freshly ground black pepper

½ cup extra virgin olive oil

1. Toast the pine nuts in a large nonstick skillet over medium heat, stirring often, for 3 to 4 minutes or until lightly browned and fragrant. Tip onto a plate and let cool.

2. Combine the pine nuts, basil, garlic, cheese, salt, and pepper in the bowl of a food processor fitted with a metal blade. Pulse until coarsely chopped. With the machine running, add the oil through the feed tube to blend into a rough paste.

3. Transfer to an airtight container. Refrigerate for up to 1 week.

> **NUTRITION PER SERVING**
>
> 71 calories
> 1 g protein
> 1 g carbohydrates
> 7 g fat
> 1 g saturated fat
> 1 mg cholesterol
> 123 mg sodium
> 1 g fiber

{ Make It a **FLAT BELLY DIET MEAL** } Serve with The Best Grilled Chicken Breast on page 205, but omit the sauce (217), and ¾ cup whole grain pasta (150). **TOTAL MEAL:** 438 calories

Asian Slaw

20 MINUTES ▪ **4 SERVINGS** ▪ **200 CALORIES** ▪ **MUFA: PEANUTS**

This colorful salad is easy to put together any time of year. Its light, refreshing flavor and solid crunch are the perfect complement to grilled scallops or chicken.

½ head green cabbage, thinly sliced (about 6 cups)

5 scallions, thinly sliced on a sharp angle

1 large carrot, shredded

1 red bell pepper, cut into thin strips

1 apple, peeled and diced

½ cup salted peanuts, coarsely chopped

3 tablespoons rice vinegar

1 tablespoon sugar

2 teaspoons sesame oil

1 teaspoon grated fresh ginger

½ teaspoon salt

Combine the cabbage, scallions, carrot, pepper, apple, and peanuts in a large bowl. Combine the vinegar, sugar, oil, ginger, and salt in a separate bowl. Pour the vinegar mixture over the cabbage mixture and toss well. Let stand 10 minutes before serving.

NUTRITION PER SERVING

200 calories
7 g protein
23 g carbohydrates
12 g fat
1.5 g saturated fat
0 mg cholesterol
330 mg sodium
6 g fiber

{ Make It a **FLAT BELLY DIET MEAL** }

Serve with the Spring Rolls and Chili Sauce on page 186, but omit the peanuts (155). **TOTAL MEAL:** 387 calories ▪ To serve as part of another *Flat Belly Diet* Meal, omit the peanuts (100).

Heirloom Tomato Salad
with Aioli and Capers

35 MINUTES **4 SERVINGS** **120 CALORIES** **MUFA: CANOLA MAYONNAISE**

Splendid tomatoes are key in a salad like this. Look for heirloom varieties at your local farmers' market, but beware—they're extremely fragile. Of course, they're also extremely delicious. So buy them—and eat them in this recipe that very night.

2 medium tomatoes, thinly sliced
1 recipe Lemon Aioli (page 177)
2 paper-thin slices red onion
¼ cup basil leaves
2 teaspoons capers, rinsed, drained, and finely chopped

Arrange the tomato slices on 4 salad plates. Use the back of a spoon to spread equal portions of the aioli on the tomatoes. Separate the onion rings and scatter over the aioli. Scatter on the basil and capers.

NUTRITION PER SERVING

120 calories
1 g protein
5 g carbohydrates
11 g fat
0.5 g saturated fat
5 mg cholesterol
152 mg sodium
1 g fiber

{ Make It a FLAT BELLY DIET MEAL }

Serve with the Mediterranean Pizza Wrap on page 112, but omit the tapenade (268).
TOTAL MEAL: 388 calories

Broccoli-Cashew Salad

▦ **15 MINUTES** ▦ **4 SERVINGS** ▦ **190 CALORIES** ▦ **MUFA: CASHEWS**

Here's a popular potluck side salad, rendered perfect for a *Flat Belly Diet* Meal. For best results, make sure the florets are cut into small, uniform pieces.

3 tablespoons canola
 mayonnaise
1 tablespoon red or
 white wine vinegar
⅛ teaspoon salt
2 cups broccoli florets
½ cup roasted unsalted
 cashews
¼ cup slivered red onion
¼ teaspoon red-pepper
 flakes

Combine the mayonnaise, vinegar, and salt in a large serving bowl. Whisk until smooth. Add the broccoli, cashews, onion, and red-pepper flakes. Toss to coat. Refrigerate until ready to serve.

**NUTRITION
PER SERVING**
190 calories
4 g protein
8 g carbohydrates
16 g fat
2 g saturated fat
5 mg cholesterol
150 mg sodium
2 g fiber

{ Make It a
FLAT
BELLY
DIET
MEAL }
Serve with the Roast Beef Panini with Avocado, Tomato, and Dijon on page 117, but omit the avocado (193).
TOTAL MEAL: 373 calories

Dilled Egg Salad Platter

20 MINUTES ▪ **4 SERVINGS** ▪ **280 CALORIES** ▪ **MUFA: CANOLA MAYONNAISE**

Try this delicious platter in lieu of a conventional egg salad sandwich. Make sure to use canola mayonnaise, which draws its MUFA status from its main ingredient, canola oil.

6 large eggs, hard-boiled and peeled (discard 3 yolks)

3 ribs celery, chopped

1/2 cup peeled and chopped hothouse cucumber

3 radishes, chopped

2 scallions, thinly sliced, or 1/4 cup chopped sweet white onion

1/4 cup canola mayonnaise

2 tablespoons snipped fresh dill

1/2 teaspoon grainy mustard

1/2 teaspoon freshly ground black pepper

1/8 teaspoon salt
Leaf lettuce, for serving

2 large tomatoes, cut into wedges

8 Wasa crisp breads, for serving

1. Coarsely chop the eggs and egg whites and place in a medium bowl. Add the celery, cucumber, radishes, scallions, mayonnaise, dill, mustard, pepper, and salt and mix well.

2. Arrange the lettuce leaves on a platter or plates. Mound the salad on top and surround with the tomato wedges. Serve with the crisp breads.

NUTRITION PER SERVING

280 calories
13 g protein
22 g carbohydrates
15 g fat
2 g saturated fat
164 mg cholesterol
390 mg sodium
5 g fiber

{ **Make It a FLAT BELLY DIET MEAL** } Serve with 4 ounces broiled shrimp (120).
TOTAL MEAL: 400 calories

salads & sides

Lentil-Walnut Salad with Goat Cheese

▇ **40 MINUTES** ▇ **4 SERVINGS** ▇ **394 CALORIES** ▇ **MUFA: WALNUT OIL**

French lentils offer a subtle pepper flavor and tend to hold their shape better than regular brown lentils. They're often available in natural food stores that carry a variety of bulk ingredients. Of course, if necessary, regular brown lentils are a worthy stand-in in this easy salad.

1 cup French lentils

3 cups reduced-sodium vegetable broth

2 bay leaves

2 whole cloves garlic, peeled

¼ cup walnut oil

2 tablespoons red wine vinegar

¼ teaspoon salt

¼ teaspoon freshly ground black pepper

1 carrot, shredded

2 tablespoons chopped parsley

1 log (4 ounces) herbed goat cheese
Ground coriander

1. Combine the lentils, broth, bay leaves, and garlic in a medium pot and bring to a boil over medium-high heat. As soon as the lentils reach the boiling point, reduce the heat so the mixture simmers. Cover and simmer for 25 to 30 minutes or until the lentils are tender. Drain any excess broth. Set aside the garlic cloves. Discard the bay leaves. Spread the lentils on a tray to cool.

2. Combine the oil, vinegar, salt, pepper, and reserved garlic cloves in a salad bowl. Whisk, smashing the garlic, until smooth. Add the lentils, carrot, and parsley. Toss to coat. Spoon the mixture onto 4 plates.

3. Cut the cheese into 4 slices. Lay flat. Dust both sides lightly with coriander. Place on a microwaveable dish. Cook in the microwave on medium for about 30 seconds or just until the cheese is warm. Set a piece of cheese on each salad.

NUTRITION PER SERVING

394 calories
17 g protein
32 g carbohydrates
22 g fat
7 g saturated fat
22 mg cholesterol
422 mg sodium
8 g fiber

{ Make It a FLAT BELLY DIET MEAL } A single serving of this recipe counts as a *Flat Belly Diet* Meal without any add-ons!

Broccoli, Cherry Tomato, and Pesto Pasta Salad

35 MINUTES ■ **4 SERVINGS** ■ **288 CALORIES** ■ **MUFA: PESTO**

At the peak of summer, using the same water to cook both pasta and a vegetable is a good way to stay cool. As a bonus, it cuts down a pot to clean! For best results, make this dish early in the day to allow time for the flavors to blend.

4 ounces rotini pasta

2 cups broccoli florets

1 cup grape tomatoes, halved

¼ red onion, thinly sliced (about ¼ cup)

¼ cup packed fresh basil, thinly sliced

¼ cup Pesto (page 122) or store-bought pesto

2 tablespoons olive oil

1. Bring a large pot of lightly salted water to a boil. Add the rotini and cook per the package directions. Add the broccoli during the last 2 minutes of cooking. Drain, rinse under cold water, and drain again. Transfer to a large bowl.

2. Add the tomatoes, onion, and basil to the bowl with the pasta. Combine the pesto and oil in a separate bowl. Stir the pesto mixture into the pasta and toss well. Refrigerate until ready to serve.

NUTRITION PER SERVING

288 calories
8 g protein
36 g carbohydrates
13 g fat
2 g saturated fat
1 mg cholesterol
105 mg sodium
3 g fiber

{ Make It a FLAT BELLY DIET MEAL } Serve with half of the Roasted Bell Pepper and Avocado Sandwich on page 115, but omit the avocado (130).
TOTAL MEAL: 418 calories

Indonesian Vegetable Salad

■ **25 MINUTES** ■ **4 SERVINGS** ■ **322 CALORIES** ■ **MUFA: PEANUT BUTTER**

This colorful platter of lightly cooked vegetables gets a *Flat Belly Diet* twist with a delish dish made with peanut sauce and water—how simple is that? Add a dash of hot sauce if the mood strikes.

2 cups green beans, trimmed

2 carrots, thinly sliced on an angle

2 cups cauliflower florets

2 cups mixed greens

1 cup bean sprouts

1 cucumber, peeled, seeded, and sliced

1 hard-boiled egg, peeled and chopped

1 cup Amazing Peanut Sauce (page 209) or store-bought peanut sauce

3–4 tablespoons water

1 tablespoon chopped peanuts (optional)

1. Bring a large pot of lightly salted water to a boil. Add the green beans and cook for 2 minutes or until crisp-tender. Remove, rinse under cold water, and drain. Return the water to a boil and repeat the same process with the carrots and cauliflower.

2. Arrange the greens and vegetables on a serving platter. Top with the chopped egg.

3. Combine the peanut sauce and water in a bowl. Stir well to thin the sauce to a pourable consistency. Pour the peanut sauce over the vegetables and serve topped with a few peanuts, if desired.

NUTRITION PER SERVING

322 calories
14 g protein
27 g carbohydrates
19 g fat
3 g saturated fat
53 mg cholesterol
420 mg sodium
8 g fiber

{ Make It a **FLAT BELLY DIET MEAL** } Serve with ½ cup fat-free Greek-style yogurt (56).
TOTAL MEAL: 378 calories

Spinach Salad with Pears, Pecans, and Goat Cheese

■ **10 MINUTES** ■ **4 SERVINGS** ■ **311 CALORIES** ■ **MUFA: PECANS**

This is a lovely salad for fall, when ripe, luscious pears are widely available. During other times of the year, strawberries, melon, or apple make suitable stand-ins.

½ cup pecans

2 tablespoons olive oil

1 tablespoon + 1 teaspoon white wine vinegar

1 tablespoon honey

½ teaspoon salt

½ teaspoon freshly ground black pepper

3 tablespoons chopped red onion

2 large red or green pears, quartered, cored, and cut into thin slices

2 tablespoons golden raisins

1 bag (6 ounces) prewashed baby spinach

3 ounces reduced-fat goat cheese, crumbled

1. Toast the pecans in a large nonstick skillet over medium heat, stirring often, for 3 to 4 minutes or until lightly browned and fragrant. Tip onto a plate and let cool.

2. Whisk the oil, vinegar, honey, salt, and pepper in a salad bowl. Stir in the onion, then the pears and raisins. Add the spinach and toss to coat.

3. Divide the salad among 4 plates and top each with the reserved pecans and goat cheese before serving.

NUTRITION PER SERVING

311 calories
6 g protein
33 g carbohydrates
20 g fat
3 g saturated fat
4 mg cholesterol
437 mg sodium
7 g fiber

{ Make It a **FLAT BELLY DIET MEAL** }

Serve with 3 ounces roasted pork tenderloin (115).

TOTAL MEAL: 426 calories

Blackened Chicken with Multicolor Slaw

■ 30 MINUTES ■ 4 SERVINGS ■ 281 CALORIES ■ MUFA: CANOLA MAYONNAISE

Blackened chicken draws on a cooking method popularized by legendary New Orleans chef Paul Prudhomme. Arranged on a colorful bed of slaw, these tender chicken bites are practically irresistible.

SLAW

- ¼ cup canola mayonnaise
- 3 tablespoons fat-free sour cream
- 3 tablespoons white wine vinegar
- 1 tablespoon sugar
- ½ teaspoon coarse-ground black pepper
- ¼ teaspoon salt
- ½ small green cabbage, cored and shredded
- ¼ small red cabbage, cored and shredded
- ½ large red bell pepper, cut into thin strips

BLACKENED CHICKEN

- 2 teaspoons paprika
- ½ teaspoon dried thyme
- ½ teaspoon freshly ground black pepper
- ¼ teaspoon salt
- ¼ teaspoon garlic powder
- ¼ teaspoon ground red pepper
- 1 pound boneless, skinless chicken breast halves, cut into 1" chunks

1. To prepare the slaw: Whisk the mayonnaise, sour cream, vinegar, sugar, pepper, and salt in a large bowl. Add the green cabbage, red cabbage, and bell pepper and toss to mix well. Let stand while cooking the chicken.

2. To prepare the chicken: Preheat the broiler. Coat a rimmed baking sheet with olive oil cooking spray.

3. Mix the paprika, thyme, black pepper, salt, garlic powder, and ground red pepper in a cup. Put the chicken on the prepared baking sheet and sprinkle with the blackened seasonings. Turn the pieces to coat them well.

4. Broil the chicken 3" to 4" from the heat for 7 to 8 minutes, turning once, or until cooked through.

5. Divide the slaw among 4 soup plates and top each with an equal portion of the blackened chicken.

NUTRITION PER SERVING

281 calories
28 g protein
13 g carbohydrates
13 g fat
1 g saturated fat
71 mg cholesterol
497 mg sodium
3 g fiber

{ Make It a FLAT BELLY DIET MEAL }

Serve with 2 slices light whole grain bread (120).
TOTAL MEAL: 410 calories

Caribbean Chicken Salad

■ **40 MINUTES** ■ **4 SERVINGS** ■ **310 CALORIES** ■ **MUFA: AVOCADO**

Jerk seasoning, traditionally used in Jamaican cooking, is a flavorful blend of allspice, thyme, garlic, onion, and habanero pepper. If you're concerned about spiciness, no worries—the sweetness of this citrus salad balances the heat.

1 pound small boneless, skinless chicken breast halves

1 tablespoon jerk seasoning

2 tablespoons + 1 teaspoon olive oil, divided

3 tablespoons freshly squeezed lime juice, divided

1 tablespoon freshly squeezed orange juice

$\frac{1}{2}$ teaspoon honey

$\frac{1}{4}$ teaspoon salt

$\frac{1}{4}$ small sweet white onion, thinly sliced

6 cups colorful mixed greens

1 mango, peeled, pitted, and sliced

1 avocado, sliced

1. Sprinkle the chicken with the jerk seasoning, 1 teaspoon of the oil, and 1 tablespoon of the lime juice. Rub in the seasonings. Let stand for 15 minutes.

2. Coat a stove-top grill pan with cooking spray. Warm over medium-high heat for 3 minutes. Add the chicken and cook, turning once, for 10 to 12 minutes or until a thermometer inserted in the thickest portion registers 165°F. Remove from the pan to a clean plate.

3. Whisk the orange juice, honey, salt, remaining 2 tablespoons oil, and remaining 2 tablespoons lime juice in a large bowl. Add the onion and greens and toss to coat well.

4. Cut the chicken into $\frac{1}{4}$" thick diagonal slices. Pour any chicken juices from the plate into the salad. Add the mango and avocado to the salad and toss gently again. Divide the salad among 4 plates and top each with equal portions of the chicken.

NUTRITION PER SERVING

310 calories
29 g protein
17 g carbohydrates
15 g fat
2 g saturated fat
66 mg cholesterol
454 mg sodium
5 g fiber

{ Make It a **FLAT BELLY DIET MEAL** }
Serve with $\frac{1}{2}$ cup of the Summery Quinoa Pilaf on page 149, but omit the hazelnuts (106).
TOTAL MEAL: 416 calories

salads & sides

Southwest Steak Salad

■ **30 MINUTES** ■ **4 SERVINGS** ■ **306 CALORIES** ■ **MUFA: AVOCADO**

This hearty salad boasts the leanest and most tender cut of beef. Though tenderloin can be costly, a little bit goes a long way here. If you're new to jicama, a mild-flavored root vegetable from Mexico, its texture and flavor are similar to a radish but without the bite; look for it in the international section of the produce aisle.

2 beef tenderloin steaks (6 ounces each)

½ teaspoon salt, divided

¼ teaspoon freshly ground black pepper

1 cup chopped avocado

½ cup fat-free Greek-style yogurt

¼ cup freshly squeezed lime juice

½ teaspoon ground cumin

6 cups mesclun or mixed greens

1 tomato, chopped

1 small jicama (about 8 ounces), peeled and cut into thin strips

1 cup frozen corn kernels, thawed

¼ cup fresh cilantro leaves

1. Sprinkle the steaks with ¼ teaspoon of the salt and the pepper. Heat a large heavy skillet coated with cooking spray over medium-high heat. Add the steaks and cook for 10 minutes for medium-rare or to the desired doneness, turning once. Place the steaks on a plate. Let stand for 15 minutes. Slice.

2. Meanwhile, combine the avocado, yogurt, lime juice, cumin, and remaining ¼ teaspoon salt in a blender or a food processor fitted with a metal blade. Process until smooth.

3. Combine the greens, tomato, jicama, corn, and cilantro in a large bowl. Toss with the avocado dressing. Divide the salad among 4 plates and top each with an equal portion of the steak.

NUTRITION PER SERVING

306 calories
26 g protein
28 g carbohydrates
12 g fat
3 g saturated fat
57 mg cholesterol
381 mg sodium
11 g fiber

{ Make It a **FLAT BELLY DIET MEAL** }

Serve with 2 corn tortillas (90).
TOTAL MEAL: 396 calories

Braised Kale with Smoked Nuts

■ **25 MINUTES** ■ **4 SERVINGS** ■ **288 CALORIES** ■ **MUFA: ALMONDS**

Chewy, crunchy, salty, and sour, this dish is guaranteed to make greens fans swoon. Kale—a relative of broccoli and cauliflower—is another super cancer-fighter.

2 tablespoons olive oil

1 large red onion, cut into thin wedges

3 tablespoons red wine vinegar

2 bunches kale (about 1½ pounds), trimmed and chopped, or 1 bag (16 ounces) prepackaged kale

¼ cup water

½ teaspoon salt

¼ teaspoon red-pepper flakes (optional)

½ cup smoked almonds, coarsely chopped

1. Heat the oil in a large pot or Dutch oven over medium-high heat. Cook the onion for 3 minutes or until lightly browned. Stir in the vinegar to deglaze the pan.

2. Meanwhile, rinse the kale, allowing the water to remain on the leaves. Add the kale and water and cook, stirring and tossing, for 3 to 4 minutes or until the kale wilts. Stir in the salt and red-pepper flakes, if using.

3. Transfer to a serving bowl and sprinkle with the nuts.

NUTRITION PER SERVING

288 calories
10 g protein
20 g carbohydrates
22 g fat
2 g saturated fat
0 mg cholesterol
580 mg sodium
6 g fiber

{ Make It a **FLAT BELLY DIET MEAL** }

Serve with 3 ounces roasted chicken breast (140).

TOTAL MEAL: 428 calories ■ To serve as part of another *Flat Belly Diet* Meal, omit the almonds (130).

Zucchini and Carrots with Walnuts

35 MINUTES ▪ **4 SERVINGS** ▪ **154 CALORIES** ▪ **MUFA: WALNUTS**

Tender ribbons of green and orange create an interesting visual medley. Topped with toasted walnuts, the combination is exquisite and just right for a spring holiday dinner.

½ cup chopped walnuts
2 medium zucchini
2 large carrots, peeled
1 tablespoon olive oil
⅛ teaspoon dried thyme
¼ teaspoon salt
⅛ teaspoon freshly ground black pepper

1. Toast the walnuts in a large nonstick skillet over medium heat, stirring often, for 3 to 4 minutes or until lightly browned and fragrant. Tip onto a plate. Wipe out the skillet.

2. Halve the zucchini lengthwise and cut the halves crosswise in 2. Cut each piece into thin strips lengthwise.

3. Use a vegetable peeler to cut long strips from the carrots, saving the core for another use.

4. Heat the oil in the same skillet over medium heat. Add the carrots and sprinkle with the thyme, salt, and pepper. Cook, tossing often, for about 3 minutes or until nearly tender. Add the zucchini and cook, tossing, for 3 to 4 minutes or until tender. Sprinkle with the walnuts.

NUTRITION PER SERVING

154 calories
4 g protein
8 g carbohydrates
13 g fat
1 g saturated fat
0 mg cholesterol
179 mg sodium
3 g fiber

{ **Make It a FLAT BELLY DIET MEAL** }

Serve with 1 turkey burger (170) on a bun (90).
TOTAL MEAL: 414 calories ▪ To serve as part of another *Flat Belly Diet* Meal, omit the walnuts (60).

Asparagus with Pine Nuts

25 MINUTES ▪ **4 SERVINGS** ▪ **180 CALORIES** ▪ **MUFA: PINE NUTS**

In spring, seeing fresh asparagus at the market is so exciting. It's a sure reminder of all the great produce that's just around the corner. Look for firm stalks with tightly closed heads. To trim, simply bend the stalk—it will break just at the point where it becomes woody.

2 pounds asparagus, trimmed and cut into 2½" pieces
½ cup pine nuts
2 cloves garlic, minced
¼ cup freshly squeezed orange juice
¼ teaspoon salt

1. Bring 1" of water to a boil in a large pot over high heat. Add the asparagus and cook for 2 minutes or until bright green. Drain and pat dry.

2. Toast the nuts in a large nonstick skillet over medium heat, stirring often, for 3 to 4 minutes or until lightly browned and fragrant. Tip onto a plate and set aside. Wipe out the skillet.

3. Coat the same skillet with olive oil cooking spray. Add the asparagus and garlic and cook over medium-high heat, stirring, for 2 minutes or until the garlic is lightly browned.

4. Add the juice and salt and cook, stirring, for 3 minutes or until thickened and the asparagus is tender.

5. Sprinkle with the reserved nuts before serving.

NUTRITION PER SERVING

180 calories
8 g protein
13 g carbohydrates
12 g fat
1 g saturated fat
0 mg cholesterol
151 mg sodium
5 g fiber

{ Make It a **FLAT BELLY DIET MEAL** }

Serve with 5 ounces roasted pork tenderloin (192).
TOTAL MEAL: 372 calories ▪ To serve as part of another *Flat Belly Diet* Meal, omit the pine nuts (45).

Bok Choy and Garlic Skillet

■ 25 MINUTES ■ 4 SERVINGS ■ 182 CALORIES ■ MUFA: OLIVE OIL

Everyone will love this combo. Loaded with a vibrant range of vegetables, this beautiful dish is easy to put together on a busy weeknight.

4 tablespoons extra virgin olive oil, divided

6 baby bok choy, quartered lengthwise

1 red bell pepper, cut into thin strips

1 carrot, cut into thin strips

3 cloves garlic, thinly sliced

1 cup snow peas, trimmed

1 tablespoon freshly squeezed lemon juice

½ teaspoon salt

¼ teaspoon freshly ground black pepper

1. Heat 2 tablespoons of the oil in a large nonstick skillet over medium-high heat.

2. Add the bok choy and cook, stirring often, for 5 to 6 minutes or until lightly browned and crisp-tender. Transfer to a plate.

3. Heat 1 tablespoon of the oil and add the bell pepper, carrot, and garlic. Cook for 1 to 2 minutes or until the garlic begins to brown.

4. Add the snow peas and cook for 1 minute longer or until the snow peas begin to turn bright green.

5. Add the bok choy, lemon juice, salt, pepper, and remaining 1 tablespoon oil and cook for 1 minute or until the bok choy is heated through.

NUTRITION PER SERVING

182 calories
4 g protein
11 g carbohydrates
15 g fat
2 g saturated fat
0 mg cholesterol
402 mg sodium
4 g fiber

{ Make It a FLAT BELLY DIET MEAL }

Serve with 4 ounces thinly sliced broiled flank steak (187).

TOTAL MEAL: 369 calories ■ To serve as part of another *Flat Belly Diet* Meal, prepare with 1 tablespoon oil (90).

Baked Green Bean Casserole

■ 40 MINUTES   ■ 6 SERVINGS   ■ 265 CALORIES   ■ MUFA: ALMONDS

Here's a new twist on that old-fashioned favorite from Thanksgivings past. Next time you're headed to a potluck, bring this covered dish and you'll have a MUFA-packed dish everyone will love.

TOPPING

1 tablespoon olive oil
1 large onion, cut into rings
¾ cup smoked almonds, divided

CASSEROLE

1 onion, chopped
1 package (5 ounces) shiitake mushrooms, sliced
1 bag (16 ounces) french-cut green beans, thawed
1 cup reduced-sodium chicken broth
8 ounces Neufchâtel cheese, cut into cubes
2 tablespoons grated Parmesan cheese
¼ teaspoon freshly grated nutmeg

1. Preheat the oven to 350°F. Coat a 1½- to 2-quart shallow baking dish with cooking spray and set aside.

2. To prepare the topping: Heat the oil in a large skillet over medium-high heat. Add the onion rings and cook, stirring occasionally, for 10 minutes or until lightly browned.

3. Meanwhile, chop ½ cup of the almonds and set aside. Grind ¼ cup of the almonds. Place on a large plate. Add the browned onion and toss with a fork to coat with the ground almonds. Set aside.

4. To prepare the casserole: Coat the same skillet with olive oil cooking spray. Cook the chopped onion and mushrooms for 8 minutes or until most of the liquid has been absorbed. Add the beans and broth and bring to a simmer. Stir in the cheese until melted. Stir in the Parmesan and nutmeg. Pour into the prepared baking dish. Sprinkle the top with the chopped almonds. Arrange the reserved onion over the nuts.

5. Bake for 25 to 30 minutes or until hot and bubbling.

NUTRITION
PER SERVING

265 calories
11 g protein
14 g carbohydrates
20 g fat
7 g saturated fat*
28 mg cholesterol
439 mg sodium
4 g fiber

*Limit saturated fat to 10% of total calories—about 17 grams per day for most women—and sodium intake to less than 2,300 milligrams.

{ Make It a FLAT BELLY DIET MEAL }   Serve with 3 ounces roast turkey (162).
TOTAL MEAL: 427 calories

Oven-Roasted Tomatoes with Pesto

■ 1 HOUR ■ 4 SERVINGS ■ 119 CALORIES ■ MUFA: PESTO

Oven roasting is a great method for intensifying the sweetness of just about any vegetable. Plum tomatoes work well with this technique because they have a firm texture and fewer seeds than beefsteaks.

12 plum tomatoes, halved lengthwise
1 tablespoon extra virgin olive oil
¼ teaspoon salt
⅛ teaspoon red-pepper flakes
¼ cup Pesto (page 122) or store-bought pesto

1. Preheat the oven to 325°F. Coat a baking sheet with cooking spray.

2. Toss the tomatoes with the oil, salt, and red-pepper flakes in a large bowl. Arrange on the prepared baking sheet.

3. Bake for 50 to 60 minutes or until the tomatoes are very soft but still hold their shape.

4. Transfer the tomatoes to a serving platter, top each with ½ teaspoon of the pesto, and serve warm or at room temperature.

NUTRITION PER SERVING
119 calories
3 g protein
8 g carbohydrates
9 g fat
1 g saturated fat
1 mg cholesterol
247 mg sodium
3 g fiber

{ Make It a FLAT BELLY DIET MEAL } Serve with the The Best Grilled Chicken Breast on page 205, and 2 cups green salad (15) with 1 tablespoon balsamic vinegar (10). **TOTAL MEAL:** 361 calories ■ To serve as part of another *Flat Belly Diet* Meal, omit the pesto (70).

Roasted Potatoes with Blue Cheese–Walnut "Butter"

■ **45 MINUTES** ■ **4 SERVINGS** ■ **242 CALORIES** ■ **MUFA: WALNUTS**

Baby potatoes come in a variety of colors, including blue, yellow, and red, each one a good source of potassium and vitamin C. All are perfectly suited to becoming a tantalizing side dish when topped with this combination of blue cheese and walnuts.

1 pound thin-skinned baby potatoes, halved
1½ teaspoons olive oil
¼ teaspoon freshly ground black pepper
⅛ teaspoon salt
½ cup coarsely chopped walnuts
2 ounces crumbled blue cheese
2 scallions, thinly sliced

1. Preheat the oven to 425°F. Coat a 9" × 9" baking dish with cooking spray or line with parchment paper. Place the potatoes in the prepared dish and toss with the oil, pepper, and salt. Turn cut side down in the pan. Roast for 30 to 35 minutes or until very tender and lightly golden on the underside.

2. Meanwhile, put the walnuts in a small baking pan or skillet and place in the oven to toast for 6 to 8 minutes. Tip into a bowl and let cool. Add the blue cheese and scallions and crumble with your fingers.

3. When the potatoes are done, turn them over and sprinkle evenly with the walnut mixture. Bake for 5 minutes longer or until the cheese is melted.

NUTRITION PER SERVING

242 calories
8 g protein
21 g carbohydrates
15 g fat
4 g saturated fat*
11 mg cholesterol
279 mg sodium
3 g fiber

*Limit saturated fat to 10% of total calories—about 17 grams per day for most women—and sodium intake to less than 2,300 milligrams.

{ Make It a **FLAT BELLY DIET MEAL** }
Serve with 4 ounces thinly sliced broiled flank steak (187).
TOTAL MEAL: 429 calories

Southwestern Fried Rice

■ **25 MINUTES** ■ **8 SERVINGS** ■ **170 CALORIES** ■ **MUFA: PUMPKIN SEEDS**

Here's a handy recipe for leftover brown rice that blends classic Asian cooking technique with the flavors of Tex-Mex cuisine. Chorizo is a type of sausage that draws its distinctive hue from mild Spanish paprika.

1 tablespoon olive oil

1 dry chorizo sausage
(1½ ounces), diced

1 teaspoon ground cumin

¼ teaspoon ground chipotle
chile pepper

1 onion, chopped
(about 1 cup)

1 red bell pepper, chopped
(about 1 cup)

3 cups cooked brown rice,
cold

1 cup pumpkin seeds,
toasted

½ teaspoon salt

2 tablespoons chopped
fresh cilantro

1 teaspoon freshly grated
lime zest

1. Heat the oil in a large nonstick skillet over medium-high heat. Add the sausage and cook for 2 minutes or until lightly browned.

2. Stir in the cumin and chile pepper and cook for 15 seconds or until fragrant.

3. Stir in the onion and bell pepper. Cook, stirring often, for 2 to 3 minutes or until crisp-tender.

4. Add the rice and cook, stirring often, for 1 to 2 minutes or until lightly toasted.

5. Stir in the pumpkin seeds and salt and cook for 1 minute longer.

6. Remove from the heat and stir in the cilantro and lime zest.

**NUTRITION
PER SERVING**

170 calories
9 g protein
24 g carbohydrates
6 g fat
1.5 g saturated fat
5 mg cholesterol
220 mg sodium
2 g fiber

{ Make It a
FLAT
BELLY
DIET
MEAL }
Serve with the Mexican Chicken with Pepita Sauce on page 199, but omit the pepitas (147), and ½ cup fresh pineapple (50). **TOTAL MEAL:** 367 calories ■ To serve as part of another *Flat Belly Diet* Meal, omit the pepitas (130).

Brown Rice Pilaf with Mushrooms

■ **1 HOUR 20 MINUTES** ■ **4 SERVINGS** ■ **311 CALORIES** ■ **MUFA: PECANS**

Mushrooms aren't the most nutrient-packed vegetable in the produce aisle but can be one of the most flavorful—as this recipe proves. Sautéed, they almost make a good substitute for red meat.

1 cup reduced-sodium, fat-free chicken broth or vegetable broth
½ cup water
½ cup pecans
1½ tablespoons olive oil
1 large onion, halved and thinly sliced
2 cloves garlic, minced
1 package (10 ounces) cremini or baby portabello mushrooms, quartered
½ teaspoon dried thyme
¼ teaspoon salt
¾ cup short- or long-grain brown rice

1. Preheat the oven to 350°F. Combine the broth and water in a small saucepan and bring to a boil over high heat. Set aside.

2. Toast the pecans in a large nonstick skillet over medium heat, stirring often, for 3 to 4 minutes or until lightly browned and fragrant. Tip onto a plate.

3. Heat the oil in a large flameproof saucepan or casserole with a lid over medium heat. Add the onion and garlic. Cover and cook, stirring often, for about 6 minutes or until tender.

4. Stir in the mushrooms, thyme, and salt (the pan will seem dry). Cover and cook, stirring often, for about 6 minutes or until the mushrooms have released their liquid and the liquid has evaporated. Stir in the rice and pecans.

5. Add the reserved broth mixture and bring to a boil. Cover and transfer to the oven. Bake for 50 to 60 minutes or until the rice is tender and the liquid has been absorbed. Let stand for 5 minutes before fluffing with a fork and serving.

NUTRITION PER SERVING

311 calories
7 g protein
37 g carbohydrates
16 g fat
2 g saturated fat
0 mg cholesterol
265 mg sodium
4 g fiber

Make It a FLAT BELLY DIET MEAL

Serve with the Squash Soup with Pecans and Greens on page 102, but omit the pecans (85). **TOTAL MEAL:** 396 calories ■ To serve as part of another *Flat Belly Diet* Meal, omit the pecans and serve ½ cup (110).

Saffron Rice

■ **30 MINUTES** ■ **4 SERVINGS** ■ **230 CALORIES** ■ **MUFA: PISTACHIOS**

Studded with pistachios, this colorful rice makes for a memorable side dish. Instant brown rice helps you get this on the table in 30 minutes. If you have more time, preparing this dish with brown basmati rice is even better.

½ teaspoon saffron threads
½ cup pistachios
2¼ cups water
  + 1 tablespoon, divided
1 teaspoon olive oil
½ teaspoon salt
1½ cups instant brown rice

1. Soak the saffron in 1 tablespoon of the water in a small bowl for 20 minutes. Use the back of a spoon to mash the threads.

2. Toast the pistachios in a large nonstick skillet over medium heat, stirring often, for 3 to 4 minutes or until lightly browned and fragrant. Tip onto a plate and let cool.

3. Heat the oil, salt, and remaining 2¼ cups water to a boil over medium-high heat. Reduce the heat to low, add the rice and the saffron mixture, and cook, covered, for 5 minutes. Turn off the heat and let the rice sit for 5 minutes.

4. Fluff the rice with a fork and stir in the pistachios.

NUTRITION PER SERVING

230 calories
6 g protein
30 g carbohydrates
10 g fat
1 g saturated fat
0 mg cholesterol
300 mg sodium
3 g fiber

{ Make It a
FLAT BELLY DIET MEAL }

Serve with the Ginger-Pork Stir-Fry on page 235, but omit the peanuts (208).
TOTAL MEAL: 437 calories ■ To serve as part of another *Flat Belly Diet* Meal, omit the pistachios (140).

Summery Quinoa Pilaf

■ **30 MINUTES** ■ **4 SERVINGS** ■ **300 CALORIES** ■ **MUFA: HAZELNUTS**

Always rinse quinoa to eliminate the soapy-tasting coating that naturally covers the grain. For an easy shortcut, pick up an assortment of melon from your grocer's salad bar.

1¼ cups water

1 cup quinoa, rinsed
and drained

2 tablespoons honey

½ lime, juiced

¼ cup chopped mint

½ pound mixed melon
pieces, finely chopped

½ cup hazelnuts, toasted
and chopped

1. Bring the water to a boil over medium-high heat. Add the quinoa, cover, and reduce the heat to low. Simmer for 12 to 15 minutes or until the water is absorbed. Uncover and allow to cool to room temperature.

2. Whisk the honey, lime juice, and mint in a large bowl. Add the melon, quinoa, and hazelnuts. Toss to combine.

**NUTRITION
PER SERVING**

300 calories
8 g protein
46 g carbohydrates
11 g fat
1 g saturated fat
0 mg cholesterol
20 mg sodium
3 g fiber

{ Make It a
**FLAT
BELLY
DIET
MEAL** }

Serve with 6 chopped dried apricots (60).

TOTAL MEAL: 377 calories ■ To serve as part of another *Flat Belly Diet* Meal, omit the hazelnuts (210).

7

Vegetarian

Zucchini Cakes with Chutney

■ 30 MINUTES ■ 4 SERVINGS (4 PANCAKES PER SERVING) ■ 380 CALORIES ■ MUFA: CANOLA OIL

Here's a way to put all those late-summer zucchini to good use. These savory pancakes are delightful with a touch of mango chutney.

- 2 pounds zucchini, coarsely shredded
- 6 scallions, thinly sliced
- 1 egg
- 1 teaspoon ground fennel
- ½ teaspoon salt
- ½ teaspoon freshly ground black pepper
- ½ cup all-purpose flour
- ¼ cup grated Romano cheese
- ¼ cup canola oil, divided
- ½ cup prepared or store-bought mango chutney

1. Place the zucchini and scallions in a large, cold, nonstick skillet and set over medium-high heat. Cook, tossing frequently, for about 5 minutes or until the zucchini give off some, if any, liquid. Transfer to a colander and drain, pressing with the back of a spoon to squeeze out excess liquid. Transfer to a mixing bowl. Set aside to cool to room temperature. Wipe out the skillet.

2. Whisk the egg, fennel, salt, and pepper in a small bowl. Add the flour and cheese to the zucchini mixture. Toss. Add the egg mixture and toss again.

3. Heat 2 tablespoons of the oil in the same skillet set over medium-high heat for about 1 minute or until sizzling. Place the zucchini mixture in 8 mounds in the pan. Flatten slightly with a spatula. Cook for about 3 minutes or until well browned on the bottom. Carefully turn the cakes and cook, reducing the heat if the cakes are browning too quickly, for about 4 minutes longer or until well browned and cooked through. Remove to a platter. Repeat with the remaining oil and zucchini mixture.

4. Serve the cakes with 2 tablespoons of the chutney per serving on the side.

NUTRITION PER SERVING

380 calories
8 g protein
47 g carbohydrates
18 g fat
3 g saturated fat
55 mg cholesterol
660 mg sodium*
4 g fiber

*Limit saturated fat to 10% of total calories—about 17 grams per day for most women—and sodium intake to less than 2,300 milligrams.

{ Make It a FLAT BELLY DIET MEAL } Serve with ½ cup fat-free Greek-style yogurt (56). **TOTAL MEAL: 436 calories**

Marinated Grilled Tofu

■ 1 HOUR ■ 4 SERVINGS ■ 380 CALORIES ■ MUFA: PEANUT BUTTER

Many cooks consider tofu the ultimate blank slate; it has a very subtle flavor, so it can be seasoned hundreds of ways. In this dish, a light Asian marinade sets the stage for a great use of peanut sauce.

1 container (14 ounces) extrafirm tofu

1 tablespoon reduced-sodium soy sauce

3 cloves garlic, minced

1 tablespoon minced fresh ginger

1 tablespoon freshly squeezed lime juice

¼ teaspoon red-pepper flakes

2 teaspoons sesame oil

2 ribs celery, sliced

4 scallions, chopped

1 red bell pepper, chopped

½ cup Amazing Peanut Sauce (page 209) or store-bought peanut sauce

¼ cup water

1. Place the tofu on top of a paper towel set on a dinner plate. Top with a second paper towel and another dinner plate. Place a medium-size can on the upper plate and leave for 20 minutes to press excess water from the tofu. Meanwhile, combine the soy sauce, half of the garlic, the ginger, lime juice, and red-pepper flakes in a shallow baking dish and mix well. Transfer the tofu to a cutting board and cut crosswise into 8 (¼" thick) slices. Arrange in the soy sauce mixture, turning to coat, and marinate for 20 minutes, turning halfway through.

2. Heat a grill pan over medium-high heat. Remove the tofu from the marinade and grill for 2 to 3 minutes per side or until well marked. Transfer to a cutting board. Cut into 1" pieces.

3. Heat the oil in a large nonstick skillet over medium-high heat. Add the celery, scallions, and bell pepper and cook for 2 to 3 minutes or until just starting to soften. Add the remaining garlic and cook for 1 minute longer. Stir in the tofu, peanut sauce, and water. Cook until heated through. Serve immediately.

NUTRITION PER SERVING

380 calories
21 g protein
21 g carbohydrates
25 g fat
4 g saturated fat*
0 mg cholesterol
525 mg sodium
5 g fiber

*Limit saturated fat to 10% of total calories—about 17 grams per day for most women—and sodium intake to less than 2,300 milligrams.

{ Make It a FLAT BELLY DIET MEAL } Serve with 1 cup steamed broccoli (20).
TOTAL MEAL: 400 calories

Walnut-Grain Burgers

■ 45 MINUTES ■ 10 SERVINGS ■ 297 CALORIES ■ MUFA: WALNUTS

These MUFA-loaded veggie burgers are so hearty, you'll hardly miss the meat. For superfast meals, keep cooked, cooled burgers frozen for up to 3 months. Simply microwave to reheat.

2 cups instant brown rice

1¾ cups low-sodium vegetable broth

½ onion, finely chopped

1 carrot, finely chopped

2 cloves garlic

1¼ cups walnuts

1 egg white

1 tablespoon salt-free seasoning blend

½ cup sesame seeds
Paprika

10 reduced-calorie hamburger buns

10 tomato slices

10 lettuce leaves

1. Combine the rice, broth, onion, carrot, and garlic in a large saucepan. Cover and bring to a boil over high heat. Reduce the heat so the mixture simmers. Cook for 5 minutes. Remove from the heat and set aside, covered, for 5 minutes. Spread on a baking sheet to cool.

2. Process the walnuts in the bowl of a food processor fitted with a metal blade until finely ground. Add the rice mixture, egg white, and seasoning. Pulse until the mixture sticks together. With wet hands, roll into 10 balls and then flatten into patties. Place the sesame seeds on a shallow plate and press the patties into them. Sprinkle with the paprika.

3. Coat a nonstick griddle or large skillet with cooking spray and heat over medium heat. Cook the patties for about 3 minutes or until golden. Turn carefully and cook for about 4 minutes longer or until heated through. Place each patty on a bun with a tomato slice and lettuce leaf.

NUTRITION PER SERVING

297 calories
9 g protein
38 g carbohydrates
14 g fat
1.5 g saturated fat
0 mg cholesterol
229 mg sodium
6 g fiber

Make It a
FLAT
BELLY
DIET
MEAL

Serve with the Smoky Tomato Soup on page 98, but omit the avocado (105).
TOTAL MEAL: 405 calories

Cuban-Style Black Beans

■ **30 MINUTES** ■ **4 SERVINGS** ■ **250 CALORIES** ■ **MUFA: AVOCADO**

Though it's tempting to rush a dish like this, the flavor improves with a slower cooking time. Packed with half of a day's fiber supply per serving, these luscious beans taste even better after a day in the refrigerator.

1 tablespoon olive oil

4 cloves garlic, finely chopped

1 onion, finely chopped

1½ teaspoons ground cumin

2 cans (15 ounces each) no-salt-added black beans, drained

½ cup freshly squeezed orange juice

1 avocado, sliced

1. Heat the oil in a large nonstick skillet over medium-high heat. Add the garlic and onion and cook, stirring frequently, for 3 minutes or until the onion softens.

2. Stir in the cumin and cook for 1 minute longer or until fragrant.

3. Add the beans and orange juice and reduce the heat to low. Simmer for 15 to 20 minutes or until the sauce begins to thicken.

4. With the back of a large silicone or wooden spoon, smash some of the beans into the sauce during the last 5 minutes of cooking.

5. Serve with the avocado on top.

NUTRITION PER SERVING

250 calories
11 g protein
34 g carbohydrates
9 g fat
1 g saturated fat
0 mg cholesterol
426 mg sodium
11 g fiber

Make It a FLAT BELLY DIET MEAL Serve with the Pumpkin Bisque on page 95, but omit the pumpkin seeds (166). **TOTAL MEAL:** 416 calories ■ To serve as part of another *Flat Belly Diet* Meal, omit the avocado (175).

Sweet Potato–Tempeh Hash

■ **25 MINUTES** ■ **4 SERVINGS** ■ **380 CALORIES** ■ **MUFA: OLIVE OIL**

This recipe landed in the vegetarian chapter (even though it would be wonderful for a weekend brunch) because it's hearty enough for a comforting supper. Like tofu, tempeh is a soybean product that lends itself well to a host of spicy flavorings. Look for tempeh in health food stores or with other refrigerated vegetarian products at your grocery.

¼ cup olive oil, divided

2 sweet potatoes, peeled and chopped

1 (8-ounce) package tempeh, chopped

1 onion, finely chopped

1 red bell pepper, finely chopped

1 tablespoon store-bought barbecue sauce

1 teaspoon Cajun Spice Mix (page 65)

¼ cup chopped fresh parsley

4 eggs

Hot-pepper sauce (optional)

1. Heat 3 tablespoons of the oil in a large nonstick skillet over medium-high heat. Add the sweet potatoes and tempeh and cook, stirring occasionally, for 5 minutes or until the mixture begins to brown. Reduce the heat to medium.

2. Add the onion and bell pepper and cook for 12 minutes longer, stirring more frequently at the end of the cooking time, until the tempeh is browned and the potatoes are tender.

3. Add the barbecue sauce, spice rub, and parsley. Toss to combine, then divide among 4 serving plates.

4. Wipe out the skillet with a paper towel. Reduce the heat to medium-low and add the remaining 1 tablespoon oil. Break the eggs into the skillet and cook to the desired doneness.

5. Slide an egg on top of each portion of the hash and serve at once. Pass hot-pepper sauce, if desired, at the table.

NUTRITION PER SERVING

380 calories
14 g protein
35 g carbohydrates
21 g fat
4 g saturated fat*
210 mg cholesterol
210 mg sodium
6 g fiber

*Limit saturated fat to 10% of total calories—about 17 grams per day for most women—and sodium intake to less than 2,300 milligrams.

{ **Make It a FLAT BELLY DIET MEAL** } A single serving of this recipe counts as a *Flat Belly Diet* Meal without any add-ons!

Chickpea Curry with Cashews

■ **20 MINUTES** ■ **4 SERVINGS** ■ **236 CALORIES** ■ **MUFA: CASHEWS**

Who needs takeout when you can put together a dish like this in 20 minutes? This toothsome Indian favorite is all the more flavorful with the addition of buttery cashew nuts.

1 tablespoon cornstarch

1 cup low-sodium vegetable broth, divided

2 teaspoons canola oil

½ onion, chopped

2 teaspoons curry powder

¼ teaspoon salt

¼ teaspoon freshly ground black pepper

1 can (15 ounces) no-salt-added chickpeas, rinsed and drained

½ cup unsalted cashews, coarsely chopped

¼ cup chopped fresh cilantro

4 tablespoons fat-free Greek-style yogurt

1. Whisk the cornstarch in a small bowl with enough of the broth to dissolve. Set aside.

2. Combine the oil, onion, curry powder, salt, and pepper in a large skillet over medium heat. Cover and cook, stirring occasionally, for 5 minutes or until the onion is softened.

3. Add the remaining broth to the pan along with the reserved cornstarch mixture. Cook, whisking constantly, until thickened. Add the chickpeas and cashews. Simmer for 5 minutes for the flavors to blend. Stir in the cilantro. Serve with a dollop of the yogurt.

NUTRITION PER SERVING

236 calories
9 g protein
26 g carbohydrates
11 g fat
2 g saturated fat
1 mg cholesterol
209 mg sodium
5 g fiber

{ **Make It a FLAT BELLY DIET MEAL** } Serve with the Saffron Rice on page 148, but omit the pistachios (140).
TOTAL MEAL: 400 calories

vegetarian

Vegetarian Picadillo

30 MINUTES ▪ **4 SERVINGS** ▪ **290 CALORIES** ▪ **MUFA: ALMONDS**

Meatless burger crumbles are a great alternative to ground beef—and faster to prepare because they're already cooked through and broken into small pieces. Look for them in the freezer case with other meatless products.

½ cup slivered almonds
1 tablespoon olive oil
1 large onion, chopped
3 cloves garlic, minced
8 ounces meatless burger crumbles
1½ teaspoons ground cumin
¼–½ teaspoon red-pepper flakes
½ teaspoon salt
1½ pounds plum tomatoes, coarsely chopped
¾ cup rinsed and drained no-salt-added canned black beans
2 tablespoons raisins
2 tablespoons chopped olives

1. Toast the almonds in a large deep skillet over medium heat, stirring often, for about 3 minutes or until lightly golden. Tip into a bowl. Wipe out the skillet.

2. Warm the oil in the same skillet over medium-high heat. Add the onion and garlic and cook, stirring often, for about 4 minutes or until tender. Stir in the crumbles, cumin, red-pepper flakes, and salt. Cook and stir for 30 seconds.

3. Add the tomatoes and stir well, scraping the bottom of the skillet. Cook for about 2 minutes or until the tomatoes start to release juice.

4. Reduce the heat to low. Stir in the beans and raisins. Cover and cook for 5 minutes or until heated and the tomatoes are cooked down. Add the olives and toasted almonds. Simmer, uncovered, for about 2 minutes or until heated.

NUTRITION PER SERVING

290 calories
21 g protein
30 g carbohydrates
14 g fat
1.5 g saturated fat
0 mg cholesterol
620 mg sodium*
10 g fiber

*Limit saturated fat to 10% of total calories—about 17 grams per day for most women—and sodium intake to less than 2,300 milligrams.

Make It a FLAT BELLY DIET MEAL

Serve with two (6") corn tortillas, warmed (90).
TOTAL MEAL: 380 calories

Creamy Barley Risotto

▨ **55 MINUTES** ▨ **4 SERVINGS** ▨ **370 CALORIES** ▨ **MUFA: OLIVE OIL**

Traditional risotto, made with Arborio rice, draws its creamy texture in part from starches released from the short Italian grain. When cooked with the same technique, barley produces similar results with far more fiber.

2 cups low-sodium vegetable broth

2 cups water

¼ cup olive oil

1 onion, chopped

1 cup pearled barley

1 cup frozen peas

3 tablespoons grated Parmesan cheese

1. Bring the broth and water to a boil in a medium saucepan. Reduce to a simmer.

2. Heat the oil in a heavy medium saucepan over medium heat. Add the onion and cook, stirring frequently, for 5 minutes or until softened. Add the barley and cook for 1 minute longer.

3. Add ½ cup of the broth and cook, stirring frequently, for about 3 minutes or until the broth is absorbed. Add the remaining broth, ½ cup at a time, allowing it to be absorbed before adding more. Cook for about 45 minutes or until the barley is tender but still firm to the bite and the risotto is creamy.

4. Stir in the peas and cheese and cook for 1 minute longer or until the peas are warmed through.

NUTRITION PER SERVING

370 calories
9 g protein
50 g carbohydrates
15 g fat
3 g saturated fat
3 mg cholesterol
240 mg sodium
11 g fiber

{ Make It a **FLAT BELLY DIET MEAL** } Serve with 2 cups mixed baby greens (15) and 1 tablespoon balsamic vinegar (10).
TOTAL MEAL: 395 calories

Penne with Mushrooms and Artichokes

▪ 20 MINUTES ▪ 4 SERVINGS ▪ 370 CALORIES ▪ MUFA: PESTO

Nothing comforts like pasta. This particular combination is quite simple to toss together when you have a batch of homemade pesto on hand.

6 ounces multigrain penne pasta

1 tablespoon extra virgin olive oil

8 ounces sliced white mushrooms

1 onion, chopped

3 cloves garlic, minced

1 pint cherry tomatoes

1 (14-ounce) can artichoke hearts, drained and chopped

¼ cup Pesto (page 122) or store-bought pesto

4 teaspoons grated Romano cheese

1. Bring a large pot of lightly salted water to a boil. Add the penne and cook per the package directions. Drain.

2. Meanwhile, heat the oil in a large nonstick skillet over medium-high heat. Add the mushrooms and onion and cook, stirring occasionally, for 7 to 8 minutes or until the mushrooms have released their liquid and start to brown slightly. Add the garlic and cook for 1 minute longer. Stir in the tomatoes and artichokes and cook for another 1 to 3 minutes or until the tomatoes just begin to soften.

3. Add the pasta and toss to combine. Remove from the heat and stir in the pesto.

4. Divide among 4 bowls and top each with 1 teaspoon of the cheese.

NUTRITION PER SERVING

370 calories
16 g protein
49 g carbohydrates
13 g fat
2 g saturated fat
5 mg cholesterol
790 mg sodium*
6 g fiber

*Limit saturated fat to 10% of total calories—about 17 grams per day for most women—and sodium intake to less than 2,300 milligrams.

{ Make It a FLAT BELLY DIET MEAL }

Serve with ½ medium pear (52).
TOTAL MEAL: 422 calories

vegetarian

Spaghetti with Roasted Cauliflower and Olives

▨ **35 MINUTES** ▨ **4 SERVINGS** ▨ **413 CALORIES** ▨ **MUFA: OLIVE OIL**

This humble spaghetti dish takes on an amazing amount of flavor with frozen cauliflower roasted to perfect sweetness. Feel free to add more garlic or hot-pepper flakes if you like.

 2 packages (10 ounces each) frozen cauliflower
¼ cup olive oil, divided
 4 cloves garlic, chopped
 8 ounces multigrain spaghetti
20 green olives, sliced (about ⅔ cup)
 2 tablespoons grated Parmesan cheese
½ teaspoon red-pepper flakes

1. Preheat the oven to 400°F.

2. Rinse the cauliflower, if necessary, to break the florets into individual pieces. Transfer to a rimmed baking sheet and drizzle with 2 tablespoons of the oil. Scatter the garlic over the cauliflower and toss with clean hands to coat. Bake for 25 minutes or until the cauliflower is well browned.

3. Meanwhile, prepare the spaghetti per the package directions. Drain and transfer to a large, shallow serving bowl. Toss with the remaining 2 tablespoons oil, then add the cauliflower mixture, olives, cheese, and red-pepper flakes. Toss until well combined.

NUTRITION PER SERVING

413 calories
14 g protein
48 g carbohydrates
19 g fat
2.5 g saturated fat
2 mg cholesterol
498 mg sodium
7 g fiber

{ **Make It a FLAT BELLY DIET MEAL** } A single serving of this recipe counts as a *Flat Belly Diet* Meal without any add-ons!

Pumpkin Kugel

55 MINUTES ▪ **12 SERVINGS** ▪ **372 CALORIES** ▪ **MUFA: PUMPKIN SEEDS**

Pumpkin seeds contribute a nice crunch to the top layer of this noodle dish. And here's an even better bonus: It's just as delicious for breakfast as it is for dinner.

- 12 ounces whole grain egg noodles
- 4 ounces Neufchâtel cheese, diced and softened
- 1 cup light sour cream
- 1 cup pumpkin puree
- 1½ cups pumpkin seeds, toasted, divided
- 2 eggs
- ½ cup sugar
- ½ cup 1% milk
- 1 teaspoon salt
- ½ teaspoon ground cinnamon
- ½ cup crushed cornflakes
- 2 tablespoons melted butter

1. Preheat the oven to 350°F. Coat an 11" × 7" baking dish with cooking spray.

2. Bring a large pot of lightly salted water to a boil. Add the noodles and cook per the package directions. Drain and transfer to a bowl.

3. Meanwhile, combine the cheese, sour cream, pumpkin puree, ¾ cup of the pumpkin seeds, the eggs, ¼ cup of the sugar, the milk, salt, and cinnamon in a bowl. Add the noodles and toss well to coat. Transfer to the prepared baking dish.

4. Combine the cornflake crumbs, butter, remaining ¾ cup pumpkin seeds, and remaining ¼ cup sugar in a bowl. Sprinkle over the noodle mixture and cover with foil that has been coated with cooking spray. Bake for 30 to 35 minutes or until heated through. Uncover and bake for 5 minutes longer or until the top is lightly crisped.

NUTRITION PER SERVING

372 calories
13 g protein
39 g carbohydrates
19 g fat
6 g saturated fat*
55 mg cholesterol
319 mg sodium
3 g fiber

*Limit saturated fat to 10% of total calories—about 17 grams per day for most women—and sodium intake to less than 2,300 milligrams.

Make It a FLAT BELLY DIET MEAL

Serve with 1 cup red grapes (60).
TOTAL MEAL: 432 calories

Eggplant Rollatini

■ 50 MINUTES   ■ 4 SERVINGS   ■ 436 CALORIES   ■ MUFA: OLIVE OIL

Baked eggplant is an easy winner when it's rolled around a delicate blend of cheeses and topped with sauce. A side of multigrain spaghetti makes the meal complete.

1 large eggplant

1 cup fat-free ricotta cheese

¼ cup grated Parmesan cheese

2 tablespoons chopped fresh basil

¼ teaspoon freshly ground black pepper

4 cups Marinara Sauce (opposite page) or store-bought reduced-sodium marinara sauce

1 ounce (¼ cup) shredded reduced-fat mozzarella cheese

4 ounces multigrain thin spaghetti

1. Preheat the broiler. Coat a large baking sheet with olive oil cooking spray. Coat a 9″× 9″ baking dish with cooking spray.

2. Peel the eggplant, if desired. Cut lengthwise into ¼″-thick slices. Place on the prepared baking sheet and coat with cooking spray. Broil 6″ from the heat for 10 minutes or until softened and lightly browned, turning once. Reduce the oven to 350°F.

3. Combine the ricotta, Parmesan, basil, and pepper in a medium bowl. Divide evenly between the eggplant, spooning onto 1 end of each slice. Roll the slices around the filling, starting from a short side. Arrange seam sides down in the prepared baking dish. Spoon 2 cups of the marinara sauce over the eggplant rolls and sprinkle with the mozzarella.

4. Cover and bake for 25 minutes or until heated through.

5. Meanwhile, cook the spaghetti per the package directions. Drain. Heat the remaining 2 cups marinara sauce in the same pot. Divide the pasta onto 4 plates and top each with ½ cup of the sauce. Serve the rollatini alongside.

NUTRITION
PER SERVING

436 calories
19 g protein
52 g carbohydrates
17 g fat
3 g saturated fat
18 mg cholesterol
433 mg sodium
11 g fiber

{ Make It a FLAT BELLY DIET MEAL }   A single serving of this recipe counts as a *Flat Belly Diet* Meal without any add-ons!

Marinara Sauce

6 HOURS 20 MINUTES ▪ **8 SERVINGS (1 CUP EACH)** ▪ **211 CALORIES** ▪ **MUFA: OLIVE OIL**

Prepared spaghetti sauces can contain over 1,000 milligrams of sodium per cup—almost half a day's allowance! This splendid sauce, on the other hand, draws its rich flavor from a classic combination of vegetables simmered with olive oil and herbs, so it tastes like you fussed over it all day, even though your slow cooker did most of the work.

½ cup olive oil

2 onions, chopped

2 large carrots, chopped

6 ounces portabella mushrooms, chopped

3 cloves garlic, chopped

1 can (28 ounces) no-salt-added diced tomatoes

1 can (15 ounces) no-salt-added tomato sauce

1 can (6 ounces) tomato paste

2 tablespoons Italian seasoning

1 tablespoon honey

1. Heat the oil in a large skillet over medium-high heat. Cook the onions, carrots, mushrooms, and garlic, stirring occasionally, for 5 to 10 minutes or until browned.

2. Spoon into a 3½- to 5-quart slow cooker. Stir in the tomatoes (with juice), tomato sauce, tomato paste, seasoning, and honey.

3. Cover and cook on low for 6 to 8 hours or until the vegetables are tender.

NUTRITION PER SERVING

211 calories
3 g protein
19 g carbohydrates
14 g fat
2 g saturated fat
0 mg cholesterol
225 mg sodium
4 g fiber

{ **Make It a FLAT BELLY DIET MEAL** }
Serve with 1 cup multigrain pasta (220).
TOTAL MEAL: 431 calories

Mexican Stuffed Peppers

■ 1 HOUR 15 MINUTES ■ 4 SERVINGS ■ 390 CALORIES ■ MUFA: PINE NUTS

If you love peppers, this dish gives you two great ways to enjoy them—rice, corn, nuts, and cheese are loaded into halved peppers and then baked on top of a zesty jalapeño tomato sauce. If you prefer a little less heat, remove the seeds from the jalapeño first.

½ cup pine nuts

1 jalapeño chile pepper, stemmed and halved

2 large cloves garlic

1 can (14½ ounces) no-salt-added stewed tomatoes

¼ cup low-sodium vegetable broth or water

2 tablespoons chili powder, divided

1½ cups cooked brown rice

¾ cup frozen corn kernels

2 plum tomatoes, chopped

½ onion, chopped

2 egg whites

¼ teaspoon salt

4 large poblano or cubanelle peppers

¾ cup shredded reduced-fat Monterey Jack cheese

1. Preheat the oven to 400°F. Put the pine nuts in a small baking dish or skillet for about 8 minutes to lightly toast while the oven heats. Tip onto a plate.

2. Combine the jalapeño pepper, garlic, stewed tomatoes with juice, broth, and 1 tablespoon plus 2 teaspoons of the chili powder in the bowl of a food processor fitted with a metal blade. Process to a medium-coarse texture. Pour into a 9" × 13" glass baking dish and set aside.

3. Mix the rice, corn, plum tomatoes, onion, egg whites, salt, toasted nuts, and remaining 1 teaspoon chili powder in a medium bowl. Halve the poblano peppers lengthwise and remove the stems and seeds. Spoon about ½ cup of the stuffing into each pepper half and place stuffed side up in the reserved sauce in the baking dish.

4. Cover the dish with foil and bake for 40 to 45 minutes or until the peppers are tender.

5. Remove the foil and sprinkle the peppers evenly with the cheese. Bake for 5 to 8 minutes longer or until the cheese has melted. Serve the peppers with the sauce.

NUTRITION PER SERVING

390 calories
15 g protein
45 g carbohydrates
20 g fat
4 g saturated fat*
15 mg cholesterol
435 mg sodium
8 g fiber

*Limit saturated fat to 10% of total calories—about 17 grams per day for most women—and sodium intake to less than 2,300 milligrams.

{ Make It a FLAT BELLY DIET MEAL } A single serving of this recipe counts as a *Flat Belly Diet* Meal without any add-ons!

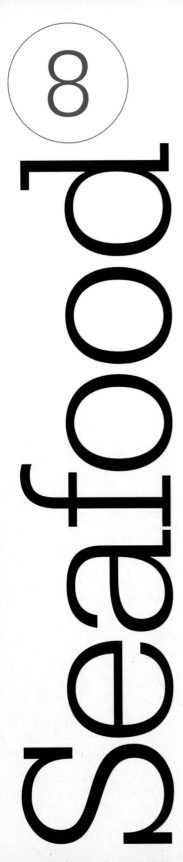

seafood

Steamed Snapper with Pesto

■ **25 MINUTES** ■ **4 SERVINGS** ■ **260 CALORIES** ■ **MUFA: PESTO**

This cooking method works equally well on the grill, which makes it perfect for hot summer evenings when you don't want to turn on the oven.

6 cups baby spinach

1 red bell pepper, thinly sliced

4 snapper fillets (6 ounces each)

½ teaspoon salt

¼ teaspoon freshly ground black pepper

4 tablespoons Pesto (page 122) or store-bought pesto

1. Preheat the oven to 450°F. Coat one side of four 12" × 20" sheets of foil with cooking spray.

2. Top half of each foil sheet with 1½ cups of the spinach, ¼ of the pepper, and 1 snapper fillet. Sprinkle with the salt and black pepper. Fold the other half of each foil sheet over the filling and crimp the edges to make a tight seal.

3. Arrange the packets on a large baking sheet. Bake for 10 to 12 minutes or until the packets are puffed. Transfer each packet to a serving plate. Carefully slit the top of each to allow the steam to escape. After a minute, peel back the foil to reveal the fish. Check to make sure the fish flakes easily when tested with a fork. Top each serving with 1 tablespoon of the pesto before serving.

NUTRITION PER SERVING

260 calories
37 g protein
6 g carbohydrates
9 g fat
1.5 g saturated fat
65 mg cholesterol
580 mg sodium
3 g fiber

{ Make It a FLAT BELLY DIET MEAL } Serve with 1 cup roasted baby red potatoes (100) and 1 cup steamed asparagus (30) tossed with 1 fresh plum tomato, chopped (12). **TOTAL MEAL:** 402 calories

■ To serve as part of another *Flat Belly Diet* Meal, omit the pesto (189).

Grilled Catfish
with Spicy Tartar Sauce

■ 20 MINUTES　■ 4 SERVINGS　■ 339 CALORIES　■ MUFA: CANOLA MAYONNAISE

Many environmental groups consider US farmed catfish to be one of the most sustainable fish species available. Spiced up and served alongside some tartar sauce with a little kick, it's clear that catfish doesn't have to be fried to taste great.

1 teaspoon paprika

½ teaspoon garlic powder

¼ teaspoon celery seed

¼ teaspoon ground cumin

½ teaspoon salt

¼ teaspoon freshly ground black pepper

4 catfish fillets (6 ounces each)

¼ cup canola mayonnaise

1 tablespoon sweet pickle relish

Scant ⅛ teaspoon ground red pepper

1. Combine the paprika, garlic powder, celery seed, cumin, salt, and black pepper in a small bowl. Rub over both sides of the catfish.

2. Combine the mayonnaise, relish, and red pepper in a bowl. Set aside.

3. Heat a grill pan over medium-high heat until hot and coat with cooking spray. Add the catfish and grill for 4 to 5 minutes per side or until the fish flakes easily when tested with a fork. Transfer to serving plates and serve with the reserved tartar sauce.

NUTRITION PER SERVING

339 calories

27 g protein

2 g carbohydrates

24 g fat

4 g saturated fat*

85 mg cholesterol

502 mg sodium

0.5 g fiber

*Limit saturated fat to 10% of total calories—about 17 grams per day for most women—and sodium intake to less than 2,300 milligrams.

{ Make It a FLAT BELLY DIET MEAL }
Serve with the Zucchini and Carrots with Walnuts on page 138, but omit the walnuts (60). **TOTAL MEAL:** 399 calories ■ To serve as part of another *Flat Belly Diet* Meal, omit the tartar sauce (234).

seafood

Roasted Monkfish with Olives

■ 50 MINUTES ■ 4 SERVINGS ■ 300 CALORIES ■ MUFA: OLIVES

Monkfish is known for its tail meat, which is dense, firm, and boneless. Its mild, sweet taste stands up well to higher temperatures in the oven or on the grill. Paired with the Mediterranean trio of fennel, tomatoes, and olives, it's a veritable feast. If the fish you see in the market has a slightly blue cast from the membrane that surrounds it, ask your fishmonger to remove it because it will make the fish tough once cooked.

2 bulbs fennel, each cut into 8 wedges

2 tablespoons olive oil, divided

40 pitted Niçoise olives (about 1⅓ cups)

2 large tomatoes, each cut into 8 wedges

4 monkfish fillets (5 ounces each)

½ teaspoon freshly ground black pepper

¼ cup chopped fresh basil (optional)

1. Preheat the oven to 400°F. Toss the fennel and 1 tablespoon of the oil in a large baking sheet with sides. Roast for 25 minutes.

2. Stir in the olives and tomatoes. Spread the vegetables to the sides of the pan and place the fish in the center. Brush the fish with the remaining 1 tablespoon oil and sprinkle with the pepper.

3. Roast for 12 to 15 minutes or until the fish flakes easily when tested with a fork. Remove the fish to a large serving plate. Stir the basil, if using, into the vegetable mixture and serve alongside the fish.

NUTRITION
PER SERVING

300 calories
29 g protein
15 g carbohydrates
15 g fat
2.5 g saturated fat
45 mg cholesterol
480 mg sodium
6 g fiber

{ Make It a FLAT BELLY DIET MEAL } Serve with ½ cup canned cannellini, rinsed, drained, and warmed with 1 clove mashed garlic and a dash of ground rosemary (100).
TOTAL MEAL: 400 calories

Five-Spice Fish with Avocado-Wasabi Sauce

■ 20 MINUTES ■ 4 SERVINGS ■ 231 CALORIES ■ MUFA: AVOCADO

Wasabi is a Japanese horseradish sold as paste and powder. You can find it near the sushi supplies in your grocery store's international section. Its distinctive fiery kick is nicely balanced by the avocado in this sauce.

1 avocado
1 tablespoon freshly
   squeezed lime juice
1 teaspoon wasabi paste
½ cup low-fat plain yogurt
4 cod or hake fillets
   (6 ounces each)
2 teaspoons olive oil
2 teaspoons Chinese
   five-spice powder
½ teaspoon salt

1. Preheat the oven to 450°F.

2. Mash the avocado, lime juice, and wasabi in a medium bowl. Whisk in the yogurt until smooth.

3. Place the fillets in a shallow baking dish. Drizzle with the oil and sprinkle with the five-spice powder and salt. Roast for 7 to 10 minutes or until the fish flakes easily when tested with a fork. Drizzle each fillet with the avocado sauce to serve.

NUTRITION
PER SERVING

231 calories
29 g protein
7 g carbohydrates
10 g fat
2 g saturated fat
66 mg cholesterol
431 mg sodium
3 g fiber

{ Make It a
FLAT
BELLY
DIET
MEAL }
Serve with the Asian Slaw on page 123, but omit the peanuts (98), and 1 cup steamed snow peas (40). **TOTAL MEAL:** 369 calories ■ To serve as part of another *Flat Belly Diet* Meal, omit the avocado-wasabi sauce (147).

Salmon Burger with Zesty Aioli

30 MINUTES ▪ **4 SERVINGS** ▪ **313 CALORIES** ▪ **MUFA: CANOLA MAYONNAISE**

These burgers are well suited to indoor grilling. For a milder burger, substitute lemon juice for the lime in the aioli; eliminate the jalapeño pepper and use parsley instead of the cumin in the patties.

AIOLI

- ¼ cup canola mayonnaise
- 1 tablespoon freshly squeezed lime juice
- ½ teaspoon freshly grated lime zest
- ½ teaspoon Dijon mustard
- 1 clove garlic, minced

BURGERS

- 2 pouches or cans (6–7 ounces each) boneless, skinless wild salmon, drained
- 2 egg whites, beaten
- 1 cup whole wheat bread crumbs
- ½ cup low-fat plain yogurt
- ½ red onion, minced
- 1 jalapeño chile pepper, seeded and finely chopped
- ½ teaspoon ground cumin
- 1 large tomato, cut into 4 slices
- 4 whole wheat buns, toasted

1. To prepare the aioli: Combine the mayonnaise, lime juice, lime zest, mustard, and garlic in a small bowl. Set aside.

2. To prepare the burgers: Mash the salmon with a fork in a medium bowl. Add the egg whites, bread crumbs, yogurt, onion, pepper, and cumin. Stir to blend. Shape into 4 burgers.

3. Coat a nonstick skillet with cooking spray. Cook the burgers over medium heat for 6 minutes, turning once, or until browned and crisp.

4. Place the bottoms of the buns on 4 plates. Top each with a tomato slice, burger, and half of the reserved aioli. Finish with the bun top.

NUTRITION PER SERVING

313 calories
27 g protein
19 g carbohydrates
16 g fat
1 g saturated fat
67 mg cholesterol
610 mg sodium*
3 g fiber

*Limit saturated fat to 10% of total calories—about 17 grams per day for most women—and sodium intake to less than 2,300 milligrams.

{ Make It a **FLAT BELLY DIET MEAL** }

Serve with a sliced apple (80). **TOTAL MEAL:** 393 calories

▪ To serve as part of another *Flat Belly Diet* Meal, omit the aioli (210).

Halibut Kebabs with Pepper Dressing

■ 1 HOUR 30 MINUTES ■ 4 SERVINGS ■ 360 CALORIES ■ MUFA: OLIVE OIL

Halibut kebabs get the royal treatment with a generous coating of this hot-and-sweet pepper dressing.

1 pound halibut fillet, cut into 16 cubes

1 tablespoon freshly squeezed lemon juice

5 tablespoons extra virgin olive oil, divided

2 tablespoons chopped shallot

1 roasted red bell pepper

1 sweet hot cherry pepper (from a jar), seeded

1 tablespoon balsamic vinegar

1 teaspoon honey

1 teaspoon Dijon mustard

½ teaspoon salt

1 small red onion, cut into 12 wedges

16 cherry tomatoes

8 cups baby spinach

1. Combine the halibut, lemon juice, 1 tablespoon of the oil, and the shallot in a bowl. Toss well and refrigerate for 1 hour.

2. Meanwhile, combine the bell pepper, hot cherry pepper, vinegar, honey, mustard, and ¼ teaspoon of the salt in a blender and puree. Transfer to a bowl and whisk in the remaining 4 tablespoons oil.

3. Prepare the grill for medium-hot direct-heat grilling. Coat the grill rack with cooking spray.

4. Bring a small saucepan of water to a boil over high heat. Add the onion wedges, return to a boil, and cook for 1 minute. Drain, rinse under cold water, and drain again.

5. Remove the halibut from the refrigerator. Thread onto each of 4 skewers, in alternating order, 4 fish cubes, 3 onion wedges, and 4 tomatoes. Sprinkle the kebabs with the remaining ¼ teaspoon salt.

6. Grill the skewers for 8 to 10 minutes, turning every 2 minutes or until the fish flakes easily when tested with a fork.

7. Place 2 cups of the spinach onto each of 4 serving plates, top with a kebab and drizzle with the pepper dressing.

NUTRITION PER SERVING

360 calories
26 g protein
18 g carbohydrates
20 g fat
3 g saturated fat
35 mg cholesterol
470 mg sodium
5 g fiber

{ Make It a FLAT BELLY DIET MEAL }

Serve with ½ cup grilled baby red potatoes (50). **TOTAL MEAL:** 410 calories

seafood

Grilled Tuna Niçoise

■ 45 MINUTES ■ 4 SERVINGS ■ 380 CALORIES ■ MUFA: TAPENADE

This elegant salad draws its inspiration and fresh flavor from the south of France. For maximum authenticity, use Niçoise olives in the tapenade.

1 tablespoon olive oil
1 tablespoon finely chopped fresh rosemary
2 zucchini
2 potatoes
1 fresh tuna steak (1½ pounds)
1 medium tomato, thickly sliced
½ cup Tapenade (opposite page) or store-bought tapenade
4 lemon wedges
   Freshly ground black pepper

1. Preheat the grill. Combine the oil and rosemary in a small bowl.

2. Cut the zucchini and potatoes into thick wedges that are roughly the same thickness and length. Slather the rosemary oil over the zucchini, potatoes, and tuna, spreading evenly.

3. Place the potatoes, zucchini, and tomatoes over direct heat. Grill for 8 minutes or until the potatoes are golden and the zucchini and tomato begin to soften, flipping halfway through. Move the vegetables away from the direct heat to cook for up to 8 minutes longer, transferring to a platter as they become tender.

4. Set the tuna over direct heat. Grill for about 3 minutes per side for rare or longer for desired doneness.

5. Transfer the tuna to a cutting board and allow to sit for 5 minutes. Cut into ½"-thick diagonal slices. Chop the cooked tomato into coarse pieces.

6. Arrange the tuna on serving plates, alternating with the zucchini and potato wedges. Place the tapenade and tomato next to the tuna and vegetables. Garnish with the lemon wedges. Pass the pepper at the table.

NUTRITION
PER SERVING

380 calories
56 g protein
14 g carbohydrates
11 g fat
2 g saturated fat
100 mg cholesterol
380 mg sodium
6 g fiber

A single serving of this recipe counts as a *Flat Belly Diet* Meal without any add-ons!

Tapenade

■ 5 MINUTES ■ 12 SERVINGS (2 TABLESPOONS EACH) ■ 60 CALORIES ■ MUFA: OLIVES

Wildly popular in many a supermarket gourmet section, this rich olive paste is incredibly easy to make at home—for a fraction of the cost.

2 cups Niçoise olives, pitted

2 teaspoons capers, rinsed and drained

3 cloves garlic

2 tablespoons olive oil

1 tablespoon freshly squeezed lemon juice

¼ teaspoon freshly ground black pepper

1. Combine the olives, capers, and garlic in the bowl of a food processor fitted with a metal blade. Pulse until coarsely chopped. Combine the oil and lemon juice in a measuring cup. With the machine running, add the oil mixture through the feed tube to blend into a rough paste. Add the pepper and pulse to combine.

2. Transfer to an airtight container. Refrigerate for up to 2 weeks.

NUTRITION PER SERVING

60 calories
0 g protein
2 g carbohydrates
5 g fat
0.5 g saturated fat
0 mg cholesterol
270 mg sodium
1 g fiber

{ Make It a FLAT BELLY DIET MEAL } Serve with 1 ½ cups cooked multigrain pasta (300) tossed with 3 sun-dried tomatoes packed in oil (30) and 1 ½ cups fresh spinach (9).
TOTAL MEAL: 399 calories

seafood

Sesame-Crusted Salmon

■ 25 MINUTES ■ 4 SERVINGS ■ 400 CALORIES ■ MUFA: SESAME SEEDS

A thick layer of sesame seeds is a great way to keep the salmon incredibly moist, even if it happens to spend a few extra minutes in the oven. Served on a bed of cooked spinach and drizzled with a simple wasabi sauce, this restaurant-worthy creation is surprisingly easy to pull together.

1 teaspoon toasted sesame oil, divided

4 salmon fillets (5 ounces each)

½ cup black sesame seeds, divided

¼ cup reduced-fat sour cream

1 teaspoon wasabi powder

1 tablespoon freshly squeezed lime juice

2 packages (10 ounces each) baby spinach, rinsed

1 tablespoon reduced-sodium soy sauce

1. Preheat the oven to 400°F. Brush a small baking dish very lightly with some of the sesame oil.

2. Pat the fillets dry with a paper towel. Spread half of the sesame seeds on a small plate and press the fish firmly onto the seeds. Transfer to the prepared dish. Bake for 10 minutes or until the fish flakes easily with a fork.

3. Combine the sour cream, wasabi, and lime juice in a small bowl. Thin with a few drops of water, if necessary, to make a smooth sauce. Set aside.

4. Heat the remaining sesame oil in a large nonstick skillet over medium-high heat. Working in batches, if necessary, add the spinach, cover, and cook for 2 to 3 minutes or until the spinach wilts. Stir in the soy sauce and remaining ¼ cup sesame seeds.

5. Divide the spinach among 4 plates. Top each with a piece of salmon and drizzle the reserved wasabi sauce around the plate.

NUTRITION PER SERVING

400 calories
40 g protein
11 g carbohydrates
23 g fat
4 g saturated fat*
95 mg cholesterol
320 mg sodium
5 g fiber

*Limit saturated fat to 10% of total calories—about 17 grams per day for most women—and sodium intake to less than 2,300 milligrams.

{ Make It a FLAT BELLY DIET MEAL } A single serving of this recipe counts as a *Flat Belly Diet* Meal without any add-ons!

Stir-Fry Walnut Shrimp

■ 40 MINUTES ■ 4 SERVINGS ■ 292 CALORIES ■ MUFA: WALNUTS

Crunchy toasted walnuts offer a wonderful contrast to the plump, juicy shrimp in this dish. Rice wine vinegar is sometimes simply labeled rice vinegar, but seasoned rice wine vinegar has a touch of added salt and sugar, so reduce the honey to 2 teaspoons if using.

2 tablespoons medium-dry sherry (optional)

1 tablespoon reduced-sodium soy sauce

1 pound peeled and deveined shrimp, thawed if frozen

½ cup walnuts, coarsely chopped

2 tablespoons canola oil

2 tablespoons chopped fresh ginger

½ cup reduced-sodium, fat-free chicken broth

3 scallions, whites thinly sliced diagonally, greens diagonally sliced 1" thick

1 tablespoon honey

1 teaspoon rice wine vinegar

1½ teaspoons cornstarch, dissolved in 1 tablespoon water

1. Mix the sherry, if using, and soy sauce in a medium bowl. Add the shrimp and toss to coat. Let stand for 10 minutes. Drain the shrimp, reserving the marinade.

2. Meanwhile, cook the walnuts in a large heavy skillet over medium heat, tossing often, for about 3 minutes or until lightly toasted. Tip into a plate. Wipe out the skillet.

3. Turn the heat up to medium-high and cook the oil and ginger in the same skillet, stirring frequently, for 1 minute or until the ginger is fragrant. Add the shrimp and stir-fry for 3 to 4 minutes or until opaque. Add the broth, scallions, and reserved marinade and bring to a boil. Boil for 1 minute.

4. Add the honey and vinegar. Stir in the cornstarch mixture and cook, stirring constantly, for about 1 minute or until thickened and bubbly. Remove from the heat and stir in the walnuts.

NUTRITION PER SERVING

292 calories
23 g protein
10 g carbohydrates
18 g fat
2 g saturated fat
151 mg cholesterol
357 mg sodium
1 g fiber

{ Make It a FLAT BELLY DIET MEAL } Serve with the Asparagus with Pine Nuts on page 139, but omit the pine nuts (45), and ⅓ cup steamed brown rice (65). **TOTAL MEAL:** 402 calories

seafood

Spanish Shrimp with Garlic Sauce

■ **25 MINUTES** ■ **4 SERVINGS** ■ **270 CALORIES** ■ **MUFA: OLIVE OIL**

This smoky shrimp dish features the tender crunch of seedless English (or hothouse) cucumbers, which have a thin skin and require no peeling.

4 tablespoons olive oil, divided

2 red bell peppers, cut into thin strips

½ seedless cucumber, thinly sliced (1½ cups)

¼ teaspoon salt, divided

4 large garlic cloves, minced

1 pound peeled and deveined shrimp, thawed if frozen

1 tablespoon smoked paprika

½ teaspoon freshly ground black pepper

2 tablespoons medium-dry sherry (optional)

2 tablespoons freshly squeezed lemon juice

1. Warm 1 tablespoon of the oil in a large, deep, heavy skillet over medium heat. Add the bell peppers, cover, and cook, stirring often, for about 5 minutes or until tender. Add the cucumber and ⅛ teaspoon of the salt, cover, and cook, stirring often, for 3 minutes or until tender and becoming translucent. Transfer the vegetables to a serving dish. Cover to keep warm.

2. Combine the garlic and remaining 3 tablespoons oil in the same skillet over medium heat. Cook, stirring, for about 1 minute or until fragrant.

3. Stir in the shrimp and sprinkle with the paprika, black pepper, and remaining ⅛ teaspoon salt. Cook, stirring often, for 5 to 7 minutes or until the shrimp are opaque. (If the pan becomes very dry, add 1 or 2 tablespoons water.)

4. Add the sherry, if using, and lemon juice. Cook, stirring, for 1 minute or until the pan juices are bubbly and thickened. Serve the shrimp over the vegetables.

NUTRITION PER SERVING

270 calories
24 g protein
8 g carbohydrates
16 g fat
2.5 g saturated fat
170 mg cholesterol
320 mg sodium
2 g fiber

{ Make It a FLAT BELLY DIET MEAL }

Serve with the Saffron Rice on page 148, but omit the pistachios (140).

TOTAL MEAL: 410 calories

Spring Rolls with Chili Sauce

■ 45 MINUTES ■ 4 SERVINGS ■ 261 CALORIES ■ MUFA: PEANUTS

Vietnamese-style spring rolls owe their seductive quality to near-translucent rice-paper wrappers, which give a tantalizing peek of plump shrimp and a wealth of fresh herbs and vegetables within. If you like, tuck a few leaves of fresh mint into the mix.

SPRING ROLLS

- 2 tablespoons freshly squeezed lime juice
- 2 teaspoons reduced-sodium soy sauce
- ½ pound cooked, medium shrimp, peeled, tails removed, and coarsely chopped
- 4 scallions, thinly sliced diagonally
- 8 sheets rice paper (about 8"–9" in diameter)
- 1 cup shredded lettuce
- ½ seedless cucumber, peeled and cut into matchsticks
- 2 carrots, coarsely grated
- 1 cup loosely packed fresh cilantro leaves
- ½ cup thinly sliced basil leaves
- ½ cup chopped dry-roasted unsalted peanuts

DIPPING SAUCE

- ½ cup sweet chili sauce
- 2 tablespoons freshly squeezed lime juice
- 1 tablespoon reduced-sodium soy sauce

1. To prepare the spring rolls: Mix the lime juice and soy sauce in a large bowl. Add the shrimp and scallions and toss to mix well.

2. Line a work surface with 2 layers of paper towels. Line a platter with paper towels and mist with water.

3. Soak a rice-paper round in warm water for about 1 minute or until pliable, then place on the paper towels. Arrange ⅛ of the lettuce along the bottom of the rice paper. Top with ⅛ of the shrimp mixture and ⅛ of the cucumber, carrots, cilantro, and basil and sprinkle with ⅛ of the peanuts. Fold the ends over and roll the rice paper up around the filling. Place on the prepared platter and cover loosely with plastic wrap to prevent drying out. Repeat with the remaining rice paper, cucumber, carrots, cilantro, and basil.

4. To prepare the dipping sauce: Mix the chili sauce, lime juice, and soy sauce in a small bowl. Serve with the rolls.

NUTRITION
PER SERVING

261 calories
20 g protein
19 g carbohydrates
13 g fat
2 g saturated fat
97 mg cholesterol
831 mg sodium*
6 g fiber

*Limit saturated fat to 10% of total calories—about 17 grams per day for most women—and sodium intake to less than 2,300 milligrams.

{ Make It a FLAT BELLY DIET MEAL } Serve with ½ cup Thai Corn and Crab Soup on page 105, prepared with 1 tablespoon oil (134). **TOTAL MEAL:** 395 calories ■ To serve as part of another *Flat Belly Diet* Meal, omit the peanuts (155).

Shrimp and Avocado Rolls

■ 45 MINUTES   ■ 4 SERVINGS   ■ 374 CALORIES   ■ MUFA: AVOCADO

With practice, these popular rolls become quite easy to make and are a great use for leftover shrimp.

1¼ cups sushi rice
1 tablespoon rice vinegar
1 tablespoon mirin
1 tablespoon honey
¼ teaspoon salt
8 sheets nori, top ¼ cut off and discarded
2 teaspoons store-bought wasabi
½ pound cooked medium shrimp (16 pieces), halved lengthwise
1 avocado, sliced
½ cucumber, peeled, seeded, and cut into thin strips

1. Cook the rice per the package directions. Meanwhile, combine the vinegar, mirin, honey, and salt in a small bowl. When the rice is cooked, stir in the vinegar mixture and let stand, covered, for 10 minutes.

2. Working one at a time, place a nori sheet on the work surface. Starting at the edge closest to you, spread the bottom half with a slightly rounded ⅓ cup of the rice. Spread ¼ teaspoon of the wasabi in a straight line across the center of the rice. Top with 4 of the shrimp halves laid end to end, ⅛ of the avocado, and ⅛ of the cucumber. Using a sushi mat, fold the end of the nori nearest you over the filling and roll. Repeat with the remaining ingredients. Cut each roll into 6 pieces to serve.

NUTRITION
PER SERVING

374 calories
19 g protein
57 g carbohydrates
7 g fat
1 g saturated fat
86 mg cholesterol
393 mg sodium
6 g fiber

{ Make It a
FLAT
BELLY
DIET
MEAL }
Serve with ¼ cup canned mandarin oranges, drained (40).
TOTAL MEAL: 414 calories

Crab Primavera with Spaghetti

■ **40 MINUTES** ■ **4 SERVINGS** ■ **414 CALORIES** ■ **MUFA: OLIVE OIL**

All the signs of spring are here—tender, sweet crab and colorful garden-fresh vegetables. *Buon appetito!*

1 red onion, cut
   into wedges
1 yellow bell pepper,
   cut into thin strips
1 zucchini, halved
   and sliced
2 cloves garlic, minced
¼ cup olive oil, divided
4 ounces multigrain
   spaghetti
1 large tomato, seeded
   and chopped
¼ cup shredded fresh basil
1 pound lump crabmeat,
   picked over
¼ cup grated Parmesan
   cheese

1. Preheat the oven to 450°F. Combine the onion, pepper, zucchini, and garlic in a 9″ × 9″ pan. Drizzle with 2 tablespoons of the oil and toss to coat. Roast for 15 minutes or until the vegetables are browned, tossing occasionally.

2. Meanwhile, prepare the pasta per the package directions, reserving ½ cup of the cooking liquid before draining.

3. Combine the roasted vegetables, pasta, tomato, basil, and crab in a large bowl. Toss to coat. Add cooking liquid a few tablespoons at a time, if needed, until moistened. Sprinkle with the cheese.

**NUTRITION
PER SERVING**

414 calories
35 g protein
28 g carbohydrates
17 g fat
3 g saturated fat
124 mg cholesterol
526 mg sodium
4 g fiber

{ Make It a **FLAT BELLY DIET MEAL** } A single serving of this recipe counts as a *Flat Belly Diet* Meal without any add-ons!

Cioppino with Lemon Aioli

■ 30 MINUTES ■ 4 SERVINGS ■ 387 CALORIES ■ MUFA: CANOLA MAYONNAISE

An Italian-style fish stew, cioppino is a versatile dish commonly made with the "catch of the day." Feel free to make some substitutions for whatever is fresh at the grocery, just be sure to use another firm whitefish in place of the tilapia.

CIOPPINO

- 2 teaspoons canola oil
- 1 onion, chopped
- 2 cloves garlic, minced
- 2 teaspoons chopped fresh oregano
- 1 can (15 ounces) crushed tomatoes
- 1 cup reduced-sodium chicken broth
- 12 ounces tilapia fillets
- ½ pound medium shrimp, peeled and deveined
- ¼ cup chopped fresh parsley
- ¼ teaspoon salt
- ¼ teaspoon freshly ground black pepper

TOAST POINTS

- 4 slices whole grain bread
  Aioli (page 177), or
  store-bought with
  lemon instead of lime

1. To prepare the cioppino: Combine the oil, onion, garlic, and oregano in a large pot over medium heat. Cover and cook, stirring occasionally, for 5 minutes or until softened. Add the tomatoes and broth. Bring to a boil, then reduce the heat to a simmer for 5 minutes for the flavors to blend.

2. Add the tilapia, shrimp, parsley, salt, and pepper. Simmer for 10 minutes or until the tilapia flakes easily when tested with a fork and the shrimp are opaque.

3. To prepare the toast points: Toast the bread. Spread with the aioli. Cut into quarters diagonally. Serve with the cioppino.

NUTRITION PER SERVING

387 calories
35 g protein
24 g carbohydrates
17 g fat
2 g saturated fat
134 mg cholesterol
744 mg sodium*
5 g fiber

*Limit saturated fat to 10% of total calories—about 17 grams per day for most women—and sodium intake to less than 2,300 milligrams.

{ Make It a FLAT BELLY DIET MEAL } A single serving of this recipe counts as a *Flat Belly Diet* Meal without any add-ons! ■ To serve as a part of another *Flat Belly Diet* Meal, omit the aioli (281).

Scallops with Avocado-Kiwi Salsa

■ **20 MINUTES** ■ **4 SERVINGS** ■ **290 CALORIES** ■ **MUFA: AVOCADO**

This vibrant green salsa is a study in creamy and tart contrast. For maximum flavor, chop the avocado and kiwifruit into fine pieces, but not so small that they become mushy when stirred.

1 avocado, diced

2 kiwifruit, peeled and finely chopped

¼ cup finely chopped red onion

¼ cup finely chopped red bell pepper

2 tablespoons chopped fresh cilantro

1 jalapeño chile pepper, seeded and finely chopped

1 tablespoon freshly squeezed lemon juice

½ teaspoon salt, divided

¼ teaspoon freshly ground black pepper, divided

1 tablespoon olive oil

1½ pounds dry (not packed in liquid) sea scallops, tough muscle removed

1. Combine the avocado, kiwi, onion, bell pepper, cilantro, chile pepper, lemon juice, ¼ teaspoon of the salt, and ⅛ teaspoon of the black pepper in a bowl.

2. Heat the oil in a large nonstick skillet over medium-high heat. Pat the scallops dry with a paper towel and sprinkle with the remaining ¼ teaspoon salt and ⅛ teaspoon black pepper. Add to the skillet and cook for 2 to 3 minutes per side or until the scallops are opaque and lightly browned. Transfer to serving plates and spoon salsa over each.

NUTRITION PER SERVING

290 calories
30 g protein
18 g carbohydrates
10 g fat
1.5 g saturated fat
55 mg cholesterol
570 mg sodium
4 g fiber

{ Make It a **FLAT BELLY DIET MEAL** } Serve with ¾ cup cooked couscous (132). **TOTAL MEAL:** 422 calories

Scallops with Lemon-Parsley Sauce

■ **15 MINUTES** ■ **4 SERVINGS** ■ **282 CALORIES** ■ **MUFA: OLIVE OIL**

Of all the herbs we commonly use, nothing could be easier than parsley. This particular sauce works nicely as a topping for grilled chicken and vegetables, too.

¼ cup chopped fresh parsley

2 tablespoons freshly squeezed lemon juice

1 clove garlic, minced

½ teaspoon salt, divided

¼ teaspoon freshly ground black pepper, divided

¼ cup extra virgin olive oil

1½ pounds dry (not packed in liquid) sea scallops, tough muscle removed

1. Combine the parsley, lemon juice, garlic, ¼ teaspoon of the salt, and ⅛ teaspoon of the pepper in a small bowl. Whisk in the oil to combine. Set aside.

2. Coat a grill pan with cooking spray and heat over medium-high heat. Pat dry the scallops with a paper towel and sprinkle with the remaining ¼ teaspoon salt and ⅛ teaspoon pepper. Add to the grill pan and grill for 2 to 3 minutes per side or until the scallops are opaque. Divide among 4 serving plates and spoon the reserved sauce over each serving.

NUTRITION PER SERVING

282 calories
29 g protein
5 g carbohydrates
15 g fat
2 g saturated fat
56 mg cholesterol
569 mg sodium
0.5 g fiber

{ **Make It a FLAT BELLY DIET MEAL** } Serve with ½ cup Brown Rice Pilaf with Mushrooms on page 147, but omit the pecans (110).
TOTAL MEAL: 392 calories

Creamy Seafood Casserole

■ **45 MINUTES** ■ **4 SERVINGS** ■ **350 CALORIES** ■ **MUFA: PISTACHIOS**

Ground pistachios create a lovely complement to the crust in this heavenly seafood creation. Panko bread crumbs, originally used in Japanese cooking, are much crispier than regular bread crumbs, so be sure to use them if available.

CASSEROLE

- ¾ cup reduced-sodium, fat-free chicken broth
- 3 medium carrots, sliced diagonally
- 1 small bunch asparagus, cut diagonally into 2″ pieces
- 1 cup 1% milk
- ¼ teaspoon salt
- ¼ teaspoon freshly ground black pepper
- 1 tablespoon cornstarch, dissolved in 2 tablespoons cold water
- 1 pound medium shrimp, thawed if frozen, peeled and deveined, tails removed
- 3 scallions, thinly sliced
- 2 tablespoons snipped fresh dill

CRUST

- ½ cup shelled pistachios, finely chopped (not ground) in a food processor
- ¼ cup Panko bread crumbs
- 2 tablespoons olive oil

1. Preheat the oven to 400°F. Spray a shallow 1½-quart baking dish with olive oil spray.

2. To prepare the casserole: Bring the broth to a boil in a large skillet over medium heat. Add the carrots and asparagus, cover, and cook, stirring often, for 3 minutes or until crisp-tender. Transfer to the prepared baking dish with a slotted spoon.

3. Add the milk, salt, and pepper to the broth in the skillet and bring to a boil. Stir the cornstarch mixture again and add to the milk mixture. Cook, stirring constantly, until thickened. Reduce the heat to medium and stir in the shrimp, scallions, and dill. Bring to a simmer and pour into the prepared baking dish.

4. To prepare the crust: Mix the pistachios and bread crumbs in a small bowl. Sprinkle evenly over the casserole. Drizzle with the oil. Bake for 15 to 20 minutes or until the shrimp are opaque and the casserole is bubbly.

NUTRITION PER SERVING

350 calories
31 g protein
20 g carbohydrates
17 g fat
3 g saturated fat
175 mg cholesterol
470 mg sodium
4 g fiber

{ Make It a FLAT BELLY DIET MEAL }
Serve with ½ medium baked potato (80).
TOTAL MEAL: 430 calories

9

Poultry

Chicken Piccata

15 MINUTES ■ **4 SERVINGS** ■ **235 CALORIES** ■ **MUFA: OLIVE OIL**

Capers are actually immature buds plucked from a small bush native to the Middle East and Mediterranean regions of the world. Pickled in vinegar brine or packed in salt, they are often displayed in small, narrow jars. To keep the sodium count under control, choose the brine-packed ones.

12 ounces boneless, skinless chicken tenders
2 tablespoons flour
4 tablespoons olive oil
2 tablespoons freshly squeezed lemon juice
2 tablespoons chopped fresh parsley
2 teaspoons capers, minced
   Freshly ground black pepper

1. Lay the tenders on a work surface. With a smooth scaloppine pounder or a rolling pin covered in plastic wrap, flatten to ¼" thickness. Dredge the cutlets lightly in the flour.

2. Heat a large skillet over medium-high heat. Add the oil to the skillet and heat until sizzling. Place the chicken in the skillet. Cook for 2 minutes per side or until lightly browned and cooked through.

3. Add the lemon juice, parsley, and capers. Bring the mixture to a boil. Reduce the heat and simmer for 2 minutes to allow the flavors to blend. Season to taste with the pepper. Serve the chicken with the pan juices.

Note: Pounding the chicken breasts to an even thickness is an important step because it allows the chicken to cook evenly so both ends are moist and delicious.

NUTRITION PER SERVING

235 calories
21 g protein
4 g carbohydrates
15 g fat
2 g saturated fat
49 mg cholesterol
108 mg sodium
0 g fiber

{ Make It a FLAT BELLY DIET MEAL }
Serve with the Spinach Salad with Pears, Pecans, and Goat Cheese on page 132, but omit the pecans (208).
TOTAL MEAL: 443 calories

Chicken with Romesco Sauce

■ 30 MINUTES ■ 4 SERVINGS ■ 340 CALORIES ■ MUFA: ALMONDS

This bold Spanish sauce is equally good as a topping for grilled fish. It's also a great dip for crudité. The MUFA power of almonds lends quite a bit of body, while the flavors of sweet roasted pepper and smoky paprika tantalize the tastebuds.

2 cloves garlic, smashed
1 slice firm whole grain bread, crust discarded and bread torn into pieces
½ cup slivered almonds
1 cup drained roasted red peppers (from a jar), coarsely chopped
1 tomato, seeded and coarsely chopped
1 tablespoon red-wine vinegar
1 teaspoon smoked paprika
½ teaspoon salt
2 tablespoons extra virgin olive oil
4 boneless, skinless chicken breast halves (5 ounces each)

1. Toast the garlic and bread in a large nonstick skillet over medium heat for 5 minutes or until lightly browned, stirring occasionally. Add the almonds and continue cooking and stirring for 3 minutes or until the almonds are toasted. Transfer to a food processor fitted with a metal blade or a blender. Add the peppers, tomato, vinegar, paprika, salt, and oil and puree. Set aside.

2. Coat the same skillet with olive oil cooking spray and return to medium heat. Add the chicken and cook, turning once, for 5 minutes or until browned. Remove to a plate. Add the reserved almond mixture and bring to a simmer over medium heat.

3. Return the chicken to the skillet. Cover and simmer for 10 minutes or until a thermometer inserted in the thickest portion registers 165°F.

NUTRITION PER SERVING

340 calories
37 g protein
11 g carbohydrates
16 g fat
2 g saturated fat
80 mg cholesterol
430 mg sodium
4 g fiber

{ Make It a FLAT BELLY DIET MEAL } Serve with 1 cup steamed asparagus (30).
TOTAL MEAL: 370 calories

Mexican Chicken with Pepita Sauce

■ 25 MINUTES ■ 4 SERVINGS ■ 175 CALORIES ■ MUFA: PUMPKIN SEEDS

Pumpkin seeds add a pleasant crunch to this spicy chicken dish. In lieu of a coating, just a spoonful of flour thickens the sauce quite nicely.

2 teaspoons canola oil
½ onion, chopped
½ red bell pepper, chopped
1 teaspoon ground cumin
1 teaspoon chopped fresh oregano
¼ teaspoon salt
1 tablespoon flour
¼ teaspoon freshly ground black pepper
1 cup reduced-sodium chicken broth
1 pound boneless, skinless chicken tenders
½ cup pumpkin seeds

1. Heat the oil in a large nonstick skillet over medium-high heat. Add the onion, bell pepper, cumin, oregano, and salt. Stir to mix. Cover and cook over medium heat, stirring occasionally, for 3 minutes or until the vegetables have softened.

2. Add the flour and black pepper. Stir so the flour thoroughly coats the vegetables. Add the broth and cook, stirring constantly, for 2 minutes or until thickened. Add the chicken. Cover and simmer for 10 minutes or until the chicken is cooked through. Add the pumpkin seeds and stir into the sauce.

NUTRITION PER SERVING

175 calories
28 g protein
7 g carbohydrates
5 g fat
0.5 g saturated fat
67 mg cholesterol
309 mg sodium
1 g fiber

{ Make It a **FLAT BELLY DIET MEAL** } Serve with the Saffron Rice on page 148, but omit the pistachios (140), and ½ cup sliced mango (55). **TOTAL MEAL:** 378 calories ■ To serve as part of a *Flat Belly Diet* Meal, omit the pepitas (147).

Mediterranean Chicken and Orzo

■ **35 MINUTES** ■ **4 SERVINGS** ■ **388 CALORIES** ■ **MUFA: OLIVES**

If your health food store carries whole wheat orzo, stock up. The flavor and texture of this rice-shaped pasta are remarkably similar to regular orzo, but the fiber boost is significant—more than 5 grams per ½-cup serving!

 4 boneless, skinless
   chicken breast halves
   (4 ounces each)
1½ cups reduced-sodium
   chicken broth
 ⅔ cup orzo, preferably
   whole wheat
 1 lemon, peeled and cut
   into chunks
 1 teaspoon dried oregano
40 pitted kalamata olives,
   chopped (about 1⅓ cups)
 2 cups baby spinach
 1 tomato, seeded and
   chopped
 ½ cup sliced roasted
   red pepper
 ¼ cup crumbled feta cheese

1. Heat a nonstick skillet coated with cooking spray over medium heat. Add the chicken and cook, turning once, for 6 minutes or until browned. Remove to a plate.

2. Add the broth and bring to a boil over high heat. Stir in the orzo, lemon, and oregano. Return the chicken to the skillet. Reduce the heat to medium-low, cover, and simmer for 10 minutes or until the orzo is tender and a thermometer inserted in the thickest portion of the chicken registers 165°F.

3. Stir in the olives, spinach, tomato, and pepper. Cook for 2 minutes, stirring, to heat through. Sprinkle with the cheese.

**NUTRITION
PER SERVING**

388 calories
35 g protein
31 g carbohydrates
14 g fat
3 g saturated fat
74 mg cholesterol
925 mg sodium*
6 g fiber

*Limit saturated fat to 10% of total calories—about 17 grams per day for most women—and sodium intake to less than 2,300 milligrams.

{ **Make It a FLAT BELLY DIET MEAL** } A single serving of this recipe counts as a *Flat Belly Diet* Meal without any add-ons!

Rotini with Chicken and Broccoli

35 MINUTES ▪ **4 SERVINGS** ▪ **421 CALORIES** ▪ **MUFA: OLIVES**

If you want to cook from scratch, use The Best Grilled Chicken Breast recipe (page 205) for your chicken breasts. If you're short on time, precooked chicken strips are a handy substitute.

6 ounces multigrain rotini pasta

½ cup chopped sun-dried tomatoes

2 cloves garlic, minced

4 tablespoons olive oil

½ pound broccoli rabe, trimmed

12 ounces boneless, skinless chicken breasts, grilled or roasted and sliced thinly

10 black olives, pitted and sliced (about ⅓ cup)

½ cup shredded fresh basil
Freshly ground black pepper
Shredded Parmesan cheese

1. Bring a large pot of water to a boil. Add the rotini and stir. Cook per the package directions for 9 to 11 minutes or until al dente. Drain the rotini, reserving ½ cup of the cooking water, and set aside.

2. Marinate the tomatoes in oil in a flat dish. Set aside for 10 minutes.

3. Heat a large skillet over medium-high heat. Add the garlic, oil, and reserved tomatoes and cook for 1 to 2 minutes or until fragrant. Add the broccoli rabe. Cover and cook, tossing occasionally, for 3 to 5 minutes or until the tomatoes soften.

4. Add the chicken, olives, and reserved pasta. Toss to combine. Add enough of the reserved water to moisten the mixture. Mix in the basil. Season to taste with the pepper and cheese.

NUTRITION PER SERVING

421 calories
28 g protein
39 g carbohydrates
17 g fat
2 g saturated fat
49 mg cholesterol
326 mg sodium
3 g fiber

{ **Make It a FLAT BELLY DIET MEAL** } A single serving of this recipe counts as a *Flat Belly Diet* Meal without any add-ons!

Walnut-Crusted Chicken Breasts with Pomegranate Syrup

■ **35 MINUTES** ■ **4 SERVINGS** ■ **403 CALORIES** ■ **MUFA: WALNUTS**

No wonder pomegranates are popular—they're a great source of antioxidants, and they taste wonderful, like a combination of apples, mixed berries, and citrus—a fruit salad in a glass! With so many pomegranate juice blends now available, feel free to experiment with your favorite in this recipe—just make sure to use a brand that's labeled 100 percent fruit juice.

1 egg
1 tablespoon water
½ cup walnuts, finely chopped
¼ cup whole grain bread crumbs
½ teaspoon salt
4 boneless, skinless chicken breast halves (5 ounces each)
2 cups pomegranate juice
1 tablespoon honey
2 teaspoons minced crystallized ginger
6 cups mesclun or mixed greens

1. Preheat the oven to 425°F. Coat a baking sheet with cooking spray.

2. Whisk the egg with the water in a shallow dish. Combine the walnuts, bread crumbs, and salt in another shallow dish. Dip the chicken into the egg and then the nut mixture. Place on the prepared baking sheet and coat with cooking spray.

3. Bake, turning once, for 15 minutes or until a thermometer inserted in the thickest portion registers 165°F. Let rest for 10 minutes, then slice the breasts.

4. Meanwhile, bring the pomegranate juice, honey, and ginger to a boil. Boil for about 15 minutes or until reduced by half. Remove from the heat and set aside.

5. Arrange the mesclun on 4 plates. Place the chicken on top and drizzle with the pomegranate syrup.

NUTRITION PER SERVING

403 calories
39 g protein
34 g carbohydrates
13 g fat
2 g saturated fat
135 mg cholesterol
496 mg sodium
3 g fiber

{ **Make It a FLAT BELLY DIET MEAL** } A single serving of this recipe counts as a *Flat Belly Diet* Meal without any add-ons!

Poached Chicken Provençal

35 MINUTES ▪ 4 SERVINGS ▪ 316 CALORIES ▪ MUFA: TAPENADE

This is an interesting dish to make because each component lends itself to another part of the recipe. The potatoes draw a deeper flavor as they cook in the poaching liquid (versus plain water). In turn, the heat from the just-cooked potatoes gently warms the tomatoes, rendering them all the more sweet.

4 boneless, skinless
  chicken breast halves
  (4 ounces each)
2 cups reduced-sodium
  chicken broth
1 teaspoon dried rosemary
1 pound small red-skinned
  potatoes, quartered
1 cup cherry tomatoes
¼ cup Tapenade (page 181)
  or store-bought tapenade
3 tablespoons freshly
  squeezed lemon juice
2 tablespoons olive oil
½ teaspoon freshly ground
  black pepper

1. Place the chicken, broth, and rosemary in a medium skillet (make sure the broth covers the chicken). Bring to a simmer over medium heat. Simmer for 10 to 12 minutes or until a thermometer inserted in the thickest portion registers 165°F. Remove the chicken to a plate and keep warm.

2. Raise the heat to medium-high and return the skillet to the stove top. Add the potatoes and bring to a simmer. Reduce the heat to low, cover, and simmer for 10 to 12 minutes or until the potatoes are tender and the liquid is absorbed. Place the potatoes in a large serving bowl. Stir in the tomatoes and tapenade. Combine the lemon juice and oil in a small bowl and stir into the potatoes. Sprinkle with the pepper. Serve with the sliced chicken.

NUTRITION PER SERVING

316 calories
32 g protein
22 g carbohydrates
11 g fat
2 g saturated fat
68 mg cholesterol
482 mg sodium
3 g fiber

{ **Make It a FLAT BELLY DIET MEAL** } Serve with
1 medium pear (104 calories).
TOTAL MEAL: 420 calories

The Best Grilled Chicken Breast

20 MINUTES **4 SERVINGS** **355 CALORIES** **MUFA: OLIVE OIL**

Chicken breasts are a wonderful partner for many of the dishes in this book, so this recipe gives you all the grilling secrets you need to know for the best results.

CHICKEN

- 4 boneless, skinless chicken breast halves (6 ounces each), trimmed
- 1 tablespoon olive oil
- ½ teaspoon salt
- ¼ teaspoon freshly ground black pepper

BALSAMICO SAUCE

- 3 tablespoons finely chopped fresh basil
- 1 tablespoon balsamic vinegar
- 1 tablespoon finely chopped shallots
- 1 teaspoon Dijon mustard
- 1 teaspoon honey
- ¼ teaspoon salt
- ¼ teaspoon freshly ground black pepper
- 4 tablespoons extra virgin olive oil

1. Prepare the grill for medium-hot direct-heat grilling (see note below).

2. To prepare the chicken, lightly pound the chicken to an even thickness using a meat mallet or the heel of your hand. Toss the chicken with the oil and sprinkle with the salt and pepper. Set over the heat on a grill rack that has been coated with oil. Grill for 5 to 6 minutes per side or until the chicken is well marked and a thermometer inserted in the thickest part registers 165°F.

3. To prepare the sauce, combine the basil, vinegar, shallots, mustard, honey, salt, and pepper in a small bowl. Whisk in the oil to combine. Spoon over sliced grilled chicken breasts.

Note: To coat the grill with a thin layer of oil, which will help prevent sticking, crumple a ball of foil, drizzle with a teaspoon of vegetable oil, and rub onto the surface of the grill with a pair of tongs.

NUTRITION PER SERVING

355 calories
39 g protein
3 g carbohydrates
19.5 g fat
3 g saturated fat
9 mg cholesterol
489 mg sodium
0 g fiber

{ **Make It a FLAT BELLY DIET MEAL** }

Serve with 2 cups mixed baby greens (15).
TOTAL MEAL: 370 calories
 To serve as part of another *Flat Belly Diet* Meal, omit the sauce (217).

Greek Grilled Chicken Breast

2 HOURS ▮ **4 SERVINGS** ▮ **308 CALORIES** ▮ **MUFA: PISTACHIOS**

This recipe uses a technique known as butterflying to make cooking even speedier. Most of the time required is for marinating. Just a quick sear on the grill and the dish is nearly done. For an especially thick yogurt cheese, drain the shredded cucumber in a colander and squeeze to remove excess liquid.

CHICKEN

- 4 boneless, skinless chicken breast halves (6 ounces each)
- 1 tablespoon olive oil
- 1 tablespoon freshly squeezed lemon juice
- 1 teaspoon dried oregano
- 1 clove garlic, minced
- ½ teaspoon salt
- ¼ teaspoon freshly ground black pepper

YOGURT CHEESE

- 1¼ cups fat-free Greek-style yogurt
- ½ cup shredded cucumber
- 1 teaspoon chopped fresh dill
- 2 cloves garlic, minced
- ½ cup shelled pistachios, coarsely chopped, divided

1. To prepare the chicken: Place a breast shiny side up with the tip facing you and the thinner side opposite your cutting hand. Place your hand on top of the breast. Hold the knife parallel to the table and carefully insert it into the thickest part of the breast, drawing it almost all the way through. Take care to keep the breast attached on 1 side. Spread the 2 halves as if opening a book and press lightly in the center to flatten. Repeat with the other 3 breast halves.

2. Combine the chicken, oil, lemon juice, oregano, and garlic in a bowl and refrigerate for 1 to 2 hours, turning occasionally.

3. To prepare the yogurt cheese: Meanwhile, place the yogurt in a coffee strainer over a bowl and set in the refrigerator for 1 to 2 hours. Combine the yogurt, cucumber, dill, garlic, and ¼ cup of the pistachios.

4. Set up the grill for medium-hot direct-heat grilling. Remove the chicken from the marinade. Sprinkle with the salt and pepper and set on a grill rack that has been coated with oil (see note, page 205). Grill for 2 to 3 minutes per side or until the chicken is well marked and cooked through. Place each breast on a serving plate, top with the yogurt cheese, and sprinkle with the remaining ¼ cup pistachios.

NUTRITION PER SERVING

308 calories
39 g protein
8 g carbohydrates
13 g fat
2.5 g saturated fat
81 mg cholesterol
397 mg sodium
2 g fiber

{ Make It a **FLAT BELLY DIET MEAL** } Serve with the Zucchini and Carrots with Walnuts on page 138, but omit the walnuts (60). **TOTAL MEAL:** 368 calories

Grilled Chicken Satay with Peanut Sauce and Cucumber Relish

■ 2 HOURS 30 MINUTES ■ 4 SERVINGS ■ 361 CALORIES ■ MUFA: PEANUT BUTTER

These tasty skewers draw their MUFA power from the easy-to-make peanut sauce on the opposite page. They're great for a party—just make a double batch.

1 pound boneless, skinless chicken breast halves, cut into 16 strips (each 2" long)
½ teaspoon curry powder
1 tablespoon freshly squeezed lime juice
1 tablespoon canola oil
1 cucumber, peeled and cut into chunks
½ red bell pepper, finely chopped
¼ red onion, finely chopped
2 tablespoons rice vinegar
3 tablespoons chopped unsalted peanuts
1 tablespoon sugar
1 tablespoon chopped fresh cilantro
½ cup Amazing Peanut Sauce (opposite page) or store-bought peanut sauce

1. Combine the chicken, curry powder, lime juice, and oil in a bowl. Refrigerate for 2 hours. Combine the cucumber, pepper, onion, vinegar, peanuts, sugar, and cilantro in a bowl. Refrigerate until ready to use.

2. Prepare the grill for medium-hot direct-heat grilling.

3. Remove the chicken from the bowl and thread 2 pieces lengthwise onto each of 8 skewers. Brush lightly with the remaining marinade mixture. Set the skewers on a grill rack that has been coated with oil (see note, page 205). Grill for 3 to 4 minutes per side or until cooked through. Meanwhile, warm the peanut sauce in a small saucepan over medium heat for 1 to 2 minutes or until hot. Serve over the skewers.

NUTRITION
PER SERVING

361 calories
29 g protein
20 g carbohydrates
18 g fat
3 g saturated fat
63 mg cholesterol
501 mg sodium
3 g fiber

{ Make It a FLAT BELLY DIET MEAL } Serve with 1 cup steamed snow peas (40).
TOTAL MEAL: 401 calories

Amazing Peanut Sauce

■ 10 MINUTES ■ 16 SERVINGS (2 TABLESPOONS EACH) ■ 117 CALORIES ■ MUFA: PEANUT BUTTER

Ginger is a spice with many healing properties and is used to relieve nausea from many causes. Prepared peanut sauce has additives to make it appear smooth at all times, so it's normal for this sauce to separate slightly. Simply give it a stir.

1 cup chunky natural unsalted peanut butter
¾ cup reduced-sodium chicken broth
⅓ cup light coconut milk
3 tablespoons packed brown sugar
2 tablespoons freshly squeezed lime juice
1 tablespoon fish sauce
1 tablespoon grated peeled fresh ginger
⅛ teaspoon red-pepper flakes

Combine the peanut butter, broth, coconut milk, brown sugar, lime juice, fish sauce, ginger, and red-pepper flakes in a small saucepan over medium heat. Cook, stirring often, for 2 to 3 minutes or until very smooth and slightly thickened.

NUTRITION PER SERVING

117 calories
4 g protein
7 g carbohydrates
8 g fat
1 g saturated fat
0 mg cholesterol
94 mg sodium
1 g fiber

{ Make It a FLAT BELLY DIET MEAL } Serve with 1½ cups cooked soba noodles (171) tossed with 1 teaspoon toasted sesame oil (40), 2 chopped scallions (20), ½ cup steamed red bell-pepper strips (20), and 1 tablespoon chopped dry-roasted peanuts (49). **TOTAL MEAL:** 417 calories

Chicken Pad Thai

15 MINUTES **4 SERVINGS** **386 CALORIES** **MUFA: PEANUTS**

In Thailand, this is the ultimate street food. There, competition among food cart cooks is fierce, so many specialize in a dish or two just to stay in business. For those who are gluten sensitive, rice noodles are a great alternative to wheat.

4 ounces flat rice noodles
4 tablespoons lower-sodium ketchup
1 tablespoon fish sauce
1 teaspoon sugar
1 tablespoon peanut oil, divided
1 egg, lightly beaten
12 ounces boneless, skinless chicken breast halves, cut into 1½" long strips
2 cloves garlic, minced
3 scallions, cut into 1" pieces
1 cup bean sprouts
½ cup unsalted peanuts, finely chopped
Lime wedges (optional)

1. Bring a pot of water to a boil and cook the noodles per the package directions.

2. Combine the ketchup, fish sauce, and sugar in a small bowl. Heat 1 teaspoon of the peanut oil in a large nonstick skillet over medium-high heat. Add the egg and cook, stirring occasionally, for about 2 minutes or until set. Transfer the egg to a bowl and reserve.

3. Return the skillet to the stove top and heat the remaining 2 teaspoons oil. Add the chicken and cook, stirring often, for 4 to 5 minutes or until lightly browned and cooked through. Add the garlic and cook for 30 seconds longer. Stir in the noodles and cook for 1 minute longer or until hot. Add the ketchup mixture and cook, tossing, for 1 minute. Stir in the scallions and reserved egg and remove from the heat.

4. Divide among 4 plates, garnishing each with ¼ cup of the bean sprouts and sprinkling with the peanuts. Serve with the lime wedges, if desired.

NUTRITION
PER SERVING

386 calories
29 g protein
36 g carbohydrates
15 g fat
2.5 g saturated fat
102 mg cholesterol
425 mg sodium
3 g fiber

{ Make It a
FLAT
BELLY
DIET
MEAL }
A single serving of this recipe counts as a *Flat Belly Diet* Meal without any add-ons!

Sesame Chicken with Snow Peas

■ 35 MINUTES ■ 4 SERVINGS ■ 347 CALORIES ■ MUFA: WALNUTS

Loaded with a colorful mix of fresh vegetables, this stir-fry combination also offers almost double the Daily Value for vitamin C.

1 pound boneless, skinless chicken breasts, cut into ½" pieces

2 tablespoons reduced-sodium soy sauce, divided

4 teaspoons cornstarch, divided

½ cup reduced-sodium chicken broth

¼ cup freshly squeezed orange juice

1 tablespoon canola oil, divided

3 cloves garlic, minced

1 onion, chopped

1 orange bell pepper, sliced

¾ cup snow peas, cut crosswise into thirds

1 can (8 ounces) sliced water chestnuts, drained and chopped

½ cup walnuts, coarsely chopped

1 teaspoon sesame oil

1. Combine the chicken, 1 tablespoon of the soy sauce, and 2 teaspoons of the cornstarch in a bowl. Combine the broth, orange juice, and remaining 1 tablespoon soy sauce and 2 teaspoons cornstarch in a separate bowl. Set aside.

2. Heat 2 teaspoons of the canola oil in a large nonstick skillet or wok over medium-high heat. Add the chicken and cook, stirring often, for 4 to 5 minutes or until cooked through. Transfer to a plate and set aside.

3. Add the remaining 1 teaspoon canola oil to the skillet. Add the garlic and cook for 15 seconds. Stir in the onion and pepper and cook for 1 to 2 minutes longer or until the vegetables just begin to soften. Stir in the snow peas and water chestnuts and cook for 1 to 2 minutes longer or until the snow peas are bright green. Add the walnuts and sesame oil and cook for 1 minute longer.

4. Stir in the reserved chicken and broth mixture. Cook for 1 to 2 minutes longer or until the sauce reaches a boil and thickens.

NUTRITION PER SERVING

347 calories
33 g protein
21 g carbohydrates
16 g fat
2 g saturated fat
66 mg cholesterol
358 mg sodium
5 g fiber

{ Make It a FLAT BELLY DIET MEAL } Serve with ⅓ cup cooked brown rice (65). **TOTAL MEAL:** 412 calories

Cashew Chicken Stir-Fry

■ **30 MINUTES** ■ **4 SERVINGS** ■ **272 CALORIES** ■ **MUFA: CASHEWS**

Chicken thighs have a meatier flavor—and slightly more fat—than breasts, so they stand up especially well to the rich cashews in this dish. If you prefer white meat, it's fine to substitute the same amount of chicken breasts.

½ cup reduced-sodium chicken broth
1 tablespoon hoisin sauce
1 tablespoon reduced-sodium soy sauce
2 teaspoons cornstarch
1 teaspoon sesame oil
2 teaspoons canola oil
12 ounces boneless, skinless chicken thighs, cut into ½" pieces
1 onion, chopped
1 tablespoon grated fresh ginger
2 cloves garlic, minced
½ red bell pepper, chopped
½ cup roasted cashews

1. Combine the broth, hoisin sauce, soy sauce, and cornstarch in a small bowl. Stir until smooth and set aside.

2. Heat the sesame oil and canola oil in a large nonstick skillet over medium-high heat. Add the chicken and cook, stirring, for about 4 minutes or until lightly browned and cooked through.

3. Add the onion, ginger, and garlic and cook, stirring, for 2 minutes longer or until the onion is slightly softened. Add the pepper and cook for 3 minutes longer or until slightly softened. Stir in the cashews and cook for 1 minute longer. Add the reserved hoisin mixture and cook for 1 to 2 minutes longer or until the sauce reaches a boil and thickens.

NUTRITION PER SERVING

272 calories
21 g protein
15 g carbohydrates
15 g fat
3 g saturated fat
71 mg cholesterol
310 mg sodium
1 g fiber

{ Make It a FLAT BELLY DIET MEAL } Serve with ½ cup Brown Rice Pilaf with Mushrooms on page 147, but omit the pecans (109). **TOTAL MEAL:** 381 calories

African Chicken Stew

4–6 HOURS ▪ 4 SERVINGS ▪ 439 CALORIES ▪ MUFA: PEANUT BUTTER

As much as possible, avoid the temptation to lift the lid when using a slow cooker. Every time you take a peek, it takes 20 to 30 minutes for the cooking temperature to return to where it was.

1 tablespoon peanut oil

12 ounces boneless, skinless chicken thighs, trimmed and cut into 24 pieces

1 onion, chopped

3 cloves garlic, minced

1 jalapeño chile pepper, seeded and chopped

1 carrot, thickly sliced

1 sweet potato, peeled and cubed

1 can (14½ ounces) reduced-sodium chicken broth

½ cup chunky natural unsalted peanut butter

2 tablespoons tomato paste

¼ teaspoon salt

¼ teaspoon freshly ground black pepper

1. Heat the oil in a large nonstick skillet over medium-high heat. Add the chicken and cook, stirring occasionally, for 3 to 4 minutes or until lightly browned. Transfer to a 4-quart slow cooker. Return the skillet to the heat and add the onion, garlic, chile pepper, and carrot. Cook for 1 minute, then transfer to the slow cooker. Stir in the sweet potato, broth, peanut butter, and tomato paste.

2. Cook on high for 3 to 4 hours or low for 5 to 6 hours or until the chicken and vegetables are very tender. Season with salt and black pepper.

NUTRITION PER SERVING

439 calories
29 g protein
32 g carbohydrates
23 g fat
4 g saturated fat*
71 mg cholesterol
615 mg sodium*
7 g fiber

*Limit saturated fat to 10% of total calories—about 17 grams per day for most women—and sodium intake to less than 2,300 milligrams.

{ Make It a FLAT BELLY DIET MEAL } A single serving of this recipe counts as a *Flat Belly Diet* Meal without any add-ons!

Chicken à l'Orange

▨ **UP TO 7 HOURS** ▨ **4 SERVINGS** ▨ **312 CALORIES** ▨ **MUFA: ALMONDS**

Tender vegetables are easy to overcook in a slow cooker, so make sure to add the asparagus in the last half hour of cooking, and then keep an eye on it. When the spears turn bright green, pull one out and take a nibble to estimate how much longer to keep the rest in.

½ cup reduced-sodium chicken broth

3 tablespoons frozen orange juice concentrate

1 teaspoon dried thyme

1 large onion, cut into wedges

1 red bell pepper, cut into strips

2 cloves garlic, chopped

4 bone-in, skinless chicken breast halves (5 ounces each)

1 pound asparagus, trimmed and cut into 3" pieces

¼ cup water

2 teaspoons cornstarch

½ cup fat-free Greek-style yogurt

½ cup slivered almonds, toasted

1. Combine the broth, orange juice concentrate, and thyme in a measuring cup. Combine the onion, pepper, and garlic in a 3- to 6-quart slow cooker. Top with the chicken. Pour the orange mixture over all.

2. Cover and cook on high for 3 to 3½ hours or on low for 6 to 7 hours.

3. Add the asparagus and turn the heat to high (if using low heat). Cover and cook for 30 minutes or until the asparagus is crisp-tender.

4. Remove the chicken and vegetables to a serving plate. Cover and keep warm.

5. Whisk together the water and cornstarch in a measuring cup. Whisk into the liquid in the slow cooker. Cook for 15 minutes or until thickened.

6. Remove from the heat and whisk in the yogurt. Pour over the chicken and vegetables. Sprinkle with the almonds.

NUTRITION PER SERVING

312 calories
37 g protein
22 g carbohydrates
9 g fat
1 g saturated fat
66 mg cholesterol
99 mg sodium
6 g fiber

{ **Make It a FLAT BELLY DIET MEAL** } Serve with 1 cup steamed whole french-cut green beans (35) and ½ cup roasted potatoes (50).
TOTAL MEAL: 397 calories

Slow Cooker Moroccan Chicken with Olives

▉ 4–6 HOURS ▉ 6 SERVINGS ▉ 388 CALORIES ▉ MUFA: OLIVE OIL

Harissa is a hot chili paste common to North African cooking. It's added to mild-flavored soups and pasta dishes like this one. If you like very spicy food, use a hotter pepper, such chile de arbol, instead of guajillo.

CHICKEN

- ½ cup reduced-sodium chicken broth
- ¼ cup all-purpose flour
- 3 tablespoons olive oil
- 2 teaspoons ground cumin
- ½ teaspoon freshly ground black pepper
- ¼ teaspoon salt
- 1 can (14½ ounces) no-salt-added stewed tomatoes
- 1 carrot, sliced
- 1 large onion
- 30 small black olives, pitted (about 1 cup)
- 3 cloves garlic, minced
- 2 pounds boneless, skinless chicken breast halves
- ½ cup chopped fresh cilantro (optional)

HARISSA

- ¾ cup dried hot red chile peppers, such as guajillo
- 2 cloves garlic, minced
- 1 teaspoon ground coriander
- 1 teaspoon ground caraway seed
- ¼ teaspoon salt
- 3 tablespoons olive oil

1. To prepare the chicken: Coat the stoneware of a slow cooker pot with cooking spray. Combine the broth, flour, oil, cumin, pepper, and salt in the pot. Whisk until smooth. Add the tomatoes (with juice), carrot, onion, olives, and garlic. Stir to mix. Tuck the chicken into the pot, covering with the other ingredients. Cover and cook on low for 5 to 6 hours or on high for 3 to 4 hours.

2. To prepare the harissa: Remove the stems and seeds from the peppers and discard. Soak the peppers in warm water for about 1 hour or until softened. Drain and transfer to a food processor fitted with a metal blade or a blender. Add the garlic, coriander, caraway seed, and salt. Process, scraping the sides of the bowl as needed, until a paste forms. Drizzle in the oil through the tube to reach a smooth consistency.

3. Stir in the cilantro (if using) just before serving. Pass the harissa at the table.

NUTRITION PER SERVING

388 calories
38 g protein
16 g carbohydrates
19 g fat
3 g saturated fat
88 mg cholesterol
530 mg sodium
4 g fiber

{ Make It a FLAT BELLY DIET MEAL } A single serving of this recipe counts as a *Flat Belly Diet* Meal without any add-ons!

Baked Chicken Parmesan

■ 30 MINUTES ■ 4 SERVINGS ■ 327 CALORIES ■ MUFA: PINE NUTS

Why fry chicken cutlets when you can enjoy an even tastier version by baking them in the oven? To make your own whole wheat bread crumbs, set out a slice of whole wheat bread in the morning. Later in the day, break it into pieces and give it a whirl in the food processor. One slice will make approximately half a cup of crumbs.

1 egg

1 tablespoon water

½ cup pine nuts, finely chopped

¼ cup whole wheat bread crumbs

½ teaspoon Italian seasoning

4 chicken cutlets (about 3 ounces each)

2 cups prepared marinara sauce

¼ cup shredded part-skim mozzarella cheese (about 2 ounces)

1. Preheat the oven to 425°F. Coat a baking sheet with cooking spray.

2. Whisk the egg with the water in a shallow dish. Combine the pine nuts, bread crumbs, and seasoning in another shallow dish. Dip the chicken into the egg and then the nut mixture. Arrange on the prepared baking sheet and coat with cooking spray.

3. Bake for 10 minutes. Turn over the breasts and top each with ½ cup of the marinara sauce and some of the cheese. Bake for 5 to 10 minutes longer or until the cheese has melted and the chicken is cooked through.

NUTRITION PER SERVING

327 calories
29 g protein
14 g carbohydrates
18 g fat
3 g saturated fat
112 mg cholesterol
673 mg sodium*
3 g fiber

*Limit saturated fat to 10% of total calories—about 17 grams per day for most women—and sodium intake to less than 2,300 milligrams.

{ **Make It a FLAT BELLY DIET MEAL** } Serve 2 cups steamed spaghetti squash (84). **TOTAL MEAL:** 411 calories. ■ To serve as part of a *Flat Belly Diet* Meal, eliminate the pine nuts and increase the bread crumbs to ¾ cup (230).

Spicy Baked Chicken with Squash and Walnuts

▨ 1 HOUR 30 MINUTES ▨ 4 SERVINGS ▨ 375 CALORIES ▨ MUFA: WALNUTS

The ancho is actually a dried poblano pepper—one of the sweetest chile peppers and very popular in authentic Mexican cuisine. It has a mild paprika flavor, with sweet to moderate heat. If ground anchos are unavailable, use 1 teaspoon paprika and ½ teaspoon ground red pepper instead.

1½ tablespoons olive oil

2 tablespoons water

2 tablespoons packed dark brown sugar

1½–2 teaspoons ground ancho chile pepper

1½ teaspoons ground cumin

½ teaspoon dried oregano

½ teaspoon salt

½ butternut squash, peeled, seeded, and cubed

4 boneless, skinless chicken breast halves (4 ounces each)

½ pound small thin-skinned potatoes, quartered

1 large sweet white onion, cut into thin wedges

½ cup walnut halves, coarsely chopped

1. Preheat the oven to 375°F. Coat a roasting pan or large casserole with olive oil spray.

2. Combine the oil, water, brown sugar, pepper, cumin, oregano, and salt in a small bowl. Brush the chicken with the mixture and place it in the roasting pan. Arrange the squash, potatoes, and onion in the prepared pan and pour remaining oil-spice mixture over. Toss with clean hands until evenly coated.

3. Bake, uncovered, for 40 minutes or until the squash and potatoes are tender. Add the walnuts and bake for 10 minutes longer or until a thermometer inserted in the thickest part registers 165°F.

NUTRITION PER SERVING

375 calories
31 g protein
31 g carbohydrates
15 g fat
2 g saturated fat
66 mg cholesterol
378 mg sodium
5 g fiber

{ Make It a FLAT BELLY DIET MEAL }

Serve with 2 cups mixed greens (15) and 1 tablespoon balsamic vinegar (10).
TOTAL MEAL: 400 calories

Orange and Herb Turkey Cutlets with Maple-Sautéed Apples

■ 55 MINUTES ■ 4 SERVINGS ■ 301 CALORIES ■ MUFA: CANOLA OIL

To protect their flavor, make sure to store apples in a plastic bag in the refrigerator, away from strongly odored foods such as cabbage or onions. Gala apples are particularly good in this recipe because they tend to hold their shape nicely when cooked.

4 tablespoons canola oil, divided

3 tablespoons freshly squeezed orange juice

1 large clove garlic, crushed through a press

1 teaspoon dried sage

½ teaspoon dried rosemary, crumbled

½ teaspoon freshly grated orange zest

½ teaspoon salt

½ teaspoon + pinch of freshly ground black pepper, divided

1 pound turkey cutlets

2 large Gala apples, quartered, cored, and thinly sliced

1 tablespoon pure maple syrup

⅛ teaspoon ground cinnamon

1. Mix 1 tablespoon of the oil, 1 tablespoon of the orange juice, the garlic, sage, rosemary, orange zest, salt, and ½ teaspoon of the pepper in a cup. Rub all over the turkey cutlets.

2. Heat 1½ tablespoons of the oil in a large nonstick skillet over medium heat. Add the apples and cook, turning often, for 9 to 10 minutes or until tender and translucent. Add the syrup, cinnamon, and remaining pinch of pepper. Toss to mix and cook for 1 minute longer. Transfer to a bowl and cover to keep warm. Rinse and dry the skillet.

3. Heat the remaining 1½ tablespoons oil in the same skillet over medium-high heat. Add the turkey (in 2 batches, if necessary) and cook, turning once, for 4 to 6 minutes or until browned and cooked through. Transfer the turkey to a warmed platter.

4. Add the remaining 2 tablespoons orange juice to the pan drippings and bring to a boil, stirring to loosen all the flavorful browned bits. Pour the pan juices over the turkey and serve with the apples.

NUTRITION PER SERVING

301 calories
28 g protein
15 g carbohydrates
15 g fat
1 g saturated fat
45 mg cholesterol
392 mg sodium
2 g fiber

{ Make It a FLAT BELLY DIET MEAL }

Serve with the Braised Kale with Smoked Nuts on page 137, but omit the almonds (130).
TOTAL MEAL: 431 calories

Turkey Sliders

20 MINUTES ■ **4 SERVINGS (2 PER SERVING)** ■ **348 CALORIES** ■ **MUFA: AVOCADO**

Looking for a burger fix? This recipe gives you not one but two juicy little burgers to enjoy. While the avocado serves as the key MUFA ingredient, feel free to add other fat-free toppings such as sliced onion or pickled hot peppers, if you like.

1 egg white, beaten
½ small red onion, minced
¼ cup minced fresh cilantro
½ teaspoon ground cumin
¼ teaspoon salt
1 pound extra-lean ground turkey breast (99% fat-free)
8 whole wheat dinner rolls, cut in half
4 leaves lettuce, halved
2 plum tomatoes, each cut into 4 slices
1 avocado, sliced

1. Whisk together the egg white, onion, cilantro, cumin, and salt in a medium bowl. Add the turkey and mix just until blended. Shape into 8 burgers, about 3" each.

2. Heat a skillet coated with cooking spray over medium heat. Cook the burgers, turning once, for 6 minutes or until well browned and a thermometer inserted in the thickest portion registers 165°F.

3. Place the bottoms of 2 dinner rolls on 4 plates. Top with 1 piece of lettuce and 1 tomato slice. Place 1 burger on each and top with the avocado and the top of the roll.

NUTRITION PER SERVING

348 calories
35 g protein
35 g carbohydrates
10 g fat
1 g saturated fat
45 mg cholesterol
502 mg sodium
8 g fiber

{ **Make It a FLAT BELLY DIET MEAL** } Serve with 1 tablespoon crumbled feta (40).
TOTAL MEAL: 388 calories

Turkey with Green Mole

45 MINUTES ▪ **4 SERVINGS** ▪ **290 CALORIES** ▪ **MUFA: PINE NUTS**

Mole (pronounced MO-lay), derived from the Aztec word for "sauce," is popular in many regions of Mexico, where it's often served with turkey. Tradition aside, this version breaks new ground with its use of bell pepper and pine nuts.

½ cup pine nuts

2 teaspoons canola oil

1 small green bell pepper, seeded and chopped

1 onion, chopped

3 cloves garlic, minced

2 teaspoons dried oregano

2 teaspoons ground cumin

¼ teaspoon salt

1 cup reduced-sodium chicken broth

¼ cup coarsely chopped fresh cilantro

4 boneless, skinless turkey breast cutlets (about 4 ounces each)

1. Place the pine nuts in a large nonstick skillet over medium-high heat. Toast, stirring occasionally, for about 5 minutes or until lightly browned. Tip onto a plate and set aside.

2. Add the oil to the skillet and return to medium-high heat. Add the pepper, onion, garlic, oregano, cumin, and salt. Cook, stirring occasionally, for 5 minutes or until softened. Remove from the heat.

3. While the vegetables are cooking, set aside 2 tablespoons of the pine nuts. Place the remaining pine nuts in a grinder or food processor fitted with a metal blade and process until finely ground. Add the vegetable mixture and broth. Process until smooth. Stir in the cilantro and set aside.

4. Wipe out the skillet and return to medium-high heat. Add the turkey and cook for 15 minutes or until cooked through. Transfer to a plate.

5. Serve with equal amounts of the sauce spooned over each portion, garnished with the reserved pine nuts.

NUTRITION PER SERVING

290 calories
32 g protein
8 g carbohydrates
15 g fat
1 g saturated fat
45 mg cholesterol
269 mg sodium
2 g fiber

{ Make It a FLAT BELLY DIET MEAL } Serve with the Southwestern Fried Rice on page 146, but omit the pumpkin seeds (130).
TOTAL MEAL: 420 calories

Rigatoni with Sardinian Sausage Sauce

■ **30 MINUTES** ■ **4 SERVINGS** ■ **430 CALORIES** ■ **MUFA: OLIVE OIL**

Large, tube-shaped pasta like rigatoni is well suited to a chunkier pasta sauce. Cooking the turkey, onions, and peppers at the same time eliminates the need for additional oil. If you prefer to use store-bought marinara, cook the turkey and vegetables in ¼ cup olive oil instead. Buy a brand that's low in sodium and contains no added sugar.

4 ounces rigatoni, preferably whole wheat

½ pound lean sweet or hot Italian turkey sausage

2 cloves garlic, chopped

1 small onion, sliced

1 red bell pepper, seeded and sliced

4 cups Marinara Sauce (page 167) or store-bought marinara sauce

1. Prepare the rigatoni per the package directions. Drain and set aside.

2. Heat a large nonstick skillet over medium-high heat. Cook the sausage, garlic, onion, and pepper for 5 minutes or until the sausage is cooked through. Stir in the sauce and bring to a simmer. Cook for 15 minutes or until the flavors blend.

3. Toss the reserved pasta with the marinara sauce just before serving.

NUTRITION PER SERVING

430 calories
17 g protein
44 g carbohydrates
21 g fat
2 g saturated fat
34 mg cholesterol
592 mg sodium
5 g fiber

{ **Make It a FLAT BELLY DIET MEAL** } A single serving of this recipe counts as a *Flat Belly Diet* Meal without any add-ons!
■ To serve as part of a *Flat Belly Diet* Meal, use store-bought marinara sauce and reduce the amount to 2 cups (260).

Turkey Meat Loaf with Walnuts and Sage

■ 1 HOUR 30 MINUTES ■ 4 SERVINGS ■ 375 CALORIES ■ MUFA: WALNUTS

Using walnuts and whole wheat bread in place of regular white bread crumbs, and lean ground turkey instead of beef, this quintessential comfort food provides the right kinds of fat—without sacrificing flavor.

2 teaspoons olive oil
1 large carrot, grated
4 scallions, thinly sliced
1 clove garlic, minced
½ cup walnuts
2 slices whole wheat bread
¼ cup fat-free milk
2 egg whites, lightly beaten
1 pound extra-lean ground turkey breast (99% fat-free)
¼ cup chopped fresh flat-leaf parsley
¼ cup grated Parmesan cheese
1 teaspoon dried sage
½ teaspoon salt
½ teaspoon freshly ground black pepper

1. Preheat the oven to 350°F. Line a rimmed baking sheet with foil and coat the foil with olive oil spray.

2. Heat the oil in a small nonstick skillet over medium heat. Add the carrot, scallions, and garlic and cook, stirring often, for about 3 minutes or until tender. Remove from the heat.

3. Meanwhile, chop the walnuts in a food processor fitted with a metal blade. Break up the bread and add to the walnuts. Pulse until both are ground to fine crumbs. Transfer to a large bowl. With a fork, stir in the milk and egg whites. Add the turkey, parsley, cheese, sage, salt, pepper, and sautéed mixture. Mix gently just until blended.

4. Shape into a free-form loaf about 7" long and 4½" wide on the prepared baking sheet. Bake for 50 to 60 minutes or until a thermometer inserted in the thickest portion registers 165°F. Let stand a few minutes before slicing.

NUTRITION PER SERVING

375 calories
28 g protein
14 g carbohydrates
27 g fat
5 g saturated fat*
116 mg cholesterol
500 mg sodium
3 g fiber

*Limit saturated fat to 10% of total calories—about 17 grams per day for most women—and sodium intake to less than 2,300 milligrams.

{ Make It a FLAT BELLY DIET MEAL } Serve with 1 cup steamed broccoli (40) sprinkled with 1 tablespoon grated Parmesan cheese (21). **TOTAL MEAL:** 436 calories

10

Meats

Korean Beef in Lettuce Leaves

30 MINUTES ▪ **4 SERVINGS (3 PER SERVING)** ▪ **379 CALORIES** ▪ **MUFA: CANOLA OIL**

Folded into a crisp lettuce leaf, these savory bundles are an ideal meal for a summer evening.

3 tablespoons 100% fruit
   orange marmalade
2 tablespoons reduced-
   sodium soy sauce
1 tablespoon hoisin sauce
1 tablespoon freshly
   grated ginger
1 clove garlic, minced
¼ cup canola oil
1 pound 93% lean
   ground beef
8 scallions, sliced
2 carrots, finely chopped
1 red bell pepper, seeded
   and finely chopped
12 Boston or Bibb lettuce
   leaves

1. Whisk together the marmalade, soy sauce, hoisin sauce, ginger, and garlic in a small bowl. Set aside.

2. Heat the oil in a large skillet over medium-high heat. Cook the beef, scallions, carrots, and pepper for 5 to 7 minutes, stirring often, or until the beef is browned and cooked through. Add the soy mixture and cook, stirring, for 5 minutes or until well blended.

3. Spoon the beef mixture into the lettuce leaves and serve, or roll like a wrap to eat.

**NUTRITION
PER SERVING**

379 calories
26 g protein
18 g carbohydrates
23 g fat
4 g saturated fat*
66 mg cholesterol
453 mg sodium
3 g fiber

*Limit saturated fat to 10% of total calories—about 17 grams per day for most women—and sodium intake to less than 2,300 milligrams.

{ **Make It a FLAT BELLY DIET MEAL** } Serve with 1 cup diced watermelon (45).
TOTAL MEAL: 415 calories

Pork and Pine Nut Meatballs

▓ 40 MINUTES ▓ 4 SERVINGS ▓ 254 CALORIES ▓ MUFA: PINE NUTS

Extra-lean ground pork is hard to find in your grocer's meat case, but its flavor is hard to pass up. Let your food processor come to the rescue and simply grind your own. Pine nuts make an especially good replacement for dried bread crumbs.

½ cup pine nuts
1 pound pork tenderloin, trimmed and cut into small chunks
1½ teaspoons crumbled dried sage
2 cloves garlic, minced
2 teaspoons red wine vinegar
¼ teaspoon salt
¼ teaspoon freshly ground black pepper
Olive oil in a spritzer

1. Preheat the oven to 375°F. Coat a large baking pan with cooking spray. Set aside.

2. Pulse the pine nuts in the bowl of a food processor fitted with a metal blade until coarsely chopped. Add the pork, sage, garlic, vinegar, salt, and pepper. Pulse until evenly ground.

3. Divide the mixture into 12 equal portions and roll into meatballs. Arrange on the prepared pan. Spritz lightly with the oil.

4. Bake for about 25 minutes or until cooked through.

NUTRITION PER SERVING

254 calories
26 g protein
3 g carbohydrates
16 g fat
2 g saturated fat
74 mg cholesterol
203 mg sodium
1 g fiber

{ Make It a **FLAT BELLY DIET MEAL** } Serve with the Zucchini and Carrots with Walnuts on page 138, but omit the walnuts (60), and tossed with ½ cup cooked whole wheat penne (105). **TOTAL MEAL:** 419 calories

Herb-Marinated Beef and Mushroom Kebabs

■ 20 MINUTES + MARINATING TIME ■ 4 SERVINGS ■ 290 CALORIES ■ MUFA: PESTO

Nothing is more luscious than beef tenderloin. And ounce for ounce, it's one of the leanest cuts, too. When making kebabs, metal skewers work best because they conduct heat better. If you prefer bamboo skewers, soak them in cold water for 30 minutes before threading.

1 pound beef tenderloin, trimmed and cut into 20 cubes

3 tablespoons chopped fresh basil

3 tablespoons chopped fresh parsley

1 tablespoon extra virgin olive oil, divided

1 clove garlic, minced

1 teaspoon dried oregano

16 white mushrooms

1 red bell pepper, seeded and cut into 16 pieces

¼ teaspoon salt

4 tablespoons Pesto (page 122) or store-bought pesto

1. Combine the beef, basil, parsley, 1 teaspoon of the oil, the garlic, and oregano in a bowl. Refrigerate for 2 hours or overnight. If using bamboo skewers, soak them in water for at least 30 minutes.

2. Preheat the broiler and coat a broiler pan with cooking spray.

3. Thread 5 beef cubes, 4 mushrooms, and 4 bell pepper wedges alternately onto each of 4 skewers. Brush the skewers with the remaining 2 teaspoons oil. Sprinkle with the salt. Broil 5" from the heat source, turning occasionally, for 8 to 10 minutes or until the beef is cooked to the desired doneness and the vegetables are tender. Brush each with the pesto and serve immediately.

NUTRITION PER SERVING

290 calories
27 g protein
6 g carbohydrates
17 g fat
4 g saturated fat*
70 mg cholesterol
320 mg sodium
2 g fiber

*Limit saturated fat to 10% of total calories—about 17 grams per day for most women—and sodium intake to less than 2,300 milligrams.

{ Make It a FLAT BELLY DIET MEAL }

Serve with ½ cup Brown Rice Pilaf with Mushrooms on page 147, but omit the pecans (110).
TOTAL MEAL: 400 calories

Pineapple and Pork Tacos with Avocado Crema

■ **45 MINUTES**   ■ **4 SERVINGS**   ■ **420 CALORIES**   ■ **MUFA: AVOCADO**

If you enjoy authentic Mexican food, you're probably already familiar with the shepherd-style tacos that inspired this recipe. Pan searing not only keeps the cooking method lean, but it also intensifies the inherent sweetness of the pineapple.

PORK AND PINEAPPLE

- 2 teaspoons sugar
- 2 teaspoons ground cumin
- ½ teaspoon ground coriander
- ¼ teaspoon ground cinnamon
- ¼ teaspoon ground red pepper
- ¼ teaspoon salt
- 12 ounces pork tenderloin, trimmed and cut into ½" cubes
- 1 tablespoon olive oil
- ¼ fresh pineapple, cored and sliced crosswise
- 2 tablespoons chopped fresh cilantro
- 12 corn tortillas (6" diameter), warmed per package directions

AVOCADO CREMA

- 1 avocado, mashed
- 2 tablespoons fat-free sour cream
- 2 tablespoons freshly squeezed lime juice
- ⅛ teaspoon salt

1. To prepare the pork and pineapple: In a cup, mix the sugar, cumin, coriander, cinnamon, pepper, and salt. Mix half of the spices with the pork, then toss with the oil. Mix the remaining spices with the pineapple. Let stand at room temperature for 15 minutes while preparing the avocado crema.

2. To prepare the avocado crema: Whisk the avocado with the sour cream, lime juice, and salt in a small bowl. Press a piece of plastic wrap directly onto the surface to keep the crema fresh looking.

3. Coat a large nonstick skillet with olive oil spray. Warm over medium-high heat for 2 minutes. Add the pork and cook, turning once or twice, for 8 minutes or until browned and cooked through. Add the cilantro and toss to combine. Transfer to a clean plate and cover loosely to keep warm.

4. Add the pineapple to the pan and cook, turning once or twice, for 3 to 4 minutes or until golden. Remove from the heat.

5. To assemble each serving, place 3 tortillas on a plate. Divide ¼ of the pork and pineapple between each tortilla. Top with the crema and roll up.

NUTRITION PER SERVING

420 calories
24 g protein
50 g carbohydrates
16 g fat
3 g saturated fat
56 mg cholesterol
310 mg sodium
9 g fiber

{ Make It a FLAT BELLY DIET MEAL }   A single serving of this recipe counts as a *Flat Belly Diet* Meal without any add-ons!

Cuban Steak with Avocado Salad

■ **30 MINUTES + MARINATING TIME** ■ **4 SERVINGS** ■ **280 CALORIES** ■ **MUFA: AVOCADO**

Mojo sauce is a garlicky, citrus-based marinade that hails from Cuba. Reserve a few tablespoons to make a superb dressing for the accompanying avocado salad. Beef is rich in iron, and pairing it with an acidic sauce will make it even easier for your body to absorb this important energy-boosting nutrient. For the most tender results, work your way across the grain when slicing.

MOJO SAUCE

- ¼ cup olive oil
- ¼ cup freshly squeezed lime juice
- 2 tablespoons freshly squeezed orange juice
- 4 cloves garlic, finely chopped
- 2 tablespoons water
- ½ teaspoon ground cumin
- ½ teaspoon dried oregano
- 2 tablespoons chopped fresh cilantro
- ½ teaspoon salt
- 1 teaspoon freshly ground black pepper

STEAK AND SALAD

- 1 pound flank steak
- 1 avocado, sliced
- ½ red onion, thinly sliced

1. To prepare the mojo sauce: Whisk the oil, lime juice, orange juice, garlic, water, cumin, oregano, cilantro, salt, and pepper in a large bowl until combined. Reserve ¼ cup of the mixture in a small bowl. Place the beef in the marinade, cover, and refrigerate for at least 2 hours or overnight.

2. Preheat a barbecue grill to medium-hot. Meanwhile, remove the steak from the marinade (discard the used marinade) and allow the steak to stand at room temperature for 30 minutes.

3. Grill the steak over direct heat, turning 2 or 3 times, for 8 minutes or until an instant-read thermometer inserted in the center registers 145°F for medium-rare/160°F for medium/165°F for well-done. Remove from the grill and let stand for 10 minutes before slicing.

4. To prepare the salad: Combine the avocado, onion, and reserved marinade in a medium bowl. Toss to coat.

NUTRITION PER SERVING

280 calories
24 g protein
6 g carbohydrates
18 g fat
4.5 g saturated fat*
45 mg cholesterol
150 mg sodium
3 g fiber

*Limit saturated fat to 10% of total calories—about 17 grams per day for most women—and sodium intake to less than 2,300 milligrams.

{ **Make It a FLAT BELLY DIET MEAL** } Serve with 2 corn tortillas (90) and 1 cup cubed papaya (55).
TOTAL MEAL: 425 calories

Ginger-Pork Stir-Fry

30 MINUTES ▪ **4 SERVINGS** ▪ **314 CALORIES** ▪ **MUFA: PEANUTS**

If you've ever wondered about baby corn, commonly available canned in the Asian section of most grocery stores, rest assured it's not a genetically altered product. They're just immature ears of real corn, grown from plants picked by hand within days of the silks emerging from the ear tips. Corn is an especially healthy food because it contains soluble fiber, which can help lower cholesterol.

12 ounces pork tenderloin, trimmed and cut into 2" × ¼" strips

3 tablespoons reduced-sodium soy sauce, divided

1 tablespoon cornstarch

1 tablespoon peanut oil, divided

1 green bell pepper, thinly sliced

1 carrot, thinly sliced

1 sweet onion, sliced

1 tablespoon freshly grated ginger

1 cup baby corn

½ cup dry-roasted unsalted peanuts

1. Toss the pork with 1 tablespoon of the soy sauce and the cornstarch.

2. Heat 2 teaspoons of the oil in a large nonstick skillet or wok over medium-high heat. Add the pork and cook for 3 to 4 minutes or until cooked through. Transfer to a plate and reserve. Return the skillet to the heat and add the remaining 1 teaspoon oil.

3. Add the pepper, carrot, onion, ginger, and corn. Cook, stirring often, for 3 to 4 minutes or until crisp-tender. Add the reserved pork, peanuts, and remaining soy sauce. Cook, stirring, for about 1 minute longer or until the pork is cooked through. Serve immediately.

NUTRITION PER SERVING

314 calories
25 g protein
20 g carbohydrates
16 g fat
3 g saturated fat
55 mg cholesterol
456 mg sodium
4 g fiber

{ **Make It a FLAT BELLY DIET MEAL** } Serve with ½ cup brown rice (98).
TOTAL MEAL: 412 calories

Mongolian Beef Stir-Fry

■ 25 MINUTES ■ 4 SERVINGS ■ 431 CALORIES ■ MUFA: ALMONDS

Slivered almonds add just the right crunch to this superquick stir-fry. As with all stir-fries, make sure you have all your ingredients prepped and ready to go before you start to cook. Oyster sauce is high in sodium but packed with flavor (and yes, it's made with oysters). Be sure to measure precisely when using.

3 ounces bean thread noodles

1 pound flank steak, cut across the grain into ¼"-thick strips

2 tablespoons reduced-sodium soy sauce

2 tablespoons dry sherry (optional), divided

1 tablespoon cornstarch

1 tablespoon peanut oil, divided

1 tablespoon minced fresh ginger

4 ounces shiitake mushrooms, stemmed and thinly sliced

1 carrot, thinly sliced diagonally

12 scallions, chopped

½ cup slivered almonds

2 tablespoons oyster sauce

1 teaspoon chili-garlic sauce

1. Prepare the noodles per the package directions, drain, and coarsely chop.

2. Combine the steak, 1 tablespoon of the soy sauce, 1 tablespoon of the sherry (if using), and the cornstarch in a bowl and mix well.

3. Heat 2 teaspoons of the oil in a large nonstick skillet or wok over high heat. Add the steak and cook, stirring often, for about 4 minutes or until no longer pink. Transfer to a plate and reserve.

4. Return the skillet to the stove top and heat the remaining 1 teaspoon oil over high heat. Add the ginger and mushrooms and cook, stirring often, for 2 to 3 minutes or until the mushrooms start to soften. Add the carrot, scallions, and almonds and cook for 2 minutes longer. Add the noodles and reserved steak and cook for 1 minute longer or until heated through.

5. Pour in the oyster sauce, chili-garlic sauce, remaining 1 tablespoon soy sauce, and remaining 1 tablespoon sherry and cook for 1 minute or until thickened. Serve immediately.

NUTRITION PER SERVING

431 calories
29 g protein
34 g carbohydrates
20 g fat
5 g saturated fat*
46 mg cholesterol
653 mg sodium*
4 g fiber

*Limit saturated fat to 10% of total calories—about 17 grams per day for most women—and sodium intake to less than 2,300 milligrams.

 Make It a FLAT BELLY DIET MEAL A single serving of this recipe counts as a *Flat Belly Diet* Meal without any add-ons!

Pistachio-Crusted Pork Scaloppine

■ **35 MINUTES** ■ **4 SERVINGS** ■ **202 CALORIES** ■ **MUFA: PISTACHIOS**

Scaloppine is traditionally cooked in a skillet, but when using a nut coating in place of flour, an oven method works better. To pound the meat evenly, be sure to start in the center of each piece and use short, flattening strokes.

12 ounces pork tenderloin, trimmed

½ cup unsalted pistachios

1 teaspoon paprika

¼ teaspoon salt

1 egg white

1 tablespoon cold water

4 lime wedges

1. Preheat the oven to 375°F. Cover a baking sheet with foil. Set aside.

2. Place the pork on a work surface. Cut into 8 slices, each ¾" thick. With a scaloppine pounder or a rolling pin covered in plastic wrap, flatten to ¼" thickness.

3. Place the pistachios in a grinder or a food processor fitted with a metal blade. Process until finely ground. Transfer to a large sheet of wax paper. Add the paprika and salt. Toss to combine. Beat the egg white and water in a bowl with a fork. With a pastry brush, coat both sides of the pork scaloppine with the egg white mixture. Sprinkle the nut mixture on both sides of the pork, pressing to adhere. Place the scaloppine in a single layer on the prepared baking sheet.

4. Bake for 15 minutes or until the pork is sizzling and cooked through. Serve with the lime wedges.

NUTRITION PER SERVING

202 calories
22 g protein
6 g carbohydrates
10 g fat
2 g saturated fat
55 mg cholesterol
204 mg sodium
2 g fiber

{ **Make It a FLAT BELLY DIET MEAL** } Serve with 1 cup steamed wild rice (150) and 1 cup broccoli florets, steamed (40) and drizzled with 1 tablespoon freshly squeezed lemon juice (5).
TOTAL MEAL: 397 calories

Pork Tenderloin with Olives and Rosemary

■ 55 MINUTES   ■ 4 SERVINGS   ■ 219 CALORIES   ■ MUFA: BLACK OLIVES

Rosemary is an especially hardy herb that grows well in warm, dry climates. If fresh rosemary isn't available, substitute 1 teaspoon ground rosemary in this dish.

1 pound pork tenderloin, trimmed

1 medium red onion, cut into eighths

1 tablespoon minced fresh rosemary

2 teaspoons olive oil

¼ teaspoon salt

¼ teaspoon freshly ground black pepper

40 black olives, pitted (about 1⅓ cups)

1. Preheat the oven to 375°F. Cover a small baking sheet with foil. Place the pork, onion, and rosemary on the pan. Drizzle the oil over all. Sprinkle with the salt and pepper. With clean hands, rub the pork and onion to coat evenly with the seasonings.

2. Roast for 20 minutes. Scatter the olives over the onions and toss to combine. Return to the oven and roast for about 15 minutes, or until an instant-read thermometer inserted in the center registers 155°F. Let stand for 10 minutes before slicing.

NUTRITION PER SERVING

219 calories
25 g protein
6 g carbohydrates
11 g fat
2 g saturated fat
74 mg cholesterol
587 mg sodium
2 g fiber

{ **Make It a FLAT BELLY DIET MEAL** }   Serve with 1 cup cooked whole wheat penne pasta (205).
TOTAL MEAL: 435 calories   ■ To serve as part of a *Flat Belly Diet* Meal, omit the olives (168).

Seville-Style Grilled Pork Chops

■ **25 MINUTES** ■ **4 SERVINGS** ■ **245 CALORIES** ■ **MUFA: GREEN OLIVES**

If you're a fan of sweet-and-salty combinations, this dish is for you. Fleshy orange sections cut from the membrane are called supremes, and they nicely balance the saltiness of firm green olives.

2 oranges
40 green olives, quartered lengthwise (about 1⅓ cups)
½ small red onion, thinly sliced
½ teaspoon cracked black pepper
½ teaspoon smoked paprika
4 boneless pork chops (about 4 ounces each)

1. Coat a grill rack or rack in a broiler pan with cooking spray. Preheat the grill or broiler.

2. Cut the peel and white pith from the oranges. Holding the oranges over a medium bowl to catch the juice, cut between the membranes to release the segments, allowing them to drop into the bowl. Squeeze the membranes to release any juices into the bowl. Add the olives, onion, and pepper to the bowl. Toss to combine.

3. Rub the paprika onto both sides of the chops. Grill or broil, turning once, for 6 to 10 minutes or until a thermometer inserted in the center of a chop registers 155°F. Serve the chops topped with the orange mixture.

NUTRITION PER SERVING

245 calories
26 g protein
10 g carbohydrates
11 g fat
2 g saturated fat
78 mg cholesterol
492 mg sodium
2 g fiber

{ Make It a **FLAT BELLY DIET MEAL** } Serve with the Saffron Rice on page 148, but omit the pistachios (140).
TOTAL MEAL: 370 calories

Chipotle Pork and Onion Casserole

■ 1 HOUR ■ 4 SERVINGS ■ 375 CALORIES ■ MUFA: OLIVE OIL

Reminiscent of enchiladas, this cheesy casserole is a real crowd pleaser. Store unused chipotle chiles and adobo sauce in the refrigerator, where they will keep for up to 3 months.

12 ounces boneless pork tenderloin, cut into ½" pieces

1 teaspoon chili powder

½ teaspoon ground cumin

¼ cup olive oil

2 onions, chopped

1 teaspoon sugar

3 cloves garlic, minced

1 carrot, chopped

1 rib celery, chopped

1 can (8.5 ounces) no-salt-added whole kernel corn, drained

1 can (15 ounces) diced tomatoes, unsalted

1 chipotle chile pepper in adobo sauce, minced

¾ cup shredded reduced-fat sharp Cheddar cheese

¼ cup fat-free sour cream

1. Preheat the oven to 350°F. Coat an 8" × 8" baking dish with cooking spray.

2. Combine the pork, chili powder, cumin, and 1 tablespoon of the oil in a bowl. Heat 2 tablespoons of the oil in a large nonstick skillet over medium heat. Add the onions and sugar and cook, stirring often, for 7 to 8 minutes or until the onions are very soft.

3. Add the garlic, carrot, and celery. Cook, stirring occasionally, for 5 to 6 minutes or until the onions are lightly browned and the vegetables are softened. Stir in the corn and cook for 2 minutes longer. Transfer to a bowl and reserve.

4. Heat the remaining 1 tablespoon oil over medium-high heat and add the pork. Cook, stirring occasionally, for 3 to 4 minutes or until the pork is no longer pink. Add the reserved onion mixture, tomatoes, and chile pepper. Cook, stirring occasionally, for 2 to 3 minutes or until slightly thickened. Transfer to the prepared baking dish and scatter the cheese on top. Cover with a sheet of foil that has been coated with cooking spray.

5. Bake for about 15 minutes or until the pork is tender and the filling is bubbling. Remove the foil and bake for 3 minutes longer or until the cheese has browned slightly. Divide among 4 serving plates and top each with 1 tablespoon of the sour cream.

NUTRITION PER SERVING

375 calories
26 g protein
19 g carbohydrates
22 g fat
6 g saturated fat*
70 mg cholesterol
321 mg sodium
4 g fiber

*Limit saturated fat to 10% of total calories—about 17 grams per day for most women—and sodium intake to less than 2,300 milligrams.

{ Make It a FLAT BELLY DIET MEAL }   Serve with 1 cup red grapes (60). **TOTAL MEAL:** 435 calories

Mexican Green Chile Pork Stew

1 HOUR 15 MINUTES ▪ **4 SERVINGS** ▪ **393 CALORIES** ▪ **MUFA: ALMONDS**

If you can't find poblano chile peppers at your grocery store, use any mildly hot green chile that's available. To ensure even cooking, make sure the vegetables are chopped to about the same size.

½ cup blanched
  slivered almonds

2 tablespoons olive oil

2½ teaspoons whole
  cumin seeds

1 large white onion,
  chopped

2 large poblano chile
  peppers, halved, seeded,
  and chopped

2 carrots, sliced

3 cloves garlic, minced

12 ounces pork tenderloin,
  cut into ¾" cubes

½ teaspoon salt

¼ teaspoon ground
  cinnamon

1 pound plum tomatoes,
  chopped

¾ cup reduced-sodium,
  fat-free chicken broth

2 zucchini, halved
  and sliced

1 sweet potato, peeled
  and chopped

1. Put ⅓ cup of the almonds in a food processor and process until ground. Reserve. Toast the remaining almonds in a small skillet.

2. Warm the oil in a Dutch oven over medium heat. Add the cumin seeds. Cook and stir for 1 minute.

3. Add the onion, peppers, carrots, and garlic and cook, stirring often, for 10 to 12 minutes or until tender. Add the pork, salt, cinnamon, and remaining almonds and cook, stirring often, for about 5 minutes or until the pork is lightly colored.

4. Add the tomatoes and broth and bring to a simmer. Reduce the heat to low, cover, and cook for 15 minutes or until the tomatoes are saucy.

5. Add the zucchini and sweet potato. Increase the heat and bring to a boil. Reduce the heat to low, cover, and cook for 20 to 25 minutes or until the pork and vegetables are tender.

6. Stir in the reserved ground almonds and cook, uncovered, for 5 minutes or until the stew is slightly thickened.

NUTRITION PER SERVING

393 calories
27 g protein
30 g carbohydrates
20 g fat
3 g saturated fat
55 mg cholesterol
478 mg sodium
9 g fiber

{ **Make It a FLAT BELLY DIET MEAL** } A single serving of this recipe counts as a *Flat Belly Diet* Meal without any add-ons!

meats

Grilled Pork with Garlic Oil and a Little Salad

■ 45 MINUTES ■ 4 SERVINGS ■ 276 CALORIES ■ MUFA: GARLIC OIL

Chopped salad is a colorful accompaniment to this lean and lovely dish. Fold the leftovers into a whole grain wrap for a quick and easy lunch. Pork tenderloin, an especially lean cut with less than 5 grams of fat per serving, also provides 62 percent of the daily value for thiamin, a B vitamin that helps cells convert carbohydrates into energy.

PORK

¼ cup Garlic-Infused Oil (page 63)

2 tablespoons freshly squeezed lemon juice

½ teaspoon dried oregano

½ teaspoon salt

½ teaspoon freshly ground black pepper

1 pound pork tenderloin, trimmed

SALAD

1 red bell pepper, coarsely chopped

½ hothouse cucumber, chopped

3 scallions, thinly sliced

¼ cup chopped fresh parsley

1. To prepare the pork: Combine the oil, lemon juice, oregano, salt, and black pepper in a small bowl. Coat the pork with 2 tablespoons of the mixture and marinate in the refrigerator for 1 to 2 hours.

2. To prepare the salad: Combine the bell pepper, cucumber, scallions, and parsley with the remaining oil mixture in a medium bowl. Cover and refrigerate until ready to serve.

3. Preheat a barbecue grill to medium-hot. Add the pork and brush with its marinade. Grill, turning 2 or 3 times, for 20 minutes or until nicely browned and an instant-read thermometer inserted in the center registers 155°F. Remove from the grill and let stand for 10 minutes.

4. Carve the pork into slices and serve with the salad.

NUTRITION PER SERVING

276 calories
25 g protein
5 g carbohydrates
18 g fat
3 g saturated fat
74 mg cholesterol
354 mg sodium
1 g fiber

{ Make It a FLAT BELLY DIET MEAL }

Serve with the Smoky Tomato Soup on page 98, but omit the avocado (100).

TOTAL MEAL: 376 calories

Spinach Steak Roulade

■ 1 HOUR ■ 6 SERVINGS ■ 320 CALORIES ■ MUFA: PINE NUTS

Here's one to impress the guests! The important thing to remember when tying meat is to keep the string tight enough to hold the shape of the cut but not so tight that it will squeeze the juices from the meat while it is cooking. Use a kitchen twine that is made from all-natural cotton or linen so that it doesn't burn or affect the flavor of the finished dish.

1½ pounds flank steak
2 cloves garlic, minced
4 cups baby spinach
¾ cup pine nuts, toasted and finely chopped
¼ cup crumbled low-fat feta cheese

1. Preheat the oven to 450°F.

2. Pound the steak between 2 sheets of plastic wrap to ½" thickness with a meat mallet or heavy skillet. Score the steak with a sharp knife on 1 side in a crosshatch pattern.

3. Heat a large nonstick skillet coated with cooking spray over medium-high heat. Add the garlic and cook for 2 minutes or until fragrant. Add the spinach and cook, stirring, for 3 minutes or until wilted. Remove from the heat and stir in the pine nuts.

4. Turn the steak over, with the short end facing you. Spread the spinach mixture over the steak, leaving a ½" border on the long sides and 2" border at the far short end. Sprinkle with the cheese. Starting from the closest side, roll up tightly. Tie the steak crosswise with kitchen twine.

5. Place seam side down in a baking dish or on a rimmed baking sheet. Cook for 35 minutes or until a thermometer inserted in the center registers 145°F for medium-rare/160°F for medium/165°F for well-done. Let stand for 10 minutes and remove the string before slicing.

NUTRITION PER SERVING

320 calories
28 g protein
4 g carbohydrates
22 g fat
5 g saturated fat*
49 mg cholesterol
169 mg sodium
1 g fiber

*Limit saturated fat to 10% of total calories—about 17 grams per day for most women—and sodium intake to less than 2,300 milligrams.

{ Make It a FLAT BELLY DIET MEAL } Serve with 1 cup roasted potatoes (100).
TOTAL MEAL: 420 calories

Moussaka

■ **45 MINUTES** ■ **6 SERVINGS** ■ **349 CALORIES** ■ **MUFA: OLIVE OIL**

Moussaka is a layered meat-and-vegetable dish that can take many forms, but this combination of eggplant and spicy beef, smothered in a blanket of sauce and topped with cheese, is hands down the most popular. Just one bite and you'll know why.

1 onion, chopped

2 cloves garlic, minced

¾ pound 97% lean ground beef

1 can (14.5 ounces) no-salt-added diced tomatoes

¼ cup tomato paste

½ teaspoon ground cinnamon

¼ teaspoon ground allspice

2 eggplants, peeled and cut lengthwise into ¼" slices

6 tablespoons olive oil

2 cups 1% milk

3 tablespoons cornstarch

½ cup grated Romano cheese

1. Heat the broiler. Coat a 9" × 9" baking dish and a large baking sheet with olive oil cooking spray.

2. Heat a large skillet coated with cooking spray over medium-high heat. Cook the onion and garlic for 3 minutes or until the onion begins to soften. Add the beef and cook for 5 to 7 minutes, stirring often, or until the beef is browned and cooked through. Stir in the tomatoes (with juice), tomato paste, cinnamon, and allspice. Bring to a boil. Reduce the heat to low and simmer for 10 minutes.

3. Place half of the eggplant on the prepared baking sheet and brush with 3 tablespoons of the oil. Broil 6" from heat for 10 minutes or until browned, turning once. Repeat with the remaining eggplant and 3 tablespoons oil.

4. Whisk together the milk and cornstarch in a small saucepan. Bring to a simmer over medium heat and cook, whisking, for 8 minutes or until thickened. Remove from the heat and stir in the cheese.

5. Layer half of the eggplant in the baking dish, then half of the meat sauce. Repeat with the eggplant and meat sauce. Spread the cheese sauce on top (don't worry if the mixture comes to the top of the pan). Broil for 3 minutes or until just starting to brown.

NUTRITION PER SERVING

349 calories
19 g protein
21 g carbohydrates
21 g fat
6 g saturated fat*
43 mg cholesterol
338 mg sodium
5 g fiber

*Limit saturated fat to 10% of total calories—about 17 grams per day for most women—and sodium intake to less than 2,300 milligrams.

{ Make It a **FLAT BELLY DIET MEAL** }

Serve with
½ multigrain pita (70).
TOTAL MEAL: 419 calories

11

Snacks

Curried Peanuts

15 MINUTES **8 SERVINGS** **120 CALORIES** **MUFA: PEANUTS**

This recipe works just as well with pecans and walnuts. Feel free to substitute those nuts if you prefer.

2 teaspoons canola oil
1 cup dry-roasted unsalted
    peanuts
1 teaspoon curry powder
¼ onion, chopped
2 tablespoons finely
    chopped fresh cilantro
⅛ teaspoon salt
    Pinch of ground red
    pepper (optional)

Heat the oil in a skillet over medium heat for 1 minute. Add the peanuts and curry powder. Cook, stirring constantly, for about 2 minutes or until golden. Add the onion, cilantro, salt, and ground red pepper, if using. Cook for about 2 minutes or until the onion is golden. Serve warm or at room temperature.

**NUTRITION
PER SERVING**

120 calories
4 g protein
5 g carbohydrates
10 g fat
1 g saturated fat
0 mg cholesterol
40 mg sodium
2 g fiber

**Make It a
FLAT
BELLY
DIET
MEAL**

Serve with the Curried Apple and Pear Soup on page 97, but omit the almonds (160), and a multigrain pita (140).
TOTAL MEAL: 420 calories

Tex-Mex Snack Mix

■ **2–3 HOURS** ■ **16 (½ CUP) SERVINGS** ■ **265 CALORIES** ■ **MUFA: CASHEWS**

If you love snack mix but hate the idea of turning on your oven in the middle of summer, pull out your slow cooker! This recipe works like a charm.

½ cup canola oil

1 tablespoon chili powder

1 teaspoon ground cumin

1 teaspoon dried oregano

½ teaspoon salt

¼ teaspoon ground red pepper

3 cups multigrain square cereal

2¼ cups unsalted whole cashews

2 cups oat or multigrain cereal

2 cups multigrain pretzel sticks

1. Combine the oil, chili powder, cumin, oregano, salt, and pepper in a small measuring cup.

2. Combine the cereal squares, cashews, oat cereal, and pretzels in a 3½- to 5-quart slow cooker. Drizzle with the oil mixture, tossing to coat well. Cover and cook on low for 2 to 3 hours, stirring twice during the cooking time. Be sure to check the mixture after 2 hours, as slow cooker times can vary.

3. Remove the lid during the last half hour of cooking to allow the mix to dry.

NUTRITION PER SERVING

265 calories
5 g protein
27 g carbohydrates
16 g fat
2 g saturated fat*
0 mg cholesterol
363 mg sodium
2 g fiber

*Limit saturated fat to 10% of total calories—about 17 grams per day for most women—and sodium intake to less than 2,300 milligrams.

{ **Make It a FLAT BELLY DIET MEAL** } Serve with ½ apple, sliced (40), and ½ cup vanilla yogurt (70).
TOTAL MEAL: 375 calories

Spicy Citrus-Spiked Olives

■ 10 MINUTES + CHILL TIME   ■ 4 SERVINGS   ■ 107 CALORIES   ■ MUFA: OLIVES

It's hard to imagine olives getting even better, but here they're dressed for success. If you prefer one citrus over the other, by all means tweak this dish to your liking.

20 kalamata olives
    (about ²/₃ cup)
20 green olives
    (about ²/₃ cup)
 2 teaspoons orange peel,
    cut into thin strips
 2 teaspoons lemon peel,
    cut into thin strips
 2 teaspoons extra virgin
    olive oil
 1 teaspoon freshly
    squeezed lemon juice
 1 teaspoon fresh thyme
    leaves
¹/₈ teaspoon red-pepper
    flakes

Combine the kalamata olives, green olives, orange peel, lemon peel, oil, lemon juice, thyme, and red-pepper flakes in a small bowl. Cover and refrigerate for at least 2 hours or overnight.

NUTRITION
PER SERVING

107 calories
0.5 g protein
2 g carbohydrates
11 g fat
1 g saturated fat
0 mg cholesterol
518 mg sodium
0.5 g fiber

{ Make It a FLAT BELLY DIET MEAL }   Serve with the Spinach Steak Roulade on page 246, but omit the pine nuts (206), and ¹/₂ cup cooked whole wheat penne (105). **TOTAL MEAL:** 418 calories

Barbecued Edamame

■ **10 MINUTES** ■ **4 SERVINGS** ■ **231 CALORIES** ■ **MUFA: EDAMAME**

The word *edamame* literally means "beans on branches," as they grow in clusters on bushy branches. These tasty legumes are a great source of fiber, too.

4 cups fresh or
  frozen edamame

1 tablespoon olive oil

½ teaspoon chili powder

½ teaspoon ground cumin

⅛ teaspoon ground red
  pepper

½ teaspoon salt

1. Bring a large pot of water to a boil over high heat. Add the edamame and cook for about 5 minutes or until bright green. Drain.

2. Heat the oil in a large nonstick skillet over medium-high heat. Add the chili powder, cumin, and red pepper and cook for 30 seconds or until fragrant. Add the edamame and cook, tossing, for about 1 minute or until hot and well coated. Add the salt and remove from the heat. Transfer to a bowl and serve warm or at room temperature.

**NUTRITION
PER SERVING**

231 calories
16 g protein
18 g carbohydrates
9 g fat
0.5 g saturated fat
0 mg cholesterol
351 mg sodium
8 g fiber

{ **Make It a
FLAT
BELLY
DIET
MEAL** }
Serve with the Five-Spice Fish with Avocado-Wasabi Sauce on page 176, but omit the avocado-wasabi sauce (147).
TOTAL MEAL: 378 calories

Sesame Crackers

1 HOUR 15 MINUTES ▪ **8 SERVINGS** ▪ **287 CALORIES** ▪ **MUFA: SESAME SEEDS**

Homemade crackers make an impressive statement, but they're actually much easier to prepare than most people might think. Once you master the basic recipe, feel free to add your own signature seasonings.

1 cup all-purpose flour
1 cup sesame seeds, toasted
1 teaspoon baking powder
1 teaspoon salt
²/₃ cup low-fat plain yogurt
¹/₃ cup canola oil
1 tablespoon toasted sesame oil

1. Combine the flour, sesame seeds, baking powder, and salt in a large bowl. Whisk together the yogurt, canola oil, and sesame oil in a small bowl. Stir into the flour mixture until a dough forms.

2. Divide the dough in half and wrap each in plastic wrap. Cover and chill for 30 minutes.

3. Preheat the oven to 375°F.

4. Roll half of the dough into a 10″ square on a lightly floured surface (don't worry if the sides are a bit rough). Cut the dough in half to form 2 pieces of 10″ × 5″ each. Cut each piece into eight 1¼″ strips, forming sixteen 1¼″ × 5″ strips total. Transfer to a large baking sheet. Bake for 20 minutes or until lightly browned, turning once. Cool on a rack. Repeat with the remaining dough.

5. Store the cooled crackers in an airtight container at room temperature for up to 1 week.

NUTRITION PER SERVING

287 calories
6 g protein
17 g carbohydrates
20 g fat
1 g saturated fat
1 mg cholesterol
355 mg sodium
0.5 g fiber

{ **Make It a FLAT BELLY DIET MEAL** } Serve with the Layered Nut-and-Cheese Spread on page 257, but omit the almonds (90).
TOTAL MEAL: 377 calories

Olive–Cream Cheese Sandwiches

■ **10 MINUTES** ■ **4 SERVINGS** ■ **370 CALORIES** ■ **MUFA: OLIVES**

Take the old crackers-and-cheese combination to a new level with this MUFA-rich spread. Using a tomato slice to top these open-faced sandwiches is another handy way to control the extra sodium.

1 package (8 ounces)
  Neufchâtel cheese,
  softened

40 pimiento-stuffed olives,
  chopped (about 1⅓ cups)

4 scallions, minced

¼ teaspoon hot-pepper
  sauce (optional)

12 lower-sodium
  wheat crackers

2 plum tomatoes,
  thinly sliced

1. Combine the cheese, olives, scallions, and hot-pepper sauce in a small bowl.

2. Spread on the crackers. Top with the tomatoes.

**NUTRITION
PER SERVING**

370 calories
10 g protein
38 g carbohydrates
21 g fat
9 g saturated fat*
40 mg cholesterol
1,280 mg sodium*
4 g fiber

*Limit saturated fat to 10%
of total calories—about
17 grams per day for most
women—and sodium intake
to less than 2,300 milligrams.

{ **Make It a
FLAT
BELLY
DIET
MEAL** } Serve with ½ cup
red grapes (30).
TOTAL MEAL: 400 calories

Layered Nut-and-Cheese Spread

15 MINUTES + CHILLING TIME ■ **8 SERVINGS** ■ **161 CALORIES** ■ **MUFA: ALMONDS**

Perfect for a party, this zippy cheese spread is reminiscent of an old-fashioned cheese ball, but it's rendered much lighter with low-fat yogurt in place of some of the cheese.

1½ cups low-fat plain yogurt

8 ounces fat-free cream cheese, softened

2 scallions, minced

1 tablespoon prepared horseradish

1 tablespoon Worcestershire sauce

1 clove garlic, minced

1 cup finely shredded reduced-fat Cheddar cheese

1 cup sliced natural almonds, toasted

1. Place 2 white paper towels in a large sieve and place over a large bowl.

2. Combine the yogurt, cream cheese, scallions, horseradish, Worcestershire, and garlic in a medium bowl. Transfer the mixture to the paper towel–lined sieve and refrigerate for 24 hours.

3. Add the Cheddar to the yogurt mixture in a large bowl and stir well to combine (the mixture will be stiff).

4. Spread half of the yogurt mixture in a shallow serving dish. Sprinkle with half of the almonds. Repeat the layers with the remaining mixture and almonds.

NUTRITION PER SERVING

161 calories
13 g protein
8 g carbohydrates
8 g fat
2 g saturated fat
6 mg cholesterol
214 mg sodium
1 g fiber

{ Make It a **FLAT BELLY DIET MEAL** } Serve with 2 ounces lean deli turkey (50) and 7 whole wheat crackers (190). **TOTAL MEAL:** 401 calories ■ To serve as part of another *Flat Belly Diet* Meal, omit the almonds (90).

Caponata

■ 30 MINUTES ■ 4 SERVINGS ■ 199 CALORIES ■ MUFA: PINE NUTS

The flavor of this traditional Italian relish improves upon keeping. Store in the refrigerator for up to 2 weeks.

½ cup pine nuts
1 pound Italian or Japanese eggplant
1 tablespoon olive oil
¼ cup minced celery
¼ cup minced onion
4 ripe plum tomatoes, peeled and coarsely chopped
2 teaspoons honey
⅛ teaspoon red-pepper flakes
1 tablespoon minced capers
1 tablespoon red wine vinegar

1. Place the pine nuts in a large nonstick skillet over medium-high heat. Cook, stirring often, for about 5 minutes or until golden. Remove and set aside.

2. Peel the eggplant and cut into ½" thick rounds. Coat the skillet with cooking spray. Place over medium-high heat for 1 minute. Place the eggplant in the pan and cook for 4 minutes on each side or until browned. Remove to a plate, cover with foil, and set aside. When cool, cut the rounds in half.

3. Return the pan to the heat. Add the oil, celery, and onion. Cook, stirring, for 3 minutes or until softened. Add the tomatoes. Cook, stirring occasionally, for 5 minutes longer or until softened.

4. Add the honey, red-pepper flakes, and reserved eggplant. Reduce the heat so the mixture simmers. Cook for 5 minutes or until the eggplant is soft. Remove from the heat. Stir in the capers, vinegar, and reserved pine nuts.

NUTRITION PER SERVING

199 calories
4 g protein
15 g carbohydrates
15 g fat
1 g saturated fat
0 mg cholesterol
76 mg sodium
6 g fiber

{ Make It a FLAT BELLY DIET MEAL } Serve as a topping over 1 cup cooked whole wheat spaghetti (200). **TOTAL MEAL:** 399 ■ To serve as part of another *Flat Belly Diet* Meal, omit the pine nuts (80).

Walnut "Pâté"

■ **30 MINUTES** ■ **8 SERVINGS** ■ **114 CALORIES** ■ **MUFA: WALNUTS**

If you're a pâté fan, chances are that once you taste this richly flavored—and cholesterol free—version, you'll never crave the real stuff again. For best results, allow to come to room temperature before serving.

1 tablespoon canola oil
1 cup walnuts
¼ onion, chopped
2 tablespoons raisins
½ teaspoon dried thyme
¼ teaspoon paprika
1 tablespoon roasted garlic (from a jar)
2 tablespoons freshly squeezed lemon juice
2 tablespoons chopped fresh parsley
⅛ teaspoon salt
Freshly ground black pepper

1. Heat the oil in a skillet over medium heat until sizzling. Add the walnuts. Cook for 3 minutes, stirring occasionally, or until toasted. Add the onion, raisins, thyme, and paprika. Cook, stirring, for 5 minutes or until the onion is softened. Add the garlic. Stir just until the garlic is incorporated. Remove from the heat. Cool to room temperature.

2. Transfer the mixture to the bowl of a food processor fitted with a metal blade or a blender. Process, scraping the bowl as needed, for about 3 minutes or until a coarse paste forms. Add the lemon juice, parsley, salt, and pepper to taste. Pulse just until combined. Serve immediately or refrigerate for up to 1 week.

NUTRITION PER SERVING

114 calories
2 g protein
5 g carbohydrates
10 g fat
1 g saturated fat
0 mg cholesterol
38 mg sodium
1 g fiber

{ Make It a **FLAT BELLY DIET MEAL** } Serve with a 4-ounce roasted center-cut pork chop (187) and 1 cup steamed butternut squash cubes (82).
TOTAL MEAL: 383 calories

snacks

Pomegranate Pepper Dip

■ 10 MINUTES ■ 8 SERVINGS ■ 167 CALORIES ■ MUFA: OLIVE OIL

Pureed roasted pepper serves as the base for this splendid dip. Pomegranate molasses is commonly available in Middle Eastern grocery stores. It's an ingredient worth seeking out, but in a pinch, a tablespoon of honey is an acceptable substitute.

2 roasted red peppers
¾ cup fresh whole grain
  bread crumbs
3 tablespoons chopped
  walnuts, toasted
1 clove garlic
1½ tablespoons freshly
  squeezed lemon juice
1 tablespoon pomegranate
  molasses
½ teaspoon ground
  coriander
¼ teaspoon ground cumin
½ teaspoon salt
½ cup extra virgin olive oil
  Carrot and celery sticks

Combine the peppers, bread crumbs, walnuts, garlic, lemon juice, molasses, coriander, cumin, and salt in a blender or food processor and process until smooth. With the blender running slowly, add the oil until combined. Serve with carrot and celery sticks.

NUTRITION PER SERVING

167 calories
1 g protein
5 g carbohydrates
16 g fat
2 g saturated fat
0 mg cholesterol
210 mg sodium
1 g fiber

{ Make It a
FLAT
BELLY
DIET
MEAL }
Serve with ½ cup carrots sticks (20), ½ cup celery sticks (10), 1 whole wheat pita toasted (120), and 1 wedge honeydew melon (58).
TOTAL MEAL: 375 calories

Southern-Style Dip

■ 10 MINUTES   ■ 4 SERVINGS   ■ 281 CALORIES   ■ MUFA: PEANUT BUTTER

Here's a dip that's like a second cousin of hummus. Plus, all the Southern favorites are here: peanuts, bacon, onion, and black-eyed peas. Add a splash of hot sauce and you're good to go.

1 slice center-cut bacon,
   such as Oscar Mayer
   30% less fat, chopped
½ sweet onion, chopped
2 cloves garlic, sliced
1 cup frozen (6 ounces)
   black-eyed peas, cooked
   per package directions
½ cup crunchy natural
   unsalted peanut butter
2 tablespoons cider vinegar
½ teaspoon hot-pepper
   sauce
¼ teaspoon salt
¼ teaspoon ground cumin
1–2 tablespoons water

1. Heat a medium nonstick skillet over medium-high heat. Add the bacon and cook for 3 to 4 minutes or until crisp. Stir in the onion and garlic and cook for 8 to 9 minutes or until softened and lightly browned.

2. Transfer to a food processor and add the black-eyed peas, peanut butter, vinegar, hot-pepper sauce, salt, and cumin. Puree and thin with the water.

NUTRITION PER SERVING

281 calories
12 g protein
21 g carbohydrates
17 g fat
2 g saturated fat
2 mg cholesterol
201 mg sodium
4 g fiber

{ Make It a FLAT BELLY DIET MEAL } Serve with ¼ cup reduced-fat shredded Cheddar cheese (81) and ½ ounce multigrain tortilla chips (70). **TOTAL MEAL:** 432 calories

Texas Caviar and Whole Grain Chips

■ **40 MINUTES + CHILL TIME** ■ **4 SERVINGS** ■ **331 CALORIES** ■ **MUFA: OLIVE OIL**

Beans are rich in complex carbohydrates, which play an important role in keeping blood sugar levels steady. You can control the heat of the finished dish by watching the amount of jalapeño seeds that are added. Naturally, for less heat, use fewer.

¼ cup olive oil, divided

2 tablespoons cider vinegar

1 fresh jalapeño pepper, with seeds, minced

1 clove garlic, crushed through a press

¼–½ teaspoon coarse-ground black pepper

¼ teaspoon salt

2 cups frozen black-eyed peas, cooked without salt per package directions

½ cup chopped roasted red peppers (from a jar), blotted dry

1 rib tender inner celery, chopped

⅓ cup chopped red onion

2 whole grain pitas (6" diameter)

1. Combine 3 tablespoons plus 1 teaspoon of the oil, the vinegar, chile pepper, garlic, black pepper, and salt in a medium bowl. Stir in the black-eyed peas, red pepper, celery, and onion.

2. Cover and chill for at least 2 hours or until ready to serve.

3. Preheat the oven to 400°F. Brush the pitas with the remaining 2 teaspoons oil and cut into 8 wedges each. Place on a baking sheet and bake for 6 to 8 minutes or until lightly toasted. Serve with the caviar.

NUTRITION PER SERVING

331 calories
11 g protein
41 g carbohydrates
15 g fat
2 g saturated fat
0 mg cholesterol
401 mg sodium
7 g fiber

{ **Make It a FLAT BELLY DIET MEAL** }

Serve with 1 medium pear (104).
TOTAL MEAL: 435 calories

Guacamole

10 MINUTES ■ **8 SERVINGS** ■ **100 CALORIES** ■ **MUFA: AVOCADO**

Guacamole, a dish with Central American roots, is traditionally prepared in a *molcajete,* a type of mortar and pestle carved from lava rock. Owing to the avocado's soft, silken texture, a bowl and fork work just fine, too. Beyond MUFAs, avocados also contain beneficial amounts of potassium and folate, two nutrients also important to heart health.

2 cups mashed avocado
1 large tomato, chopped
¼ white onion, diced
¼ cup chopped fresh
   cilantro
¼ cup freshly squeezed
   lime juice
1 or 2 fresh jalapeño chile
   peppers, minced
¾ teaspoon salt
½–1 teaspoon green or
   red Tabasco (optional)

Combine the avocado, tomato, onion, cilantro, lime juice, peppers, salt, and Tabasco (if using) in a medium bowl. Stir until combined. Serve immediately.

**NUTRITION
PER SERVING**

100 calories
1 g protein
7 g carbohydrates
8.5 g fat
1 g saturated fat
0 mg cholesterol
224 mg sodium
4 g fiber

{ Make It a
FLAT
BELLY
DIET
MEAL }
Serve with ½ cup canned drained black beans, warmed, mashed, and seasoned with ½ teaspoon chile powder (90); 1 ounce feta cheese (80); and 1 ounce multigrain tortilla chips (140). **TOTAL MEAL:** 410 calories

Mashed Avocado Snack

■ **5 MINUTES** ■ **1 SERVING** ■ **161 CALORIES** ■ **MUFA: AVOCADO**

If you love guacamole, give this superquick spread a try. This delicious pineapple-avocado combination is something new and different.

¼ avocado, mashed
¼ cup chopped fresh or canned, drained, juice-packed crushed pineapple
½ teaspoon hot-pepper sauce
  Pinch of salt
2 multigrain Wasa crisp breads

Mix the avocado, pineapple, hot-pepper sauce, and salt. Spread over the crisp breads.

NUTRITION PER SERVING

161 calories
3 g protein
26 g carbohydrates
6 g fat
1 g saturated fat
0 mg cholesterol
254 mg sodium
7 g fiber

Make It a
FLAT BELLY DIET MEAL

Serve with 6 Ry Krisp crackers (150), 2 tablespoons fat-free sour cream (30), and ½ cup sliced banana (70).
TOTAL MEAL: 411 calories

Tropical Fruit Dip

■ **15 MINUTES** ■ **4 SERVINGS** ■ **380 CALORIES** ■ **MUFA: BRAZIL NUTS**

It's hard to feel deprived with this luscious fruit plate in front of you. Enjoy whatever is in season. Star fruit, also known as carambola, is a sweet-tart fruit with 5 large ribs that, when cut crosswise, appears star-shaped. As far as flavor goes, kiwi would make a fine substitute.

1 package (8 ounces) Neufchâtel cheese, softened

3 tablespoons honey

1 tablespoon finely chopped crystallized ginger

¼ teaspoon ground cardamom

1 cup strawberries

1 small papaya, peeled, seeded, and cut into chunks

1 small star fruit, sliced

½ pineapple, cored, trimmed, and cut into spears

½ cup Brazil nuts, chopped

1. Stir together the cheese, honey, ginger, and cardamom until well blended. If time permits, refrigerate for at least 2 hours to blend the flavors.

2. Divide the cheese mixture, strawberries, papaya, star fruit, pineapple, and nuts into 4 portions. Dip the fruit into the cheese mixture, then into the nuts.

NUTRITION PER SERVING

380 calories
10 g protein
35 g carbohydrates
24 g fat
11 g saturated fat*
40 mg cholesterol
240 mg sodium
4 g fiber

*Limit saturated fat to 10% of total calories—about 17 grams per day for most women—and sodium intake to less than 2,300 milligrams.

{ Make It a FLAT BELLY DIET MEAL }

A single serving of this recipe counts as a *Flat Belly Diet* Meal without any add-ons!

Stuffed Dried Plums

■ **25 MINUTES** ■ **4 SERVINGS** ■ **344 CALORIES** ■ **MUFA: ALMONDS**

Dried plums, also known as prunes, offer the perfect chewy sweetness to complement the sour lemon flavor of the filling and pack a serious amount of fiber in every bite. But take note: These little gems are for serious lemon-lovers only.

½ cup slivered almonds, toasted

4 ounces goat cheese

1 tablespoon freshly squeezed lemon juice

½ teaspoon freshly grated lemon zest

32 pitted dried plums

1. Combine the almonds, cheese, lemon juice, and lemon zest in a food processor fitted with a metal blade. Process until smooth.

2. Cut a slit in each plum with a small sharp knife. Spoon about 1 teaspoon of the almond mixture into each plum.

NUTRITION PER SERVING

344 calories
10 g protein
47 g carbohydrates
16 g fat
6 g saturated fat*
22 mg cholesterol
148 mg sodium
6 g fiber

*Limit saturated fat to 10% of total calories—about 17 grams per day for most women—and sodium intake to less than 2,300 milligrams.

{ Make It a **FLAT BELLY DIET MEAL** } Serve with 2 ounces roasted pork tenderloin (80). **TOTAL MEAL:** 424 calories

Peanut Butter Spirals

■ **10 MINUTES** ■ **2 SERVINGS** ■ **390 CALORIES** ■ **MUFA: PEANUT BUTTER**

What an easy alternative to the standard PB&J, made all the more dressy with a hint of vanilla and dash of cinnamon. Of course, as far as crunchy or creamy goes, the choice is up to you.

¼ cup natural peanut butter

2 tablespoons vanilla low-fat yogurt

2 (8") whole-wheat tortillas

1 ripe banana

2 teaspoons honey

1 tablespoon honey-crunch wheat germ

Ground cinnamon

1. Combine the peanut butter and yogurt in a small bowl, stirring until smooth. Spread equal amounts on each tortilla, leaving a ½" border.

2. Slice the banana into the same bowl. Drizzle with the honey and toss to coat.

3. Arrange the banana slices over each tortilla. Sprinkle with the wheat germ and cinnamon.

4. Roll up and slice each roll into 6 pieces.

NUTRITION PER SERVING

390 calories
13 g protein
54 g carbohydrates
17 g fat
2.5 g saturated fat
0 mg cholesterol
300 mg sodium
6 g fiber

{ **Make It a FLAT BELLY DIET MEAL** } A single serving of this recipe counts as a *Flat Belly Diet* Meal without any add-ons!

Tostones

■ 15 MINUTES   ■ 2 SERVINGS   ■ 230 CALORIES   ■ MUFA: CANOLA OIL

Plantains are a staple food in the tropics, similar to potatoes with a neutral flavor. By using a non-stick skillet and carefully controlling the amount of fat used, this recipe is considerably lighter than the traditional Puerto Rican snack that inspires it.

2 tablespoons canola oil, divided

1 unripe (green) plantain banana, peeled and sliced into 1″ pieces (see Note)

1 clove garlic, chopped

⅛ teaspoon salt

Dash of freshly squeezed lime juice

1. Heat 1 tablespoon of the oil in a nonstick skillet over medium-high heat.

2. Cook the plantain for 5 minutes, turning pieces as necessary until they begin to brown. Turn off the heat, transfer the plantain to a plate, and allow to cool slightly.

3. Use the flat bottom of a drinking glass to press and flatten the cut side of each piece.

4. Return the skillet to the stove and heat the remaining tablespoon of oil over medium-high heat with the garlic. Cook the plantain for 5 minutes longer, turning the pieces as necessary until they are crisped and brown.

5. Sprinkle with the salt and lime juice just before serving.

Note: To peel a plantain, cut both ends off, then run a knife along the length of the plantain, cutting through the peel only. Make a few lengthwise slits like this through the peel, then carefully pull it away from the flesh.

NUTRITION PER SERVING

230 calories
1 g protein
29 g carbohydrates
14 g fat
1 g saturated fat
0 mg cholesterol
150 mg sodium
2 g fiber

{ **FLAT BELLY DIET MEAL** } Make It a

Serve with the Cuban-Style Black Beans on page 156, but omit the avocado (175).
TOTAL MEAL: 405 calories

Sesame-Scallion Pancakes with Chutney

■ 15 MINUTES ■ 2 SERVINGS (2 PANCAKES EACH) ■ 285 CALORIES ■ MUFA: SESAME SEEDS

For great flavor and color in your finished dish, use both the white and green parts of the scallion in these savory pancakes. Scallions are higher in folate and vitamin C than regular, full-size onions.

2 eggs

2 tablespoons fat-free milk

3 tablespoons whole wheat pastry flour

5 scallions, thinly sliced

⅛ teaspoon hot-pepper sauce

¼ cup sesame seeds

¼ cup prepared or store-bought mango chutney

1. Beat the eggs and milk with a fork in a bowl. Whisk in the flour until smooth. Stir in the scallions and hot-pepper sauce.

2. Coat a nonstick griddle or large skillet with cooking spray. Place over medium-high heat. Dollop the mixture in 4 portions onto the griddle or pan. Flatten slightly if needed. Sprinkle the sesame seeds evenly over the tops. Cook for 3 minutes or until browned on the bottom. Flip and cook for 3 minutes longer or until cooked through. Serve with 2 tablespoons of the chutney.

NUTRITION
PER SERVING

285 calories
12 g protein
30 g carbohydrates
14 g fat
3 g saturated fat
212 mg cholesterol
100 mg sodium
5 g fiber

{ Make It a FLAT BELLY DIET MEAL } Serve with 2 ounces of roasted skinless chicken breast (100).
TOTAL MEAL: 385 calories

Stuffed Mushrooms

■ **45 MINUTES** ■ **4 SERVINGS** ■ **242 CALORIES** ■ **MUFA: PECANS**

These mushrooms make a perfect snack, but they can go the distance for a party, too. Simply dress them up a bit with a small sliver of roasted pepper or a sprig of parsley on top.

24 large cremini or white mushrooms

1 small red onion, chopped

1 clove garlic, minced

½ teaspoon dried thyme

½ cup pecans, toasted and finely chopped

½ cup whole wheat bread crumbs

6 ounces Jarlsberg light cheese, shredded

1. Preheat the oven to 350°F. Coat a baking sheet with sides with cooking spray.

2. Remove the stems from the mushrooms and finely chop. Set aside the caps.

3. Heat a medium skillet coated with cooking spray over medium heat. Add the chopped mushroom stems, onion, garlic, and thyme. Cook for 6 minutes or until the liquid evaporates.

4. Remove from the heat and stir in the pecans, bread crumbs, and cheese. Fill the reserved mushroom caps with the mixture, mounding slightly. Place on the prepared baking sheet. Bake for 20 to 25 minutes or until the filling is browned and the mushrooms are tender.

NUTRITION PER SERVING

242 calories
15 g protein
13 g carbohydrates
16 g fat
4 g saturated fat*
14 mg cholesterol
82 mg sodium
3 g fiber

*Limit saturated fat to 10% of total calories—about 17 grams per day for most women—and sodium intake to less than 2,300 milligrams.

{ Make It a **FLAT BELLY DIET MEAL** } Serve with ⅔ cup cooked brown rice (130) and 1 cup steamed baby carrots (50).
TOTAL MEAL: 422 calories ■ To serve as part of another *Flat Belly Diet* Meal, omit the pecans (180).

Micro-Roasted Potatoes with Tapenade

■ **15 MINUTES** ■ **2 SERVINGS** ■ **175 CALORIES** ■ **MUFA: TAPENADE**

Tender new potatoes cook much faster than baked potatoes, even in the microwave. If you prefer, use Greek-style yogurt in place of the sour cream.

8 small thin-skinned red or white potatoes

2 tablespoons fat-free sour cream

4 tablespoons Tapenade (page 181) or store-bought tapenade

1. Pierce each potato several times with a skewer and place on a piece of paper towel in a microwave oven. Microwave on high for 5 to 6 minutes or until soft when gently squeezed with a gloved hand. Let stand for 5 minutes.

2. Halve each potato lengthwise and arrange on a plate. Top each with equal parts of the sour cream and tapenade.

NUTRITION PER SERVING

175 calories
6 g protein
14 g carbohydrates
9 g fat
1 g saturated fat
0 mg cholesterol
219 mg sodium
6 g fiber

{ Make It a **FLAT BELLY DIET MEAL** }

Serve with the Spinach Salad with Pears, Pecans, and Goat Cheese on page 132, but omit the pecans (210).
TOTAL MEAL: 385 calories

Roasted Tomatoes with Garlic

■ 30 MINUTES ■ 1 SERVING ■ 238 CALORIES ■ MUFA: OLIVE OIL

Grape tomatoes, already naturally sweet, take on a new intensity when roasted with a little olive oil and garlic. This recipe can be easily doubled or tripled. It's important to enjoy all the MUFAs, so make sure to mop up the delicious juices with the toast.

1 pint grape tomatoes

1 tablespoon olive oil

1 large clove garlic, cut into thin slivers

¼ teaspoon dried basil, crumbled

¼ teaspoon freshly ground black pepper

⅛ teaspoon salt

1 slice crusty whole grain bread, toasted

1. Preheat the oven to 400°F. Combine the tomatoes, oil, garlic, basil, pepper, and salt in a small baking dish. Stir to mix.

2. Roast the tomatoes, stirring once or twice, for 22 to 25 minutes or until they have mostly collapsed and are tender and juicy. Serve hot or cold with the toast.

NUTRITION PER SERVING

238 calories
5 g protein
27 g carbohydrates
15 g fat
2 g saturated fat
0 mg cholesterol
386 mg sodium
9 g fiber

{ Make It a **FLAT BELLY DIET MEAL** }
Serve with the Pork Tenderloin with Olives and Rosemary on page 239, but omit the olives (168).
TOTAL MEAL: 406 calories

Nutty Chicken Nuggets

■ 25 MINUTES ■ 4 SERVINGS ■ 348 CALORIES ■ MUFA: SESAME SEEDS

You can make this recipe ahead and just bake what you need. Simply line a paper plate with wax paper and place the crumbed chicken on the paper, then in a ziplock freezer bag, and freeze. Bake from frozen, following the instructions but adding about 5 minutes.

CHICKEN

2 tablespoons canola oil, divided

1 slice whole wheat bread

3 tablespoons slivered almonds

½ cup sesame seeds

2 egg whites

1 pound chicken tenders

½ teaspoon salt

¼ teaspoon coarse-ground black pepper

DIP

⅓ cup fat-free plain Greek-style yogurt

1 tablespoon honey

1 teaspoon grainy mustard

1. To prepare the chicken: Preheat the oven to 400°F. Coat a heavy baking sheet with 1 tablespoon of the oil.

2. Place the bread and almonds in a food processor fitted with a metal blade and pulse to make fine crumbs. Tip onto a pie plate and mix with the sesame seeds. In another pie plate, lightly beat the egg whites.

3. Season the chicken with the salt and pepper. One piece at a time, dip the chicken into the egg whites, letting the excess drip off. Roll in the crumbs, pressing so they adhere. Put the coated chicken onto the prepared baking sheet. When all have been coated, sprinkle any leftover crumb mixture over the chicken. Drizzle evenly with the remaining 1 tablespoon oil.

4. Bake, without turning, for 12 to 15 minutes or until the crumbs are lightly browned and the chicken is cooked through in the thickest part.

5. To prepare the dip: Meanwhile, mix the yogurt, honey, and mustard in a small bowl. Serve with the chicken.

NUTRITION PER SERVING

348 calories
35 g protein
12 g carbohydrates
19 g fat
1 g saturated fat
67 mg cholesterol
456 mg sodium
3 g fiber

{ Make It a FLAT BELLY DIET MEAL }

Serve with ½ cup carrots sticks (20), ½ cup celery sticks (10), and 1 cup raw broccoli florets (20).
TOTAL MEAL: 398 calories

White Pita Pizzas

■ 15 MINUTES ■ 4 SERVINGS ■ 257 CALORIES ■ MUFA: PESTO

Offering the perfect blend of gooey cheese and garlic, these white pizzas are so quick to prepare, you can have them out of the oven faster than a delivery driver could knock at your door.

2 whole wheat pitas, split horizontally into 2 halves each

1 cup fat-free ricotta cheese

¾ cup shredded reduced-fat mozzarella cheese

¼ cup grated Parmesan cheese

1 clove garlic, minced

4 tablespoons Pesto (page 122) or store-bought pesto

1. Preheat the oven to 425°F. Coat a baking sheet with cooking spray.

2. Place the pita halves on the prepared baking sheet and bake for 4 minutes. Remove from the oven and cool for 5 minutes.

3. Meanwhile, combine the ricotta, mozzarella, Parmesan, and garlic in a bowl. Spread ¼ over each pita. Spread 1 tablespoon of the pesto over the cheese on each pita. Bake for 6 to 7 minutes or until the cheese is melted.

NUTRITION PER SERVING

257 calories
16 g protein
19 g carbohydrates
12.5 g fat
4 g saturated fat*
29 mg cholesterol
515 mg sodium
2 g fiber

*Limit saturated fat to 10% of total calories—about 17 grams per day for most women—and sodium intake to less than 2,300 milligrams.

{ **Make It a FLAT BELLY DIET MEAL** } Serve with the Stuffed Mushrooms on page 272, but omit the pecans (180).
TOTAL MEAL: 436 calories

snacks

Whole Wheat Pizza Margherita

■ **45 MINUTES** ■ **4 SERVINGS** ■ **393 CALORIES** ■ **MUFA: OLIVE OIL**

You can have pizza made from scratch, even for weeknight meals, by planning ahead. Make the dough in the morning and refrigerate it for a slow rise, or make several crusts on a weekend and freeze them to bake (no need to thaw) for a quick weeknight meal.

Thin Pizza Crust
(opposite page)
1 tomato, thinly sliced
3 ounces fresh mozzarella,
  thinly sliced
¼ cup slivered fresh basil
1 tablespoon olive oil

1. Prepare the dough for the crust: Coat a 12" round pizza pan with cooking spray. Punch down the dough. Transfer to a lightly floured surface. Let stand for 5 minutes. With floured hands or a rolling pin, pat or roll into a 12" circle. Transfer to the prepared pan. Pinch the edges to make a border. Cover with plastic wrap and let stand for 15 minutes.

2. Preheat the oven to 375°F. Pat dry the tomatoes and mozzarella. Arrange the tomatoes on the crust. Sprinkle with the basil. Cover with the mozzarella, then drizzle with the oil.

3. Bake for 15 to 18 minutes or until the cheese starts to color. Cut into 4 wedges.

NUTRITION PER SERVING (¼ PIZZA)

393 calories
13 g protein
46 g carbohydrates
18 g fat
5 g saturated fat*
15 mg cholesterol
214 mg sodium
6 g fiber

*Limit saturated fat to 10% of total calories—about 17 grams per day for most women—and sodium intake to less than 2,300 milligrams.

{ Make It a **FLAT BELLY DIET MEAL** } A single serving of this recipe counts as a *Flat Belly Diet* Meal without any add-ons!

Thin Pizza Crust

14 MINUTES + 45 MINUTES RISING TIME ■ **4 SERVINGS (EACH ¼ OF 12″ DIAMETER CRUST)**
295 CALORIES ■ **MUFA: OLIVE OIL**

White whole wheat flour has all the fiber and nutrition of traditional whole wheat, but with milder flavor and lighter color. If desired, this dough can be prepared in a bread dough machine according to the manufacturer's directions.

⅔ cup warm water
(105°F to 115°F)
1 envelope (¼ ounce)
active dry yeast
(2¼ teaspoons)
2 cups whole wheat flour,
preferably white whole
wheat, divided
¼ teaspoon salt
3 tablespoons olive oil

1. Coat a large bowl with cooking spray and set aside. Mix the water and yeast in a glass measuring cup until the yeast dissolves. Combine 1½ cups of the flour and the salt in the bowl of a food processor. Pulse to mix. With the machine running, add the yeast mixture and oil through the feed tube. Process to mix. Pulse in enough of the remaining ½ cup flour so the mixture forms a ball. The dough should be soft but not sticky.

2. Transfer to a lightly floured surface. With your hands, knead for about 1 minute or until the dough is smooth. Use only scant amounts of any remaining flour, if necessary, to prevent it from sticking to the surface. Place in the prepared bowl and coat lightly with cooking spray. Cover with plastic wrap. Set aside to rise for about 45 minutes or until doubled in size.

3. Punch down the dough. Shape into a ball, transfer to a work surface, and let stand for 5 minutes. Shape, add toppings, and bake per the recipe directions. To freeze the crust before baking: Roll or pat the dough per the recipe directions. Place on a pizza pan dusted with cornmeal. Cover tightly with plastic wrap, then foil. Freeze for up to 1 month. To bake, remove the wrappings, top the frozen crust, and bake per the recipe directions.

NUTRITION PER SERVING

295 calories
9 g protein
45 g carbohydrates
10 g fat
1 g saturated fat
0 mg cholesterol
148 mg sodium
5 g fiber

{ Make It a
**FLAT
BELLY
DIET
MEAL** }
Serve with the Caponata on page 258, but omit the pine nuts (80), and top with 1 tablespoon grated Parmesan cheese (21).
TOTAL MEAL: 396 calories

Chocolate-Zucchini Snack Cake

45 MINUTES   **12 SERVINGS**   **361 CALORIES**   **MUFA: CHOCOLATE**

Three cheers for chocolate! Allowing the chips to melt on a warm cake results in a lovely chocolate spread that helps this otherwise lean cake stay moist.

1¾ cups whole wheat
    pastry flour

1½ teaspoons baking powder

½ teaspoon baking soda

¼ teaspoon salt

2 eggs

½ cup sugar

½ cup low-fat vanilla yogurt

⅓ cup canola oil

1 teaspoon vanilla extract

1½ cups shredded zucchini

3 cups semisweet chocolate
    chips, divided

1. Preheat the oven to 350°F. Coat an 11″ × 8″ baking pan with cooking spray.

2. Combine the flour, baking powder, baking soda, and salt in a large bowl.

3. Whisk the eggs, sugar, yogurt, oil, and vanilla extract in a medium bowl. Whisk in the zucchini and 1½ cups of the chips. Stir into the flour mixture just until blended. Spread into the prepared pan and bake for 30 minutes or until lightly browned and a wooden toothpick inserted in the center comes out clean.

4. Remove from the oven and sprinkle the remaining 1½ cups chips over the cake. Spread with a small spatula as they melt to form an icing, placing back into the warm oven, if needed, for about 1 minute.

NUTRITION PER SERVING

361 calories
5 g protein
47 g carbohydrates
20 g fat
8 g saturated fat*
36 mg cholesterol
175 mg sodium
4 g fiber

*Limit saturated fat to 10% of total calories—about 17 grams per day for most women—and sodium intake to less than 2,300 milligrams.

{ Make It a **FLAT BELLY DIET MEAL** }
Serve with ¾ cup fat-free milk (60).
TOTAL MEAL: 421 calories

Chocolate-Cranberry Quesadilla

▥ **5 MINUTES** ▥ **1 SERVING** ▥ **332 CALORIES** ▥ **MUFA: CHOCOLATE**

This quesadilla is guaranteed to stop a chocolate attack in its tracks. Tart cranberries and cinnamon offer just the right contrast to rich melted chocolate.

1 whole wheat tortilla
(8" diameter)
¼ cup chopped semisweet
chocolate chips
1 tablespoon dried
unsweetened cranberries
Cinnamon

Place a skillet over medium-high heat. Place the tortilla in the pan. Toast for 1 minute on each side or until warm but still pliable. Sprinkle on the chips and cranberries. Dust lightly with cinnamon. Fold over like an omelet. Flip and cook for 30 seconds or until the chocolate starts to melt. Cut into 4 wedges.

**NUTRITION
PER SERVING**

332 calories
4 g protein
54 g carbohydrates
14 g fat
6 g saturated fat*
0 mg cholesterol
241 mg sodium
4 g fiber

*Limit saturated fat to 10%
of total calories—about
17 grams per day for most
women—and sodium intake
to less than 2,300 milligrams.

{ **Make It a
FLAT
BELLY
DIET
MEAL** } Serve with ½ cup
pineapple tidbits (60).
TOTAL MEAL: 392 calories

Chocolate-Drizzled Popcorn

■ **40 MINUTES** ■ **4 SERVINGS** ■ **392 CALORIES** ■ **MUFA: CASHEWS**

Thinking about a movie night? Whip up a batch of this luscious popcorn and you're sure to have a new favorite feature.

12 cups air-popped popcorn
½ cup roasted cashews, unsalted
1 cup semisweet chocolate chips

1. Spread the popcorn and cashews on a large baking sheet.

2. Bring a small saucepan of water to a simmer over medium heat. Place the chips in a small bowl and set over the simmering water, being careful to keep the water from touching the bowl containing the chocolate. Stir often until the chocolate is melted. While hot, use a spoon to drizzle the chocolate over the popcorn in a back-and-forth motion. Let cool at room temperature for about 20 minutes or until the chocolate sets.

NUTRITION PER SERVING

392 calories
7 g protein
51 g carbohydrates
22 g fat
9 g saturated fat*
0 mg cholesterol
9 mg sodium
6 g fiber

*Limit saturated fat to 10% of total calories—about 17 grams per day for most women—and sodium intake to less than 2,300 milligrams.

{ **Make It a FLAT BELLY DIET MEAL** } A single serving of this recipe counts as a *Flat Belly Diet* Meal without any add-ons!

Peanut Butter and Yogurt Smoothie

■ **5 MINUTES** ■ **1 SERVING** ■ **410 CALORIES** ■ **MUFA: PEANUT BUTTER**

Natural peanut butter lends a somewhat coarse texture to this hearty breakfast drink. If you prefer a smoother smoothie, a trans-free blend of regular peanut butter will do the trick.

½ cup fat-free milk

½ cup fat-free plain yogurt

2 tablespoons creamy natural unsalted peanut butter

¼ very ripe banana

1 tablespoon honey

4 ice cubes

Combine the milk, yogurt, peanut butter, banana, honey, and ice cubes in a blender. Process until smooth. Pour into a tall glass and serve.

NUTRITION PER SERVING

410 calories
19 g protein
50 g carbohydrates
16 g fat
2 g saturated fat
5 mg cholesterol
289 mg sodium
3 g fiber

{ **Make It a FLAT BELLY DIET MEAL** } A single serving of this recipe counts as a *Flat Belly Diet* Meal without any add-ons!

Mocha–Peanut Butter Cooler

5 MINUTES ■ **1 SERVING** ■ **363 CALORIES** ■ **MUFA: PEANUT BUTTER**

Still wishing for an afternoon pick-me-up from your local coffee stand? Try whizzing up a MUFA-rich cooler instead. This refreshing blend will leave your cravings in the dust.

3/4 cup fat-free milk

2 tablespoons creamy natural unsalted peanut butter

5 teaspoons packed dark brown sugar

1 1/2 teaspoons unsweetened cocoa powder

1/8 teaspoon instant coffee powder or granules

1/4 teaspoon vanilla extract

6 ice cubes

Combine the milk, peanut butter, brown sugar, cocoa powder, instant coffee, vanilla extract, and ice cubes in a blender. Puree and serve.

NUTRITION PER SERVING

363 calories
14 g protein
40 g carbohydrates
17 g fat
2 g saturated fat
2 mg cholesterol
108 mg sodium
2 g fiber

{ **Make It a FLAT BELLY DIET MEAL** }

Serve with 1/2 cup vanilla yogurt (70).
TOTAL MEAL: 433 calories

12

Desserts

desserts

Mediterranean Sesame-Honey Candy

■ 45 MINUTES ■ 12 SERVINGS ■ 179 CALORIES ■ MUFA: SESAME SEEDS

Candy making is a simple pursuit—after all, just 5 basic ingredients go into this recipe—but it's important that you use the right equipment because time and temperature are critical for consistent results. If you don't have a candy thermometer, look into the new digital tools. Some come preset for incredibly accurate readings.

1½ cups toasted sesame seeds
½ cup orange blossom honey
½ cup sugar
1 teaspoon vanilla extract
½ teaspoon salt

1. Line an 8" × 8" glass baking pan with parchment paper and coat with cooking spray. Set aside.

2. Toast the sesame seeds in a large deep skillet over medium heat, stirring often, for about 3 minutes or until lightly golden. Tip into a bowl and set aside.

3. Bring the honey and sugar to a boil in a heavy-bottomed saucepan over medium heat, stirring constantly, for about 10 minutes. Cook until the mixture registers 250°F on a candy thermometer. Stir in the reserved sesame seeds, vanilla extract, and salt and continue cooking for about 4 minutes or until the mixture reaches 275°F on the candy thermometer. Pour into the prepared pan and let stand for 15 to 20 minutes or until still warm but cool enough to handle. Turn the candy out onto a cutting board and cut into 24 pieces. Cool completely.

NUTRITION PER SERVING

179 calories
3 g protein
24 g carbohydrates
9 g fat
1 g saturated fat
0 mg cholesterol
99 mg sodium
2 g fiber

{ Make It a
FLAT
BELLY
DIET
MEAL }
Serve with 1 apple (80)
and 4 cups light popcorn (100).
TOTAL MEAL: 359 calories

Orange, Date, and Walnut Drops

■ 3½ HOURS ■ 6 SERVINGS (5 DROPS PER SERVING) ■ 343 CALORIES ■ MUFA: WALNUTS

Dried dates are naturally rich, chewy, and intensely sweet, so they marry well with oranges and walnuts in these easy candies. If you find the mixture sticky to work with, rub a little canola oil on your hands before rolling the balls.

1¼ cups sugar

¼ cup water

1 cup pitted dates, finely chopped

1–2 tablespoons freshly grated orange zest

¼ teaspoon vanilla extract

¾ cup walnuts, finely chopped, divided

1. Combine the sugar and water in a small saucepan over medium-high heat. Bring to a boil and cook for 5 to 6 minutes or until the sugar melts and the syrup is thick enough to coat the back of a spoon.

2. Remove from the heat and stir in the dates, orange zest, and vanilla extract. Let stand for about 20 minutes or until still warm but not hot. Add ¼ cup of the walnuts and stir until combined. Chill for 1 hour.

3. Divide the mixture into 30 equal portions and roll each into a small ball. Place the remaining ½ cup walnuts in a bowl and roll each ball in the nuts to coat. Cover and chill for 2 hours to allow to set.

NUTRITION PER SERVING

343 calories
3 g protein
66 g carbohydrates
10 g fat
1 g saturated fat
0 mg cholesterol
0 mg sodium
4 g fiber

{ Make It a FLAT BELLY DIET MEAL }

Serve with ½ cup nonfat cottage cheese (80).
TOTAL MEAL: 423 calories

Peanut Butter No-Bake Bars

■ 65 MINUTES   ■ 6 SERVINGS (1 BAR PER SERVING)   ■ 324 CALORIES   ■ MUFA: PEANUTS

Think of these treats as a cross between two childhood classics—s'mores and Rice Krispies Treats. Unlike those favorites, however, these are made with whole grain cereal, so you get the benefit of 5 grams of fiber per serving. Now that's what makes growing up worth it! Keep in an airtight container in a cool spot for up to 3 days.

1 tablespoon trans-free margarine

3 cups standard-size marshmallows (20–22)

1 tablespoon creamy natural unsalted peanut butter

3 cups wheat square cereal

½ cup dry-roasted peanuts

¼ cup semisweet chocolate chips

1. Coat an 8″ × 8″ baking pan with cooking spray.

2. Melt the margarine in a large saucepan over medium heat. Add the marshmallows and cook, stirring, for 4 to 5 minutes or until melted. Stir in the peanut butter, stirring until well combined and smooth. Remove the saucepan from the heat, add the cereal and peanuts, and stir until well coated.

3. Transfer to the prepared pan, using a rubber spatula if needed. Place a piece of wax paper coated with cooking spray over the top and press down with your hand to flatten. Cool for 20 minutes.

4. Remove the cereal square from the pan and set on a rack over a baking pan. Place the chocolate chips in a small bowl and microwave in 5-second increments, stirring with a spoon in between each, for 20 to 25 seconds or until melted. Using a small spoon, drizzle the chocolate in a quick back-and-forth motion over the cereal square. Cool completely for 30 to 35 minutes or until the chocolate sets.

NUTRITION PER SERVING

324 calories
7 g protein
53 g carbohydrates
11 g fat
2.5 g saturated fat*
0 mg cholesterol
298 mg sodium
5 g fiber

*Limit saturated fat to 10% of total calories—about 17 grams per day for most women—and sodium intake to less than 2,300 milligrams.

{ Make It a FLAT BELLY DIET MEAL } Serve with ¾ cup fat-free milk (60). **TOTAL MEAL:** 384 calories

Cherry-Almond Granola Bars

■ 50 MINUTES   ■ 12 SERVINGS   ■ 240 CALORIES   ■ MUFA: ALMONDS

Just about any dried fruit will work in this recipe, though cranberries and apricots would make the best substitutes if dried cherries aren't your style. Many studies have shown that people with high cholesterol benefit from eating oats and other foods high in fiber.

1½ cups slivered almonds, divided
1½ cups oatmeal
1 tablespoon whole wheat pastry flour
⅔ cup chopped dried unsweetened cherries
2 eggs
1 cup packed light brown sugar
1 tablespoon canola oil
1 teaspoon ground cinnamon
¼ teaspoon salt
1 teaspoon vanilla extract

1. Preheat the oven to 325°F. Line a 9" × 9" pan with foil, allowing about a 1" overhang from the sides. Coat with cooking spray.

2. Place ½ cup of the almonds and the oatmeal on a large baking sheet with sides. Bake for 10 minutes or until toasted, stirring once. Set aside.

3. Place the flour and remaining 1 cup oatmeal in a food processor fitted with a metal blade. Process until smooth. Transfer to a medium bowl and combine with the cherries and the reserved almonds and oatmeal.

4. Whisk together the eggs, brown sugar, oil, cinnamon, salt, and vanilla extract in a large bowl. Stir in the oatmeal-almond mixture until well blended. Spread in the prepared pan.

5. Bake for 30 minutes or until golden brown. Remove from the pan, using the foil as a guide, and cool completely on a rack. Cut into 12 rectangles with a serrated knife.

NUTRITION PER SERVING

240 calories
7 g protein
34 g carbohydrates
9 g fat
1 g saturated fat
35 mg cholesterol
69 mg sodium
3 g fiber

{ Make It a FLAT BELLY DIET MEAL }

Serve with 1 cup soy milk (127) and ½ cup fresh raspberries (32).
TOTAL MEAL: 399 calories

Sweet Peanut Sauce

■ 10 MINUTES ■ 8 SERVINGS (2 TABLESPOONS EACH) ■ 130 CALORIES ■ MUFA: PEANUT BUTTER

Use this topping to render your favorite low-fat dessert a MUFA-laden treat—puddings, cheese-cakes, and cookies, not to mention fresh fruit are good choices.

½ cup creamy natural
  unsalted peanut butter
½ cup fat-free evaporated
  milk
2 tablespoons honey

Heat the peanut butter, milk, and honey in a small saucepan over low heat. Stir constantly until melted and smooth. Serve warm.

NUTRITION PER SERVING

130 calories
5 g protein
10 g carbohydrates
8 g fat
1 g saturated fat
0 mg cholesterol
20 mg sodium
1 g fiber

{ Make It a **FLAT BELLY DIET MEAL** }

Serve with 1 apple, sliced (80), ¼ cup unsweetened raisins (130), and 1 tablespoon peanuts (55).
TOTAL MEAL: 395 calories

Decadent Dark Chocolate Sauce

■ 10 MINUTES ■ 4 SERVINGS (3 TABLESPOONS EACH) ■ 180 CALORIES ■ MUFA: CHOCOLATE

Here's a great way to enjoy the antioxidant benefits chocolate has to offer. Use this as an alternative to Sweet Peanut Sauce, above.

4 ounces bittersweet or
  semisweet chocolate
½ cup whole milk
2 tablespoons packed
  brown sugar

Heat the chocolate, milk, and brown sugar in a small saucepan over low heat. Stir constantly until melted and smooth. Serve warm.

NUTRITION PER SERVING

180 calories
2 g protein
26 g carbohydrates
9 g fat
6 g saturated fat*
5 mg cholesterol
20 mg sodium
2 g fiber

{ Make It a **FLAT BELLY DIET MEAL** }

Serve with 1 cup sliced mango (110) and ½ cup sliced banana (70).
TOTAL MEAL: 360 calories

*Limit saturated fat to 10% of total calories—about 17 grams per day for most women—and sodium intake to less than 2,300 milligrams.

Cookie Crisps

■ 35 MINUTES ■ 10 SERVINGS (3 COOKIES PER SERVING) ■ 200 CALORIES

Flaxseed is rich in alpha-linolenic acid, a type of plant-derived omega-3 fatty acid similar to those found in fish. In many studies, flaxseed has been shown to play a role in fighting heart disease by lowering cholesterol.

2 cups whole wheat pastry flour
2 tablespoons flaxseed
½ teaspoon baking soda
¼ teaspoon salt
1 teaspoon ground cinnamon
½ teaspoon ground ginger
4 tablespoons trans-free margarine, softened
2 tablespoons canola oil
⅓ cup packed dark brown sugar
⅓ cup honey
1 large egg

1. Preheat the oven to 350°F. Coat 2 baking sheets with cooking spray.

2. Combine the flour, flaxseed, baking soda, salt, cinnamon, and ginger in a medium bowl. Set aside.

3. Cream the margarine, oil, brown sugar, honey, and egg with a hand mixer. Add the reserved dry ingredients and stir until combined.

4. Drop by rounded tablespoons on the prepared baking sheets and bake for 10 to 12 minutes or until golden. Let cool on the trays for 5 minutes. Transfer to a rack to cool completely.

NUTRITION PER SERVING

200 calories
3 g protein
31 g carbohydrates
8 g fat
1 g saturated fat
20 mg cholesterol
170 mg sodium
3 g fiber

{ Make It a FLAT BELLY DIET MEAL } Serve with the Sweet Peanut Sauce on page 293 (130) and ½ pear (52).
TOTAL MEAL: 382 calories

Chocolate-Almond Macaroons

■ **50 MINUTES** ■ **6 SERVINGS (5 COOKIES PER SERVING)** ■ **193 CALORIES** ■ **MUFA: ALMONDS**

Sometimes macaroons blur the line between candy and cookie, but with the addition of ground almonds, these light and crunchy treats are rendered even more satisfying.

¾ cup blanched almonds
½ cup sugar, divided
4 egg whites
¼ cup unsweetened cocoa powder
1 teaspoon vanilla extract
½ teaspoon almond extract
¼ teaspoon salt

1. Preheat the oven to 325°F. Line 2 large baking sheets with parchment paper.

2. Toast the almonds in a large deep skillet over medium heat, stirring often, for about 3 minutes or until golden. Tip into the bowl of a food processor fitted with a metal blade.

3. Add 1 tablespoon of the sugar. Process until the almonds are finely ground.

4. Beat the egg whites with an electric mixer on high speed until the whites hold soft peaks. Gradually beat in the remaining sugar until the whites hold stiff peaks. Beat in the cocoa, vanilla extract, almond extract, and salt. Gently fold in the almonds.

5. Drop the mixture by rounded tablespoons onto the prepared baking sheets, leaving 1" between each macaroon. Bake for 27 to 30 minutes or until very lightly browned. Place baking sheets on a rack and let macaroons cool until firm.

NUTRITION PER SERVING

193 calories
7 g protein
22 g carbohydrates
10 g fat
1 g saturated fat
0 mg cholesterol
140 mg sodium
3 g fiber

{ Make It a **FLAT BELLY DIET MEAL** }
Serve with the Decadent Dark Chocolate Sauce on page 293 (180).
TOTAL MEAL: 373 calories

Almond Biscotti

■ **65 MINUTES** ■ **12 SERVINGS (2 COOKIES PER SERVING)** ■ **181 CALORIES** ■ **MUFA: ALMONDS**

Perhaps biscotti are extra fun to make because they're literally baked twice—the cookie dough is first baked into a long loaf, then cut into individual slices and baked again. A serrated knife works well for cutting biscotti, but an electric knife works even better.

1¼ cups whole wheat
    pastry flour
1 teaspoon baking powder
¼ teaspoon salt
1 egg
¼ cup canola oil
¼ cup granulated sugar
3 tablespoons packed dark
    brown sugar
1 teaspoon vanilla extract
½ teaspoon almond extract
1½ cups chopped almonds

1. Preheat the oven to 325°F. Line a large baking sheet with parchment paper.

2. Mix the flour, baking powder, and salt in a medium bowl. Whisk the egg, oil, granulated sugar, brown sugar, vanilla extract, and almond extract in a small bowl. Stir in the almonds. Pour over the dry ingredients and stir to mix well (the mixture will feel crumbly).

3. Shape into a 1"-thick loaf on the prepared baking sheet. Bake for 30 to 45 minutes or until golden and firm. Let cool for 10 minutes. Remove from the baking sheet and slice diagonally into 1"-thick pieces. Arrange cut side up on the baking sheet. Bake for 5 minutes longer or until lightly browned. Transfer to a rack to cool completely.

**NUTRITION
PER SERVING**

181 calories
4 g protein
17 g carbohydrates
11 g fat
1 g saturated fat
18 mg cholesterol
89 mg sodium
2 g fiber

Make It a FLAT BELLY DIET MEAL

Serve with 8 ounces cappuccino made with 1% milk (73) and 1 cup sliced strawberries (53) mixed with 1 small banana, sliced (90).
TOTAL MEAL: 397 calories

Sesame-Oat Cookies

■ **25 MINUTES** ■ **8 SERVINGS (3 COOKIES PER SERVING)** ■ **337 CALORIES** ■ **MUFA: TAHINI**

Who needs butter for baking? In this recipe, use tahini instead of butter and avoid 5 grams of saturated fat per serving! Another benefit? Oats contain soluble fiber, which helps keep blood sugar levels in balance.

1½ cups oatmeal

¼ cup whole wheat
   pastry flour

 1 teaspoon ground
   cinnamon

½ teaspoon salt

 1 cup tahini

½ cup packed dark brown
   sugar

¼ cup honey

 2 tablespoons warm water

 2 egg whites

1. Preheat the oven to 325°F. Coat 2 baking sheets with cooking spray.

2. Mix the oats, flour, cinnamon, and salt in a medium bowl. Set aside.

3. Combine the tahini, brown sugar, honey, water, and egg whites in a large bowl. Whisk until smooth. Add the oatmeal mixture and stir until blended.

4. Drop by heaping tablespoons onto the prepared baking sheets. Bake for 12 to 15 minutes or until golden brown. Remove from the oven and let cool on sheets for 5 minutes. Transfer to a rack to cool completely.

**NUTRITION
PER SERVING**

337 calories
9 g protein
41 g carbohydrates
17 g fat
2 g saturated fat
0 mg cholesterol
176 mg sodium
3 g fiber

{ Make It a
FLAT
BELLY
DIET
MEAL }

Serve with
1 apple (80).
TOTAL MEAL: 417 calories

Baklava

■ **55 MINUTES** ■ **24 SERVINGS** ■ **193 CALORIES** ■ **MUFA: PISTACHIOS**

Though not always easy to find, whole wheat pastry dough also works well in this recipe and will add a touch more fiber to this deliciously flaky dessert. Look for it in health food stores.

3 cups unsalted pistachios, coarsely chopped

⅓ cup sugar

2 teaspoons freshly grated orange zest

¼ teaspoon ground cloves

⅛ teaspoon salt
  Butter-flavored cooking spray

24 sheets (17″ × 12″ each) frozen phyllo dough, thawed and halved crosswise

1 tablespoon water

¾ cup honey

¼ cup freshly squeezed orange juice

1 tablespoon freshly squeezed lemon juice

½ teaspoon ground cardamom

1. Preheat the oven to 350°F. Combine the pistachios, sugar, orange zest, cloves, and salt in a medium bowl and set aside.

2. Lightly coat a 9″ × 13″ baking dish with the cooking spray. Working with 1 phyllo sheet at a time, place the sheet lengthwise in the bottom of the dish, allowing 1 end to extend over the edges of the dish, and lightly coat with the cooking spray. Repeat the procedure with 5 phyllo sheets and cooking spray for a total of 6 layers. Sprinkle evenly with ⅓ of the reserved nut mixture (about 1 cup). Repeat the procedure with 6 phyllo sheets, cooking spray, and nut mixture 2 more times. Top the last layer of the nut mixture with the remaining 6 phyllo sheets, each lightly coated with cooking spray. Lightly coat the top sheet with cooking spray and press the baklava gently into the dish. Sprinkle the surface with the water.

3. Make 4 even lengthwise cuts and 6 even crosswise cuts to form 24 portions, using a sharp knife. Bake for 30 minutes or until the phyllo is golden brown. Remove from the oven.

4. Meanwhile, combine the honey, orange juice, lemon juice, and cardamom in a medium saucepan over low heat. Cook for 2 minutes or until the honey is completely dissolved.

5. Drizzle the honey mixture over the baklava. Place the pan on a rack and cool completely.

NUTRITION PER SERVING

193 calories
5 g protein
26 g carbohydrates
9 g fat
1 g saturated fat
0 mg cholesterol
106 mg sodium
2 g fiber

{ Make It a **FLAT BELLY DIET MEAL** }

Serve with 1 cup red grapes (104) and 1 cup 1% milk (118).
TOTAL MEAL: 415 calories

desserts

Cherry-Pear Strudel

■ 50 MINUTES ■ 8 SERVINGS ■ 253 CALORIES ■ MUFA: WALNUTS

Pears ripen from the inside out, so don't wait until the flesh around the middle feels soft before slicing. To test for ripeness, press near the stem. It will give under gentle pressure when it's ready.

Butter-flavored
cooking spray
1 cup walnuts
3 pears, peeled and
coarsely chopped
¼ cup dried unsweetened
cherries, cranberries,
or raisins
⅓ cup sugar
10 sheets (9″ × 14″ each)
frozen phyllo dough,
thawed
1 teaspoon canola oil
¼ teaspoon ground
cinnamon

1. Preheat the oven to 350°F. Coat a baking sheet with the cooking spray.

2. Toast the walnuts in a large deep skillet over medium heat, stirring often, for about 3 minutes or until lightly golden. Tip into a bowl and set aside. When cooled, finely chop.

3. Combine the pears, cherries, sugar, and ¼ cup of the reserved walnuts in a bowl.

4. Place 1 sheet of the phyllo dough on a work surface with the wide edge toward you. Coat lightly with the cooking spray. Repeat with 2 more phyllo sheets and the cooking spray to create a stack of 3 sheets. Sprinkle 2 tablespoons of the chopped nuts over the phyllo. Top with another phyllo sheet and coat with the cooking spray. Repeat layering 1 sheet of the phyllo, cooking spray, and chopped nuts 5 more times. Top with the last sheet of the phyllo. Brush with the oil.

5. Spread with the pear filling, leaving a 2″ border on all sides. Starting at the long side, sprinkle with the cinnamon and roll to form a cylinder, tucking under the sides. Place seam side down on the prepared baking sheet and coat with cooking spray.

6. Bake for 30 minutes or until browned and crisp. Place baking sheet on a rack and cool for 15 minutes.

NUTRITION PER SERVING

253 calories
5 g protein
35 g carbohydrates
12 g fat
1 g saturated fat
0 mg cholesterol
116 mg sodium
3 g fiber

{ Make It a
FLAT
BELLY
DIET
MEAL }

Serve with ½ cup slow-churned reduced-fat caramel ice cream (120).
TOTAL MEAL: 373 calories

Red Fruit Crumble

■ **1 HOUR** ■ **6 SERVINGS** ■ **332 CALORIES** ■ **MUFA: WALNUTS**

Intensely fruity, this lovely dessert is bursting with flavor and so easy to put together, it's a great one to make with kids. One serving provides almost ¼ of a day's fiber.

FRUIT

  1 pound strawberries,
    hulled and thickly sliced
  3 ripe plums, cut into
    1" pieces (¾ pound)
  1 cup fresh or frozen
    raspberries
  ¼ cup all-fruit raspberry
    or strawberry preserves,
    stirred smooth

TOPPING

  1 cup oatmeal
  ⅓ cup whole wheat
    pastry flour
  ⅓ cup firmly packed dark
    brown sugar
  ½ teaspoon ground
    cinnamon
  ⅛ teaspoon salt
  3 tablespoons trans-free
    margarine, cut into
    small pieces
  ¾ cup chopped walnuts

1. Preheat the oven to 375°F.

2. To prepare the fruit: Combine the strawberries, plums, raspberries, and fruit preserves in an 8″ × 8″ glass baking dish and mix gently with a spatula.

3. To prepare the topping: Mix the oats, flour, brown sugar, cinnamon, and salt in a medium bowl, crumbling the mixture with your hands to break up the lumps of sugar. Add the margarine and crumble until well incorporated. Stir in the walnuts. Sprinkle over the fruit.

4. Bake, uncovered, for 35 to 40 minutes or until the fruit is tender and bubbly and the topping is lightly browned. Place baking dish on a rack and let cool for at least 30 minutes before serving.

NUTRITION PER SERVING

332 calories
6 g protein
46 g carbohydrates
14 g fat
1.5 g saturated fat
0 mg cholesterol
95 mg sodium
6 g fiber

{ Make It a **FLAT BELLY DIET MEAL** } Serve with ½ cup slow-churned reduced-fat vanilla ice cream (100).
TOTAL MEAL: 432 calories

Fruit Crepes with Chocolate Sauce

■ 15 MINUTES   ■ 4 SERVINGS   ■ 370 CALORIES   ■ MUFA: CHOCOLATE

If you're short on time, store-bought crepes are a handy alternative to making fresh. However, these crepes are a little sturdier than most because of the whole grains in the pancake mix. As with making pancakes, a hot skillet is essential. For best results, throw a drop of water on the skillet—if it bounces, the pan's hot enough.

CREPES

- ½ cup Easy Pancake Mix (page 83)
- 1 egg
- ¼ cup 1% milk
- ¼ cup water
  Dash of salt
- 1 tablespoon trans-free margarine, melted

FILLING

- ¼ cup fat-free Greek-style yogurt
- 1 tablespoon honey
- ⅛ teaspoon cinnamon
- 2 kiwifruit, peeled and cut into chunks
- 1 banana, sliced
- ½ cup fresh pineapple chunks
- ½ cup chopped fresh strawberries
- 1 recipe Decadent Dark Chocolate Sauce (page 293), warmed

1. To prepare the crepes: Whisk together the pancake mix and egg in a medium mixing bowl. Gradually add the milk and water, stirring to combine. Add the salt and margarine and stir until smooth.

2. Coat a small nonstick skillet with cooking spray and place over medium-high heat. Pour or scoop about ¼ cup batter into the pan. Tilt the pan with a circular motion so that the batter coats the surface evenly. Cook the crepe for 1 to 2 minutes or until the bottom is lightly browned. Loosen with a spatula, turn, and cook the other side for 1 minute longer. Repeat to make 3 more crepes.

3. To prepare the filling: Whisk the yogurt, honey, and cinnamon in a small bowl until smooth. Add the kiwi, banana, pineapple, and strawberries. Stir gently just to combine. Set aside.

4. Place each crepe on a dessert plate. Spoon the reserved fruit mixture down the center of each crepe. Roll into a tube and place seam side down on the plate. Drizzle with the chocolate sauce and serve immediately.

NUTRITION PER SERVING

370 calories
8 g protein
61 g carbohydrates
6 g fat
6 g saturated fat*
55 mg cholesterol
270 mg sodium
5 g fiber

*Limit saturated fat to 10% of total calories—about 17 grams per day for most women—and sodium intake to less than 2,300 milligrams.

{ Make It a FLAT BELLY DIET MEAL }   A single serving of this recipe counts as a *Flat Belly Diet* Meal without any add-ons!

Irresistible Brownies

■ 35 MINUTES ■ 8 SERVINGS ■ 305 CALORIES ■ MUFA: WALNUTS

If you first measure the oil and stir together all the other wet ingredients in your measuring cup, these brownies are easy to put together using only 1 mixing bowl.

½ cup unbleached
   all-purpose flour
⅓ cup unsweetened cocoa
   powder, sifted if lumpy
¼ teaspoon baking powder
⅛ teaspoon salt
⅔ cup packed dark brown
   sugar
¼ cup canola oil
1 large egg + 1 large egg
   white
1 teaspoon vanilla extract
¼ cup miniature semisweet
   chocolate chips
1 cup chopped walnuts

1. Preheat the oven to 350°F. Coat an 8" × 8" or 9" × 9" baking pan with cooking spray.

2. Combine the flour, cocoa, baking powder, and salt in a large bowl.

3. Combine the brown sugar, oil, egg and egg white, and vanilla extract in a small bowl. Whisk until smooth. Pour into the flour mixture and stir until blended. Stir in the chocolate chips and walnuts (the batter will be stiff).

4. Spread the batter in a thin layer in the prepared pan. Bake for 20 to 22 minutes or until firm at the edges and a wooden toothpick inserted off center comes out with a few moist crumbs. Place pan on a rack and let cool completely. Cut into 8 bars.

NUTRITION PER SERVING

305 calories
5 g protein
31 g carbohydrates
22 g fat
2 g saturated fat
26 mg cholesterol
73 mg sodium
2 g fiber

{ Make It a
FLAT
BELLY
DIET
MEAL }

Serve with ½ cup slow-churned reduced-fat vanilla ice cream (100).
TOTAL MEAL: 405 calories

Cherry-Berry Almond Fruit Cake

■ 1 HOUR 30 MINUTES ■ 16 SERVINGS ■ 360 CALORIES ■ MUFA: ALMONDS

Frozen fruit is so much cheaper than fresh for most of the year. To freeze berries when in season, spread fruit in a single layer on baking tray and place in freezer. Transfer to freezer bags when solid.

CAKE

2 cups blanched almonds, divided
1½ cups sugar, divided
2 cups all-purpose flour
1 tablespoon baking powder
½ teaspoon baking soda
½ teaspoon salt
1 cup buttermilk
2 eggs
3 egg whites
⅓ cup canola oil
¼ cup freshly squeezed lemon juice
1 teaspoon almond extract
1 cup frozen unsweetened blueberries
1 cup frozen unsweetened raspberries
1 cup frozen unsweetened cherries

GLAZE

1½ cups confectioners' sugar
3–4 tablespoons buttermilk

1. Preheat the oven to 350°F. Coat a 12-cup Bundt pan with cooking spray, then dust with flour.

2. To prepare the cake: Toast the almonds in a large deep skillet over medium heat, stirring often, for about 3 minutes or until lightly golden. Tip into a bowl and set ½ cup aside.

3. Combine 1½ cups of the almonds and ½ cup of the sugar in a food processor fitted with a metal blade. Process until the almonds are finely ground. Combine the ground almonds, flour, baking powder, baking soda, salt, and remaining 1 cup sugar in a large bowl. Add the buttermilk, eggs, egg whites, oil, lemon juice, and almond extract. Whisk until well combined. Fold in the blueberries, raspberries, and cherries. Pour the batter into the prepared pan.

4. Bake in the center of the oven for 65 to 70 minutes or until a wooden toothpick inserted into the cake comes out clean. Place pan on a rack and let cool for 15 minutes. Remove the cake from the pan, transfer to the rack, and let cool completely.

5. To prepare the glaze: Combine the confectioners' sugar and buttermilk in a bowl and stir until dissolved. Spoon over the cake. Coarsely chop the reserved ½ cup almonds and sprinkle over the top of the cake onto the glaze. Let set at least 15 minutes before serving.

NUTRITION
PER SERVING

360 calories
8 g protein
52 g carbohydrates
15 g fat
1 g saturated fat
27 mg cholesterol
231 mg sodium
4 g fiber

{ Make It a
FLAT
BELLY
DIET
MEAL }

Serve with ½ cup fresh raspberries (32).
TOTAL MEAL: 392 calories

Pumpkin Cream Roll

■ 1 HOUR 20 MINUTES   ■ 16 SERVINGS   ■ 229 CALORIES   ■ MUFA: WALNUTS

One whiff of this cake baking is all you need to get ready for autumn. Each slice reveals a tantalizing spiral of maple-sweetened cake and luscious cream cheese filling. Our lightened-up version uses Neufchâtel cheese and yogurt in place of regular cream cheese, saving 50 calories per serving.

¾ cup + 1 tablespoon
   all-purpose flour, divided
¾ cup whole wheat
   pastry flour
1 teaspoon ground
   pumpkin pie spice
1 teaspoon baking powder
¼ teaspoon salt
5 egg whites
3 egg yolks
1 cup pure maple syrup,
   divided
1¼ cups canned pumpkin
1½ cups chopped walnuts
1 package (8 ounces)
   Neufchâtel cheese
½ cup low-fat vanilla yogurt

1. Preheat the oven to 375°F. Lightly coat a 15½" × 10½" × 1" jelly-roll pan with cooking spray. Line with wax paper. Lightly coat the paper with cooking spray and sprinkle with 1 tablespoon of the all-purpose flour.

2. Combine the pastry flour, pumpkin pie spice, baking powder, salt, and remaining ¾ cup all-purpose flour in a medium bowl.

3. Beat the egg whites and ¼ cup of the syrup in a large mixing bowl with an electric mixer on high speed until stiff, glossy peaks form. Transfer to a clean bowl.

4. Beat the egg yolks and remaining ¾ cup syrup in the same mixing bowl with the same beaters on medium speed until lemony in color and slightly thickened. Beat in the pumpkin until blended. Whisk ¼ of the beaten egg whites into the whole egg mixture. Sprinkle half of the flour mixture over the top and fold with a rubber spatula until just blended. Fold in the remaining beaten whites, then the remaining flour mixture.

5. Spread into the pan. Sprinkle evenly with the walnuts. Bake for 15 minutes or until the cake springs back when touched.

6. Lay a clean kitchen towel on the counter. Invert the cake onto the towel. Carefully remove the wax paper. Fold 1 side of the towel over 1 long side of the cake, then roll up the cake and towel, jelly-roll style. Transfer to a rack and let cool for 30 minutes.

7. Beat the cheese and yogurt in a large bowl with an electric mixer on high speed for 8 minutes or until light, fluffy, and stiff. (Don't worry if the mixture looks curdled in the beginning; it will come together upon beating.)

8. Carefully unroll the cake and remove the towel. Spread the cream cheese mixture over the cake. Reroll the cake, using the towel as a guide. Place on a serving platter.

NUTRITION PER SERVING

229 calories
7 g protein
26 g carbohydrates
11 g fat
3 g saturated fat
50 mg cholesterol
160 mg sodium
2 g fiber

{ Make It a **FLAT BELLY DIET MEAL** } Serve with 1 medium pear, sliced (104) and 8 ounces cappuccino made with 1% milk (73). **TOTAL MEAL:** 406 calories

desserts

Super-Rich Chocolate Cake with Maple Frosting

■ 1 HOUR 30 MINUTES ■ 16 SERVINGS ■ 276 CALORIES ■ MUFA: CANOLA MAYONNAISE

Here's a cake guaranteed to win rave reviews in the flavor department. Beating the egg whites while they cook over a double boiler renders a marshmallow-like frosting that's pure heaven. It's best to enjoy this cake on the day that it's made; cover and refrigerate until ready to serve.

CAKE

- 1 cup sugar
- 1 cup canola mayonnaise
- 1 cup buttermilk
- 1 tablespoon vanilla extract
- 1½ cups whole wheat pastry flour
- 1 cup all-purpose flour
- ½ cup cocoa powder
- 1½ teaspoons baking soda
- ¼ teaspoon salt

FROSTING

- ¾ cup maple syrup
- 3 egg whites
- ½ teaspoon cream of tartar

1. To prepare the cake: Preheat the oven to 350°F. Coat two 9″ round cake pans with cooking spray.

2. Beat the sugar and mayonnaise in a large bowl with an electric mixer at medium speed until well blended. Beat in the buttermilk and vanilla extract. Add the pastry flour, all-purpose flour, cocoa, baking soda, and salt and beat just until blended.

3. Spread the batter into the pans. Bake for 45 minutes or until a wooden pick comes out clean. Place the pans on a rack and let cool completely.

4. To prepare the frosting: Combine the syrup, egg whites, and cream of tartar in the top of a double boiler. Beat with an electric mixer until well blended. Place over rapidly boiling water. Beat for 7 minutes or until stiff peaks form. Remove the top of the double boiler from the water and continue beating for 5 minutes or until thickened and fluffy.

5. Place 1 cake layer on a serving plate. Spread 1 cup of the frosting over the cake. Top with the second cake layer. Spread the remaining frosting over the top and sides of the cake.

NUTRITION PER SERVING

276 calories
4 g protein
39 g carbohydrates
14 g fat
0.5 g saturated fat
6 mg cholesterol
272 mg sodium
2 g fiber

{ Make It a **FLAT BELLY DIET MEAL** } Serve with
1 cup 1% milk (118).
TOTAL MEAL: 394 calories

desserts

Lemon Cupcakes with Citrus Icing

■ **55 MINUTES** ■ **12 SERVINGS** ■ **316 CALORIES** ■ **MUFA: SAFFLOWER OIL**

Infused with intense lemon flavor, just one bite and you'll know why these cupcakes were our hands-down favorite for the cover of this cookbook. Serve these delightful little cakes for any spring-time celebration.

CUPCAKES

- 1²/₃ cups unbleached all-purpose flour
- 1 cup sugar
- 2 teaspoons baking powder
- ½ teaspoon baking soda
- ¼ teaspoon salt
- ¾ cup safflower oil
- 2 eggs
- ⅓ cup fat-free milk
- ¼ cup freshly squeezed lemon juice
- 1 teaspoon freshly grated lemon zest
- 1 teaspoon lemon extract
- ½ teaspoon vanilla extract

ICING

- 1½ cups confectioners' sugar
- 2 tablespoons freshly squeezed orange juice
- 1 teaspoon freshly grated orange zest

1. Preheat the oven to 350°F. Line a 12-cup muffin pan with paper liners.

2. To prepare the cupcakes: Combine the flour, sugar, baking powder, baking soda, and salt in a bowl. Combine the oil, eggs, milk, lemon juice, lemon zest, lemon extract, and vanilla extract in a separate bowl. Add to the flour mixture and stir until smooth.

3. Spoon the batter into the muffin cups and bake for 17 to 19 minutes or until lightly golden and the cupcakes are springy when gently touched. Place pan on a rack and let cool for 5 minutes. Remove the cupcakes from the pan, transfer to the rack, and let cool completely.

4. To prepare the icing: Combine the confectioners' sugar, orange juice, and orange zest in a bowl and stir until smooth. Spread some of the glaze over each cupcake with a small spatula and let stand for at least 10 minutes before serving.

NUTRITION PER SERVING

316 calories
3 g protein
45 g carbohydrates
15 g fat
1 g saturated fat
35 mg cholesterol
183 mg sodium
0.5 g fiber

{ Make It a **FLAT BELLY DIET MEAL** }
Serve with
1 cup 1% milk (118).
TOTAL MEAL: 434 calories

Peach and Blueberry Tart with Pecan Crust

■ 2 HOURS + COOLING TIME   ■ 8 SERVINGS   ■ 322 CALORIES   ■ MUFA: PECANS

If you prefer your peaches skinned, by all means go ahead and peel them for this tasty tart. Instead of blanching, a serrated peeler makes quick work of soft-skinned fruits. Look for one in your kitchen supply store.

CRUST

1 cup pecan halves
1 cup whole wheat
   pastry flour
2 teaspoons freshly
   grated lemon zest
⅛ teaspoon salt
1 egg white, beaten
2 tablespoons canola oil
1–2 tablespoons cold water

FILLING

¾ cup all-fruit peach
   preserves
1½ tablespoons cornstarch
1¼ pounds ripe but firm
   peaches, sliced
¾ cup fresh blueberries

TOPPING

1 cup fat-free Greek-style
   yogurt
3 tablespoons wildflower
   honey

1. To prepare the crust: Preheat the oven to 375°F. Coat a 10″ fluted removable bottom tart pan or springform pan with cooking spray.

2. Set aside 8 pecan halves. Place the remaining pecans in the bowl of a food processor fitted with a metal blade or a blender. Process until finely ground. Add the flour, lemon zest, and salt. Process briefly to blend. Combine the egg white, oil, and water in a measuring cup. With the machine running, drizzle the liquid mixture into the bowl. Add up to 1 tablespoon water if needed. Turn off the machine as soon as the ingredients start to bind together.

3. Turn the mixture onto a lightly floured work surface. Pat into a disk (the mixture will be soft). Transfer to the bottom of the prepared pan. Press into the bottom and ½″ up the side. Refrigerate for 15 minutes.

4. To prepare the filling: Combine the preserves and cornstarch in a small bowl. Add the peaches and blueberries and toss gently to mix. Spoon into the prepared crust. Bake for about 1 hour 15 minutes or until the juices are bubbling. Place pan on a rack to cool completely.

5. To prepare the topping: Whisk the yogurt with the honey in a bowl. Spoon on top of each serving and top with a reserved pecan half.

NUTRITION PER SERVING

322 calories
6 g protein
44 g carbohydrates
15 g fat
1.5 g saturated fat
1 mg cholesterol
52 mg sodium
3 g fiber

{ Make It a
FLAT
BELLY
DIET
MEAL }

Serve with 8 ounces cappuccino made with 1% milk (73).
TOTAL MEAL: 395 calories

Ginger-Macadamia Nut Cheesecake with Praline Topping

■ **3 HOURS + CHILL TIME** ■ **12 SERVINGS** ■ **339 CALORIES** ■ **MUFA: MACADAMIA NUTS**

If you're planning to celebrate a special occasion with a Southern menu, this is the dessert to make. Macadamia nuts, used in both the crunchy topping and the crust, provide more MUFA than any other nut or seed.

CRUST
- ¾ cup gingersnap crumbs
- 1 cup macadamia nuts
- 2 tablespoons sugar
- 1 tablespoon finely chopped crystallized ginger
- 2 tablespoons trans-free margarine, melted

FILLING
- 1½ cups fat-free vanilla yogurt
- 2 packages (8 ounces each) fat-free cream cheese
- ¾ cup sugar
- 3 eggs
- 3 tablespoons all-purpose flour

PRALINE
- ½ cup macadamia nuts, chopped
- ¼ teaspoon salt
- 2 tablespoons trans-free margarine
- ½ cup sugar

1. Preheat the oven to 350°F. Coat a 9" springform pan with cooking spray.

2. To prepare the crust: Combine the cookie crumbs, macadamia nuts, sugar, and ginger in the bowl of a food processor. Process until the mixture is fine crumbs, transfer to a bowl, and stir in the margarine. Press into the bottom and partway up the side of the prepared pan. Bake for 7 to 8 minutes or until set. Remove from the oven and cool.

3. To prepare the filling: Drain the yogurt in a colander lined with cheesecloth or paper towels for 1 to 2 hours or until thick. Place the cream cheese, yogurt, sugar, and eggs in a large bowl and beat with an electric mixer on medium-high speed until smooth. Beat in the flour.

4. Pour into the crust and bake for 50 to 55 minutes. Remove from the oven and run a knife around the sides to loosen. Place pan on a rack and let cool for 45 minutes. Remove the cake from the pan and chill for 3 to 4 hours.

5. To prepare the praline: Meanwhile, coat a baking sheet with cooking spray. Stir together the macadamia nuts and salt in a small bowl. Melt the margarine in a heavy-bottomed saucepan over medium heat. Add the sugar and cook, stirring with a fork, for about 5 minutes or until melted. Continue cooking, without stirring, for 7 to 8 minutes or until a golden caramel. Stir in the macadamia nuts and stir to coat. Spoon onto the prepared baking sheet and press with a rubber spatula to create a thin layer of praline. Cool completely.

6. Transfer the praline to a cutting board and break into small to medium pieces. Randomly press ³⁄₄ of the pieces into the top of the cheesecake, point side up. Finely chop the remaining praline and sprinkle over the cheesecake.

NUTRITION
PER SERVING

339 calories
10 g protein
39 g carbohydrates
16 g fat
3 g saturated fat
60 mg cholesterol
403 mg sodium
2 g fiber

{ Make It a
FLAT
BELLY
DIET
MEAL }
Serve with ³⁄₄ cup
fat-free milk (60).
TOTAL MEAL: 399 calories

Chocolate-Raspberry Cheesecake

4 HOURS ■ **12 SERVINGS** ■ **390 CALORIES** ■ **MUFA: CHOCOLATE**

A true showstopper, this cheesecake redefines healthy decadence. A layer of sweetened raspberries provides a refreshing surprise with every bite.

1 cup graham cracker crumbs

2 tablespoons trans-free margarine, melted

⅔ cup + 2 tablespoons sugar

1 cup fresh raspberries + additional for garnish

3 cups bittersweet chocolate chips, divided

2 packages (8 ounces each) fat-free cream cheese

1 cup light sour cream

3 eggs

3 tablespoons all-purpose flour

2 teaspoons vanilla extract

1 teaspoon instant coffee granules

2 tablespoons half-and-half

1. Preheat the oven to 350°F. Coat a 9" springform pan with cooking spray and set aside.

2. Combine the graham cracker crumbs, margarine, and 1 tablespoon of the sugar in a bowl and mix together. Press into the bottom of the prepared pan and refrigerate until ready to use. Toss the raspberries with 1 tablespoon of the sugar.

3. Melt 2 cups of the chocolate chips in the top of a double boiler, taking care to keep the water from touching the bottom of the pan containing the chips. Remove from the heat and set aside.

4. Meanwhile, beat together the cream cheese, sour cream, eggs, and remaining ⅔ cup sugar with an electric mixer until smooth. Slowly beat in the flour, vanilla extract, and coffee. Add the reserved chocolate and beat on high speed until well incorporated.

5. Pour half of the chocolate batter into the pan and top with the raspberry mixture. Gently pour the remaining batter over the raspberries.

6. Bake for 48 to 52 minutes. Remove from the oven and run a knife around the edge of the sides to loosen. Place pan on a rack and let cool for 45 minutes. Remove the cake from the pan and chill for 3 hours or up to overnight.

7. When the cake is chilled, melt the remaining 1 cup chocolate chips in the top of a double boiler and stir in the half-and-half. Cool slightly and pour onto the top of the cake. Spread with a spatula to the edge so that some of the chocolate runs down the side of the cake. Garnish with additional raspberries. Chill until ready to serve.

NUTRITION PER SERVING

390 calories
11 g protein
53 g carbohydrates
18 g fat
9 g saturated fat*
65 mg cholesterol
300 mg sodium
1 g fiber

*Limit saturated fat to 10% of total calories—about 17 grams per day for most women—and sodium intake to less than 2,300 milligrams.

{ Make It a FLAT BELLY DIET MEAL } A single serving of this recipe counts as a *Flat Belly Diet* Meal without any add-ons!

Sweet and Sour Blueberry Parfait

■ **5 MINUTES** ■ **4 SERVINGS** ■ **248 CALORIES** ■ **MUFA: AVOCADO**

When blueberry season strikes, enjoy this supereasy recipe. Ounce for ounce, blueberries provide more antioxidants than any other fresh fruit or vegetables. Plus, they're grown with far fewer pesticides than many other crops.

1 lime
1 avocado
1 cup part-skim
   ricotta cheese
5 tablespoons honey,
   divided
1 cup fresh blueberries
1 tablespoon finely
   chopped fresh mint
   leaves + 4 sprigs
   for garnish

1. Grate the lime zest from the lime. Squeeze the juice from the lime and set both aside.

2. Combine the avocado, cheese, 3 tablespoons honey, reserved lime juice, and reserved lime zest in the bowl of a food processor fitted with a metal blade or a blender. Pulse 12 times. Scrape down the sides of the bowl. Process, scraping the sides of the bowl as needed, for about 2 minutes or until smooth. Chill before serving, if desired.

3. Place the remaining 2 tablespoons honey in a microwaveable bowl. Microwave for 10 seconds or until softened. Add the blueberries. Toss to coat.

4. Add the chopped mint to the avocado mixture and stir to combine. Divide a third of the blueberries in the bottoms of 4 parfait or dessert dishes. Dollop with half of the avocado mixture. Top with another third of the blueberries, followed by the remaining avocado mixture. Top with the remaining blueberries. Garnish with the mint sprigs.

NUTRITION PER SERVING

248 calories
8 g protein
35 g carbohydrates
10 g fat
4 g saturated fat*
19 mg cholesterol
82 mg sodium
3 g fiber

*Limit saturated fat to 10% of total calories—about 17 grams per day for most women—and sodium intake to less than 2,300 milligrams.

{ **Make It a FLAT BELLY DIET MEAL** } Serve with 1 ounce low-fat graham crackers (120). **TOTAL MEAL:** 368 calories

Strawberry Panna Cotta

■ **4 HOURS** ■ **4 SERVINGS** ■ **250 CALORIES** ■ **MUFA: SWEET PEANUT SAUCE**

Panna cotta literally translates as "cooked cream" in Italian. These softly set and creamy Italian puddings are so silky smooth, they're perfect draped in Sweet Peanut Sauce (page 293).

1½ teaspoons unflavored
    gelatin
1½ tablespoons water
  1 cup 1% milk
  ½ cup buttermilk
  ¼ cup honey
1½ cups sliced strawberries
  ½ cup Sweet Peanut Sauce
    (page 293)

1. Sprinkle the gelatin over the water and mix. Set aside for 10 minutes to soften.

2. Heat the milk over medium heat, whisking constantly, for 3 to 5 minutes or until the mixture is steaming hot but not boiling. Remove from the heat and whisk in the reserved gelatin. Stir until completely dissolved. Let cool slightly. Add the buttermilk and honey and whisk to dissolve. Cool to room temperature. Stir in the strawberries.

3. Divide the mixture among 4 custard cups or ramekins. Refrigerate for 4 hours or up to overnight until set.

4. Run a knife blade around the inside of the cups to loosen each panna cotta. Gently shake each one onto a dessert plate. Drizzle with the peanut sauce before serving.

NUTRITION PER SERVING

250 calories
9 g protein
31 g carbohydrates
9 g fat
1.5 g saturated fat
5 mg cholesterol
90 mg sodium
2 g fiber

{ **Make It a FLAT BELLY DIET MEAL** } Serve with the Almond Biscotti on page 296 (181). **TOTAL MEAL:** 431 calories

Choco-Nut Sundae

■ 15 MINUTES ■ 4 SERVINGS ■ 393 CALORIES ■ MUFA: PEANUT BUTTER

Here, all the flavors you expect in a classic ice cream sundae are reversed: Instead of a crunchy topping, warm peanut butter sauce flows over rich chocolate ice cream. Colorful strawberry halves offer a healthy fiber boost.

1 recipe Sweet Peanut Sauce (page 293)
1 teaspoon vanilla extract
2 cups slow-churned light chocolate ice cream
1 cup strawberries, halved

1. Prepare the peanut sauce per the recipe directions, adding the vanilla extract at the end of cooking time. Stir until well blended.

2. Scoop ½ cup of the ice cream into each of 4 dishes. Drizzle with the peanut sauce and top with the strawberries.

NUTRITION PER SERVING

393 calories
13 g protein
39 g carbohydrates
21 g fat
5 g saturated fat*
23 mg cholesterol
88 mg sodium
3 g fiber

*Limit saturated fat to 10% of total calories—about 17 grams per day for most women—and sodium intake to less than 2,300 milligrams.

{ Make It a FLAT BELLY DIET MEAL } A single serving of this recipe counts as a *Flat Belly Diet* Meal without any add-ons!

The-Best-for-Last Chocolate Mousse

■ 10 MINUTES ■ 4 SERVINGS ■ 271 CALORIES ■ MUFA: CHOCOLATE

As a garnish, pretty chocolate curls turn a humble fruit cup into a restaurant-worthy confection. Making them is as easy as drawing a vegetable peeler along the edge of a bar of chocolate. Use the short wide edge to make small tubular curls; use the longer, narrower edge for thinner, longer shavings.

12 ounces soft silken tofu, drained
2 teaspoons vanilla extract
⅛ teaspoon almond extract
1 cup semisweet chocolate chips, melted
½ cup fat-free Greek-style yogurt

1. Place the tofu, vanilla extract, and almond extract in a food processor and blend until smooth. Add the chocolate and blend for 1 minute. Scrape the sides with a rubber spatula and blend for 1 minute longer or until incorporated. Pour into a large bowl.

2. Fold in the yogurt just until blended. Refrigerate until ready to serve.

Note: For chocolate semifreddo, place the mixture in a 9" loaf pan lined with foil. Cover and freeze for 3 to 4 hours or until just set. Serve immediately.

NUTRITION
PER SERVING
───────────
271 calories
11 g protein
40 g carbohydrates
18 g fat
10 g saturated fat
0 mg cholesterol
19 mg sodium
4 g fiber

{ Make It a
FLAT
BELLY
DIET
MEAL }
Serve with ½ cup fresh raspberries (30) and 8 ounces cappuccino made with 1% milk (73).
TOTAL MEAL: 374 calories

{ 14-DAY MEAL PLANS }

Day 1

BREAKFAST

Cranberry Pecan Scone, page 88

Mango Surprise Smoothie, page 73, prepared without the avocado

LUNCH

Broccoli Cherry Tomato and Pesto Pasta Salad, page 129

5 whole wheat crackers

¼ cup sliced pears, canned in natural juices

DINNER

Chicken Piccata, page 196

Bok Choy and Garlic Skillet, page 141

SNACK

1 medium apple cut into wedges and topped with 2 tablespoons natural peanut butter

4 cups light trans fat-free microwaved popcorn

{ **NUTRITION FOR TOTAL DAY**: 1,625 calories, 69 g protein, 203 g carbohydrate, 65 g fat, 10 g sat fat, 86 mg cholesterol, 1,401 mg sodium, 25 g fiber }

Day 2

BREAKFAST

Granola Parfait, page 68

LUNCH

Chicken pasta salad made with ¼ cup cooked and chilled whole wheat penne tossed with 1 tablespoon Pesto sauce on page 122 or prepared pesto, 3 ounces chopped cooked chicken breast, 1 cup grape tomatoes, ¾ cup shredded carrots, and 2 tablespoons shredded Parmesan cheese

DINNER

Chickpea Curry with Cashews, page 158

½ cup cooked brown rice

1 cup steamed broccoli

SNACK

1 cup canned pineapple chunks in natural juice mixed into 1 cup nonfat cottage cheese and sprinkled with 2 tablespoons walnuts

{ **NUTRITION FOR TOTAL DAY:** 1,655 calories, 112 g protein, 200 g carbohydrate, 51 g fat, 9 g sat fat, 97 mg cholesterol, 850 mg sodium, 36 g fiber }

Day 3

BREAKFAST

Huevos Rancheros, page 76

LUNCH

Sandwich made with 1 100% whole wheat English muffin, 1 tablespoon pesto sauce, 2 ounces organic natural turkey breast, 3 large Romaine leaves, and ½ cup roasted red peppers

1 cup grape tomatoes

2 fresh pineapple rings

DINNER

Southwest Steak Salad, page 136

Fresh melon wedge

½ slice whole wheat bread

SNACK

Lemon smoothie prepared with 1 cup skim milk blended with 6 ounces nonfat lemon yogurt, 1 medium orange, sectioned, and a handful of ice. Stir in 1 tablespoon cold-pressed flaxseed oil before serving.

{ **NUTRITION FOR TOTAL DAY:** 1,566 calories, 85 g protein, 208 g carbohydrate, 50 g fat, 8 g sat fat, 300 mg cholesterol, 1,635 mg sodium, 37 g fiber }

Day 4

BREAKFAST

Eggs Florentine with Sun-Dried Tomato Pesto, page 81

2 slices cooked turkey bacon

1 cup freshly squeezed 100% orange juice

LUNCH

Salad prepared with 2 cups mixed baby greens and topped with 2 tablespoons low-fat Asian dressing, ⅔ cup shelled edamame, ½ cup mandarin orange segments, and 2 tablespoons almonds

DINNER

Eggplant Rollatini, page 166

SNACK

Strawberry-chocolate sundae made with 1 cup sliced strawberries, ¼ cup semisweet chocolate chips, and ½ cup nonfat ricotta cheese

{ **NUTRITION FOR TOTAL DAY:** 1,577 calories, 68 g protein, 180 g carbohydrate, 72 g fat, 19 g sat fat, 265 mg cholesterol, 1,693 mg sodium, 35 g fiber }

Day 5

BREAKFAST

Banana Pancakes with Walnut Honey, page 84

LUNCH

1 cup cooked whole wheat spaghetti topped with 1 cup Marinara Sauce, page 167, and 6 store-bought veggie meatballs, microwaved

DINNER

Halibut Kebabs with Pepper Dressing, page 179

SNACK

Red Fruit Crumble, page 301

1 cup skim milk

{ **NUTRITION FOR TOTAL DAY:** 1,541 calories, 70 g protein, 185 g carbohydrate, 63 g fat, 8 g sat fat, 80 mg cholesterol, 1,556 mg sodium, 28 g fiber }

Day 6

BREAKFAST

Granola, page 70

6 ounces fat-free vanilla yogurt

LUNCH

Half of a multigrain pita filled with 3 ounces chunk light tuna in water, 2 diced sun-dried tomatoes, 2 tablespoons chopped walnuts, and 2 tablespoons crumbled feta cheese

DINNER

Mongolian Beef Stir-Fry, page 236

SNACK

3 rye crispbread crackers spread with 2 tablespoons natural almond butter and topped with 1 medium sliced apple

{ **NUTRITION FOR TOTAL DAY:** 1,584 calories, 82 g protein, 168 g carbohydrate, 67 g fat, 13 g sat fat, 124 mg cholesterol, 1,495 mg sodium, 25 g fiber }

Day 7

BREAKFAST

2 slices whole grain low-sodium Ezekiel sprouted bread, toasted, topped with ½ cup nonfat ricotta cheese, 2 tablespoons walnuts

½ cup freshly squeezed 100% orange juice

LUNCH

Spicy Olive and Turkey Pita Sandwich, page 110

1 cup carrot and celery sticks

DINNER

Spanish Shrimp with Garlic Sauce, page 184

Cuban-Style Black Beans, page 156, prepared without the avocado

SNACK

Chocolate-Zucchini Snack Cake, page 281

{ **NUTRITION FOR TOTAL DAY:** 1,544 calories, 77 g protein, 179 g carbohydrate, 63 g fat, 13 g sat fat, 248 mg cholesterol, 2,260 mg sodium, 30 g fiber }

Day 8

BREAKFAST

1½ cups 100% whole grain puffs cereal served with 1 cup skim milk and topped with 2 tablespoons chopped pecans and 3 tablespoons raisins

1 cup freshly squeezed 100% orange juice

LUNCH

Roast Beef Panini with Avocado, Tomato, and Dijon, page 117

1 apple

DINNER

Mexican Stuffed Peppers, page 169

SNACK

Tropical Fruit Dip, page 267

{ **NUTRITION FOR TOTAL DAY:** 1,630 calories, 59 g protein, 221 g carbohydrate, 66 g fat, 18 g sat fat, 92 mg cholesterol, 1,433 mg sodium, 27 g fiber }

Day 9

BREAKFAST

1 100% whole wheat English muffin, toasted and spread with 2 tablespoons natural peanut butter and ½ cup sliced bananas

LUNCH

Penne with Mushrooms and Artichokes, page 163

1 cup marinated artichokes, drained

DINNER

Pork and Pine Nut Meatballs, page 230

1 cup green beans cooked with 1 teaspoon oil and tossed with 1 teaspoon balsamic vinegar and 4 chopped fresh basil leaves

SNACK

Pomegranate Pepper Dip, page 260

10 rice bran crackers

1 cup cauliflower florets

{ **NUTRITION FOR TOTAL DAY:** 1,566 calories, 68 g protein, 161 g carbohydrate, 79 g fat, 9 g sat fat, 76 mg cholesterol, 2,247 mg sodium, 33 g fiber }

Day 10

BREAKFAST

¾ cup dry 1-minute oatmeal, cooked in water per package instructions, and topped with 1 cup frozen blueberries, warmed in microwave 1 minute, and 2 tablespoons cashews

LUNCH

Caribbean Chicken Salad, page 134

DINNER

Walnut-Grain Burger, page 155

1 pear, sliced

SNACK

Cherry-Berry Almond Fruit Cake, page 305

{ **NUTRITION FOR TOTAL DAY:** 1,539 calories, 63 g protein, 215 g carbohydrate, 60 g fat, 8 g sat fat, 93 mg cholesterol, 1,179 mg sodium, 32 g fiber }

Day 11

BREAKFAST

Blueberry Breakfast Sandwich, page 74

½ cup freshly squeezed 100% orange juice

LUNCH

Smoky Tomato Soup, page 98

1 string cheese stick (1 ounce)

1 slice whole wheat bread

DINNER

Blackened Chicken with Multicolor Slaw, page 133

1 cup cantalope cubes

SNACK

Peanut Butter No-Bake Bars, page 290

1 cup skim milk

{ **NUTRITION FOR TOTAL DAY:** 1,570 calories, 82 g protein, 222 g carbohydrate, 50 g fat, 10 g sat fat, 94 mg cholesterol, 2,073 mg sodium, 26 g fiber }

Day 12

BREAKFAST

Peanut Butter and Yogurt Smoothie, page 284

LUNCH

Asparagus Frittata, page 78

2 cups mixed greens salad topped with 2 tablespoons reduced-calorie all-natural caesar salad dressing

4 pieces rye crispbread

DINNER

Spaghetti with Roasted Cauliflower and Olives, page 164

1-ounce slice of whole wheat or whole grain baguette

SNACK

Sweet and Sour Blueberry Parfait, page 318

½ ounce dark chocolate

{ **NUTRITION FOR TOTAL DAY:** 1,582 calories, 57 g protein, 192 g carbohydrate, 70 g fat, 14 g sat fat, 240 mg cholesterol, 1,671 mg sodium, 24 g fiber }

Day 13

BREAKFAST

1 slice Nutty Quick Bread, page 91, topped with ¼ cup nonfat ricotta cheese and drizzled with 1 teaspoon honey

LUNCH

Mediterranean Pizza Wrap, page 112

2 tablespoons store-bought hummus

1 cup celery sticks

DINNER

Grilled Catfish with Spicy Tartar Sauce, page 173

½ cup cooked brown rice

SNACK

3 tablespoons Layered Nut-and-Cheese Spread, page 257

6 rye crisps

{ **NUTRITION FOR TOTAL DAY:** 1,594 calories, 72 g protein, 187 g carbohydrate, 71 g fat, 12 g sat fat, 145 mg cholesterol, 1,899 sodium, 27 g fiber }

Day 14

BREAKFAST

Cinnamon-Pecan Waffles, page 86

½ cup fresh blueberries

LUNCH

2 cups mixed organic greens topped with 2 tablespoons fat-free vinaigrette dressing, ½ fresh sliced plum tomato, 3 ounces uncured Black Forest ham, ½ cup no-salt-added black beans, and 2 tablespoons pumpkin seeds

DINNER

Rotini with Chicken and Broccoli, page 201

SNACK

Tex-Mex Snack Mix, page 251

2 cups air-popped popcorn

{ **NUTRITION FOR TOTAL DAY:** 1,629 calories, 77 g protein, 189 g carbohydrate, 68 g fat, 11 g sat fat, 205 mg cholesterol, 2,068 mg sodium, 27 g fiber }

{ Your MUFA SERVING CHART }

FOOD	SERVING	CALORIES
Almond butter	2 Tbsp	200
Almonds	2 Tbsp	109
Avocado, California (Hass)	1/4 cup	96
Avocado, Florida	1/4 cup	69
Black olive tapenade	2 Tbsp	88
Brazil nuts	2 Tbsp	110
Canola oil	1 Tbsp	124
Cashew butter	2 Tbsp	190
Cashews	2 Tbsp	100
Flaxseed oil (cold-pressed organic)	1 Tbsp	120
Green olive tapenade	2 Tbsp	54
Green or black olives	10 large	50
Hazelnuts	2 Tbsp	110
Macadamia nuts	2 Tbsp	120
Natural peanut butter, crunchy	2 Tbsp	188
Natural peanut butter, smooth	2 Tbsp	188
Olive oil	1 Tbsp	119
Peanut oil	1 Tbsp	119
Peanuts	2 Tbsp	110
Pecans	2 Tbsp	90
Pesto sauce	1 Tbsp	80
Pine nuts	2 Tbsp	113
Pistachios	2 Tbsp	88
Pumpkin seeds	2 Tbsp	148
Safflower oil (high oleic)	1 Tbsp	120
Semisweet chocolate chips	1/4 cup	207
Sesame or soybean oil	1 Tbsp	120
Soybeans (edamame), shelled and boiled	1 cup	298
Sunflower oil (high oleic)	1 Tbsp	120
Sunflower seed butter	2 Tbsp	190
Sunflower seeds	2 Tbsp	90
Tahini (sesame seed paste)	2 Tbsp	178
Walnut oil	1 Tbsp	120
Walnuts	2 Tbsp	82

{ RECOMMENDED PORTIONS OF FOOD }

	AMOUNT	CALORIES

Beans & Legumes

Adzuki beans, cooked	½ cup	147
Baked beans	⅓ cup	113
Baked beans, vegetarian	⅓ cup	113
Bean sprouts (mung beans)	½ cup	13
Black-eyed peas (cowpeas), cooked	½ cup	90
Black turtle beans, cooked	½ cup	120
Broad beans (fava beans), cooked	½ cup	62
Butter beans (lima), cooked	½ cup	105
Butter beans (lima), raw	½ cup	88
Cannellini beans, cooked	½ cup	100
Chickpeas (garbanzo beans), cooked	½ cup	134
Cranberry beans, cooked	½ cup	120
Edamame, out of shell, cooked	½ cup	100
French beans, cooked	½ cup	114
French beans, raw	3 ounces	30
Great Northern beans, cooked	½ cup	104
Hummus	⅛ cup	56
Kidney beans, red, cooked	½ cup	110
Lentils, brown, cooked	½ cup	115
Navy beans, cooked	½ cup	127
Pinto beans, cooked	½ cup	122
Refried beans	½ cup	119
Split peas, cooked	½ cup	115

Beef and Pork

Beef, bottom round, trimmed, boneless, braised	3 ounces	108
Beef, chuck roast, lean, braised	3 ounces	179
Beef, eye round, lean, roasted	3 ounces	138
Beef, filet mignon, lean, broiled	3 ounces	179
Beef, flank steak, lean, broiled	4 ounces	187
Beef, steak, top sirloin, lean, broiled	3 ounces	166
Beef, tip sirloin, lean, roasted	3 ounces	152
Canadian bacon, grilled	1 ounce	52

	AMOUNT	CALORIES

Beef and Pork—continued

Ham, low-sodium, 96% fat-free	1 ounce	31
Pork, chop, center-cut, roasted	4 ounces	187
Pork tenderloin, roasted	3 ounces	115

Beverages

Cappuccino, with low-fat milk	1 cup	73
Chai, with soy milk	1 cup	130
Coffee, iced latte, with fat-free milk	1 cup	47
Iced tea, unsweetened	1 cup	0
Milk, fat-free	1 cup	90
Milk, low-fat 1%	1 cup	118
Soy milk, unsweetened	1 cup	80
Soy milk, vanilla	1 cup	100
Tomato-vegetable juice, low-sodium	1 cup	53

Eggs, Cheese, and Yogurt

Cheddar cheese, reduced-fat, shredded	¼ cup	81
Cottage cheese, fat-free	½ cup	96
Eggs	1 large	75
Egg white	¼ cup	29
Feta, crumbled	1 tablespoon	40
Parmesan cheese, grated	1 tablespoon	21
Provolone, reduced-fat	1 slice (1 ounce)	77
Ricotta cheese, fat-free	¼ cup	50
Sour cream, fat-free	1 tablespoon	15
Yogurt, fat-free Greek-style	½ cup	56
Yogurt, low-fat vanilla	½ cup	90

Fruit

Apple	1 medium	80
Applesauce, canned, unsweetened	⅓ cup	33
Apricot	1 medium	17
Apricot, dried	6	60

	AMOUNT	CALORIES
Avocado	¼ cup	58
Banana	1 large (8")	121
Blackberries	1 cup	62
Blueberries	½ cup	41
Cantaloupe, balled	1 cup	60
Cantaloupe, wedged	⅛ of large	35
Cherries, sweet	½ cup	50
Clementine, mandarin orange	1 medium	40
Date, medjool, pitted	1 medium	66
Fig	1 large	47
Grapefruit	½ of medium	60
Grapes, green or red	1 cup	60
Guava	1 medium	61
Honeydew, balled	1 cup	64
Honeydew, wedged	⅛ of medium	58
Kiwifruit (Chinese gooseberry), peeled	1 medium	46
Mandarin oranges, canned	½ cup	80
Mango, sliced	1 cup	110
Nectarine	1 medium	70
Orange	1 large (3¹⁄₁₆")	86
Papaya, cubed	1 cup	55
Peach	1 medium	38
Pear	1 medium	104
Pineapple, sliced	1 cup	100
Pineapple, tidbits	½ cup	60
Plantain	¼ of medium	55
Plum	1 (2⅛")	30
Plum, sliced	½ cup	47
Pomegranate	½ of 3⅜"	53
Pummelo, sectioned	½ cup	36
Raspberries, red	1 cup	64
Rhubarb, diced	1 cup	26
Star fruit (carambola)	1 medium	28
Tangerine	1 medium	50
Watermelon, chopped	1 cup	45

	AMOUNT	CALORIES

Pasta, Bread, and Grain

* Note: For most pasta shapes, 1 ounce of dry pasta makes approximately ½ cup cooked.

	AMOUNT	CALORIES
Angel hair pasta, semolina, dry	1 ounce	102
Angel hair pasta, whole grain, dry, organic	1 ounce	106
Bagel, whole grain	1 ounce	75
Barley, pearled, cooked	¼ cup	48
Basmati rice, uncooked	¼ cup	150
Biscuit, buttermilk	½ of 2.5″ biscuit	105
Bread, French, whole grain	1 slice (1 ounce)	90
Bread, pita, whole wheat	½ of 6.5″ pita	85
Bread, whole grain	1 slice (1 ounce)	75
Bread, whole grain	1 slice	60
Bread crumbs, dry	1 ounce	112
Bulgur, cooked	⅓ cup	50
Bun, hamburger, whole grain	1 bun (1 ounce)	90
Corn bread	1 ounce	89
Couscous, cooked	¾ cup	132
Cracker, crispbread, rye	¾ ounce	78
Cracker, wheat	¾ ounce	80
Elbow pasta, semolina, dry	1 ounce	102
Hominy, canned, white	½ cup	59
Oats, rolled, dry	2 tablespoons	38
Oats, unprocessed whole grain	2 tablespoons	76
Pilaf, 7-grain whole, cooked	¼ cup	85
Quinoa, cooked	¼ cup	81
Rice, brown, long grain, cooked	⅓ cup	65
Rice, brown, medium grain, cooked	⅓ cup	66
Rice, wild, cooked	⅓ cup	50
Roll, dinner, whole wheat	1 roll (1 ounce)	77
Soba noodle	1½ cups	171
Spaghetti pasta, brown rice, dry	1 ounce	106
Spaghetti pasta, lentil bean, wheat-free, gluten-free, dry	1 ounce	95

	AMOUNT	CALORIES
Spaghetti pasta, semolina, dry, organic	1 ounce	106
Spaghetti pasta, whole wheat, dry, organic	1 ounce	100
Tortilla, corn	6"	45
Tortilla, wheat or corn	11" (3.5 oz)	175
Tortilla, wheat or corn	6" (1 ounce)	73
Tortilla chip, multigrain	½ ounce	70
Whole wheat English muffin	1	120

Poultry

Chicken, drumstick, without skin, cooked	3 ounces	146
Chicken, ground, before cooking	4 ounces	150
Chicken, thigh, boneless, without skin, cooked	3 ounces	166
Chicken breast, roasted	3 ounces	140
Turkey, deli	2 ounces	50
Turkey, drumstick, without skin, cooked	3 ounces	159
Turkey, roasted	3 ounces	162
Turkey burger, 90% lean, or organic	3 ounces	170
Turkey jerky	1 ounce	81
Turkey pepperoni, sliced	1 ounce	69
Turkey sausage, Italian, cooked, lean	2 ounces	95

Seafood

Cod, Atlantic, baked	3 ounces	89
Crab, Alaskan, king crab leg, steamed	3 ounces	83
Crab, blue, cooked	3 ounces	101
Crab, imitation (surimi)	3 ounces	87
Flounder, baked	3 ounces	99
Grouper, baked	3 ounces	100
Halibut, baked	3 ounces	119
Lobster, cooked	3 ounces	81
Mahi mahi, baked	3 ounces	93
Salmon, Alaskan Chinook, smoked, canned	3 ounces	128
Salmon, pink, canned, drained	3 ounces	116

	AMOUNT	CALORIES
Seafood—continued		
Shrimp, broiled	4 ounces	120
Swordfish, baked	3 ounces	132
Tilapia, baked or broiled	3 ounces	109
Tuna, chunk light, packed in water	3 ounces	120
Tuna, yellow fin, baked	3 ounces	118
Sweeteners and Condiments		
Apple butter	1 tablespoon	29
Barbecue sauce	1 tablespoon	12
Fruit spread, black cherry	1 tablespoon	40
Fruit spread, blackberry, seedless	1 tablespoon	40
Fruit spread, blueberry	1 tablespoon	40
Fruit spread, boysenberry	1 tablespoon	40
Fruit spread, concord grape	1 tablespoon	40
Fruit spread, harvest berry	1 tablespoon	40
Fruit spread, orange marmalade	1 tablespoon	40
Fruit spread, peach	1 tablespoon	40
Fruit spread, raspberry	1 tablespoon	40
Honey	1 teaspoon	30
Horseradish sauce	1 tablespoon	30
Ketchup	1 tablespoon	16
Mayonnaise, canola	1 tablespoon	100
Mustard	1 tablespoon	10
Mustard, Dijon, coarse-grain	1 tablespoon	20
Salsa, medium	2 tablespoons	10
Soy sauce	1 tablespoon	11
Vinegar, balsamic or red wine	1 tablespoon	10
Worcestershire sauce	1 tablespoon	11
Vegetables		
Alfalfa sprouts	½ cup	5
Artichoke	1 medium	60

	AMOUNT	CALORIES
Artichoke hearts, cooked, drained	½ cup	42
Arugula (rocket)	4 ounces	28
Asparagus, cooked	1 cup	30
Beets, cooked	½ cup	37
Beets, pickled, whole, canned	½ cup	65
Bell pepper, chopped	1 cup	39
Broccoli, florets	1 cup	20
Broccoli raab, cooked	1 cup	28
Brussels sprouts, cooked	1 cup	65
Cabbage	¼ medium head	54
Cabbage, bok choy, cooked, drained	1 cup	20
Carrot	1 medium	25
Carrots, cooked, drained	½ cup	27
Cauliflower	¼ large head	53
Cauliflower, florets, cooked	1 cup	39
Celery	1 medium stalk	9
Celery, chopped	1 cup	17
Cherry tomatoes, red	1 cup	27
Collard greens, chopped, cooked, drained	1 cup	49
Corn, sweet white or yellow	1 large ear	123
Corn, sweet white or yellow	½ cup	66
Cucumber	1 (8")	45
Eggplant, cubed, cooked, drained	1 cup	35
Fennel bulb, sliced	1 cup	27
Garlic	1 clove	4
Garlic, chopped	1 teaspoon	4
Gingerroot, grated	1 tablespoon	5
Grape tomatoes, red	1 cup	30
Green beans	1 cup	35
Kale, curly, cooked	1 cup	36
Lettuce, bibb	1 5" head	21
Lettuce, bibb	4 large leaves	8
Lettuce, mixed baby	2 cup	15
Lettuce, romaine	5 inner leaves	9

	AMOUNT	CALORIES

Vegetables—continued

	AMOUNT	CALORIES
Lettuce, romaine, chopped	1 cup	8
Mushrooms, brown Italian	5 medium	15
Mushrooms, portobello	2 ounces	15
Mushrooms, portobello, grilled	3 ounces	29
Onion, green (scallions), top and bulb, chopped	½ cup	16
Onion, red, chopped	½ cup	46
Onion, red or yellow	1 medium	46
Onion, red or yellow, sliced	1 large slice	16
Onion, yellow, chopped	½ cup	34
Peas, green, cooked	½ cup	62
Peas, snow, steamed	1 cup	40
Pepper, ancho, dried	1 medium	47
Potato, baby, roasted	1 cup	100
Potato, baked, with skin	1 medium	162
Potato, russet, baked, with skin	1 medium	160
Potatoes, new	3 ounces	54
Sauerkraut, canned, low-sodium	1 cup	31
Shallots, chopped	¼ cup	29
Spaghetti squash, baked	1 cup	42
Spinach, baby	1 cup	6
Spinach, cooked	1 cup	41
Squash, acorn, cooked, mashed	½ cup	42
Squash, butternut, cubed, baked	1 cup	82
Squash, summer	1 medium	31
Squash, summer, sliced, cooked	1 cup	36
Squash, winter acorn, cubed, baked	½ cup	57
Sweet potato, baked, without skin	1 medium	103
Sweet potato, cooked, mashed	½ cup	125
Swiss chard, chopped, cooked, drained	1 cup	35
Tomatillo	1 medium	11
Tomatillo, chopped	½ cup	21

	AMOUNT	CALORIES
Tomato, plum	1 medium	12
Tomato, red	1 medium	35
Tomato, red, chopped	½ cup	19
Tomato, red, crushed, canned	½ cup	39
Tomato, red, sliced	1 slice	6
Tomato paste	1 tablespoon	13
Zucchini	1 medium	35
Zucchini, sliced, steamed	1 cup	25

Flat Belly Diet Recipes

	AMOUNT	CALORIES
African Chicken Stew, page 214	1 serving	439
Almond Biscotti, page 296	2 cookies	181
Amazing Peanut Sauce, page 209	2 tablespoons	117
Apple and Cashew Butter Sandwich, page 75	1 serving	345
Asian Slaw, page 123	1 serving	200
Asian Slaw, page 123, prepared without the peanuts	1 serving	100
Asparagus Frittata, page 78	1 serving	218
Asparagus with Pine Nuts, page 139	1 serving	180
Asparagus with Pine Nuts, page 139, prepared without the pine nuts	1 serving	45
Baked Chicken Parmesan, page 218	1 serving	327
Baked Chicken Parmesan, page 218, prepared without pine nuts, and 3/4 cup bread crumbs	1 serving	230
Baked Green Bean Casserole, page 142	1 serving	265
Baklava, page 298	1 serving	290
Banana Pancakes with Walnut Honey, page 84	3 pancakes	280
Barbecued Edamame, page 253	1 serving	231
Beefy Onion Soup, page 100	1¼ cups	310
Best Grilled Chicken Breast, The, page 205	1 serving	355
Best Grilled Chicken Breast, The, page 205, prepared without the Balsamico Sauce	1 breast	217
Blackened Chicken with Multicolor Slaw, page 133	1 serving	281
Blueberry Breakfast Sandwich, page 74	1 serving	360
Bok Choy and Garlic Skillet, page 141	1 serving	182

Recommended Portions of Food

	AMOUNT	CALORIES
Flat Belly Diet Recipes—continued		
Braised Kale with Smoked Nuts, page 137	1 serving	288
Braised Kale with Smoked Nuts, page 137, prepared without the almonds	1 serving	130
Broccoli, Cherry Tomato, and Pesto Pasta Salad, page 129	1 serving	288
Broccoli-Cashew Salad, page 126	1 serving	190
Brown Rice Pilaf with Mushrooms, page 147	1 serving	311
Brown Rice Pilaf with Mushrooms, page 147, prepared without the pecans	½ cup	110
Caponata, page 258	1 serving	199
Caponata, page 258, prepared without the pine nuts	1 serving	85
Caribbean Chicken Salad, page 134	1 serving	310
Cashew Chicken Stir-Fry, page 213	1 serving	272
Cherry-Almond Granola Bars, page 291	1 serving	265
Cherry-Berry Almond Fruit Cake, page 305	1 serving	360
Cherry-Pear Strudel, page 300	1 serving	253
Chicken à l'Orange, page 215	1 serving	312
Chicken Avocado Sandwich, page 107	1 serving	260
Chicken Pad Thai, page 211	1 serving	386
Chicken Piccata, page 196	1 serving	235
Chicken Piccata, page 196, prepared with 1 tablespoon oil	1 serving	210
Chicken with Romesco Sauce, page 198	1 serving	340
Chicken-Barley Soup with Vegetables and Pesto, page 106	1¾ cups	260
Chickpea Curry with Cashews, page 158	1 serving	260
Chipotle Pork and Onion Casserole, page 242	1 serving	375
Chocolate-Almond Macaroons, page 295	5 cookies	193
Chocolate-Cranberry Quesadilla, page 282	1 serving	332
Chocolate-Drizzled Popcorn, page 283	1 serving	392
Chocolate-Raspberry Cheesecake, page 316	1 serving	390
Chocolate-Zucchini Snack Cake, page 281	1 serving	361
Choco-Nut Sundae, page 321	1 serving	393

	AMOUNT	CALORIES
Cinnamon-Pecan Waffles, page 86	1 waffle	395
Cioppino with Lemon Aioli, page 189	1 serving	380
Cioppino with Lemon Aioli, page 189, prepared without the aioli	1 serving	281
Colorful Bok Choy and Garlic Skillet, page 141, prepared with 1 tablespoon oil	1 serving	90
Cookie Crisps, page 294	3 cookies	200
Crab Primavera with Spaghetti, page 188	1 serving	414
Cranberry-Pecan Scones, page 88	1 scone	210
Creamy Barley Risotto, page 161	1 serving	370
Creamy Broccoli Soup, page 99	1½ cups	200
Creamy Seafood Casserole, page 193	1 serving	350
Cuban Steak with Avocado Salad, page 234	1 serving	280
Cuban-Style Black Beans, page 156	1 serving	250
Cuban-Style Black Beans, page 156, prepared without the avocado	1 serving	175
Curried Apple and Pear Soup, page 97	1½ cups	97
Curried Apple and Pear Soup, page 97, prepared without the almonds	1½ cups	155
Curried Peanuts, page 250	1 serving	120
Decadent Dark Chocolate Sauce, page 293	3 tablespoons	180
Dilled Egg Salad Platter, page 127	1 serving	280
Easy Pancake Mix, page 83	⅓ cup	130
Eggplant Rollatini, page 166	1 serving	436
Eggs Florentine with Sun-Dried Tomato Pesto, page 81	1 serving	175
Five-Spice Fish with Avocado-Wasabi Sauce, page 176	1 serving	231
Five-Spice Fish with Avocado-Wasabi Sauce, page 176, prepared without the sauce	1 serving	147
Fruit Crepes with Chocolate Sauce, page 302	1 serving	370
Ginger-Macadamia Nut Cheesecake with Praline Topping, page 314	1 serving	300
Ginger-Pork Stir-Fry, page 235	1 serving	314
Granola, page 70	¾ cup	294
Granola Parfait, page 68	1 serving	420

	AMOUNT	CALORIES

Flat Belly Diet Recipes—continued

Greek Grilled Chicken Breast, page 206	1 serving	308
Greek Salad Wrap, page 114	1 serving	230
Grilled Catfish with Spicy Tartar Sauce, page 173	1 serving	339
Grilled Catfish with Spicy Tartar Sauce, page 173, prepared without the tartar sauce	1 serving	234
Grilled Chicken Satay with Peanut Sauce and Cucumber Relish, page 208	1 serving	361
Grilled Pork with Garlic Oil and a Little Salad, page 244	1 serving	276
Grilled Tuna Nicoise, page 180	1 serving	380
Guacamole, page 264	1 serving	100
Halibut Kebabs with Pepper Dressing, page 179	1 serving	360
Ham and Avocado Omelet, page 79	1 serving	313
Heirloom Tomato Salad with Aioli and Capers, page 124	1 serving	120
Herb-Marinated Beef and Mushroom Kebabs, page 231	1 serving	290
Huevos Rancheros, page 76	1 serving	331
Hummus, page 113	¼ cup	126
Indonesian Vegetable Salad, page 131	1 serving	322
Irresistible Brownies, page 303	1 serving	305
Korean Beef in Lettuce Leaves, page 228	1 serving	370
Layered Nut-and-Cheese Spread, page 257	1 serving	161
Layered Nut-and-Cheese Spread, page 257, prepared without the almonds	1 serving	90
Lemon Cupcakes with Citrus Icing, page 310	1 serving	316
Lentil-Walnut Salad with Goat Cheese, page 128	1 serving	394
Mango Surprise Smoothie, page 73	1 serving	268
Mango Surprise Smoothie, page 73, prepared without the avocado	1½ cups	210
Maple-Walnut Oatmeal, page 71	¾ cup	321
Marinara Sauce, page 167	1 serving	211
Marinated Grilled Tofu, page 153	1 serving	380
Mashed Avocado Snack, page 265	1 serving	161
Mediterranean Chicken and Orzo, page 200	1 serving	388
Mediterranean Pizza Wrap, page 112	1 serving	300

	AMOUNT	CALORIES
Mediterranean Sesame-Honey Candy, page 288	1 serving	179
Mexican Chicken with Pepita Sauce, page 199	1 serving	183
Mexican Chicken with Pepita Sauce, page 199, prepared without the pepitas	1 serving	147
Mexican Green Chile Pork Stew, page 243	1 serving	393
Mexican Stuffed Peppers, page 169	1 serving	390
Micro-Roasted Potatoes with Tapenade, page 273	1 serving	175
Mocha–Peanut Butter Cooler, page 285	1 serving	355
Mom's Turkey Breakfast Sausage, page 82	2 patties	100
Mongolian Beef Stir-Fry, page 236	1 serving	418
Moussaka, page 247	1 serving	349
Nutty Chicken Nuggets, page 275	1 serving	348
Nutty Quick Bread, page 91	1 serving	340
Old-Fashioned Peanut Soup, page 94	1¼ cups	300
Olive Bread, page 108	1 serving	290
Olive–Cream Cheese Sandwiches, page 256	1 serving	370
Orange and Herb Turkey Cutlets with Maple-Sautéed Apples, page 220	1 serving	301
Orange, Date, and Walnut Drops, page 289	1 serving	343
Oven-Roasted Tomatoes with Pesto, page 143	1 serving	119
Oven-Roasted Tomatoes with Pesto, page 143, prepared without the pesto	1 serving	70
Peach and Blueberry Tart with Pecan Crust, page 313	1 serving	322
Peanut Butter and Yogurt Smoothie, page 284	1 serving	410
Peanut Butter No-Bake Bars, page 290	1 serving	410
Peanut Butter Spirals, page 269	1 serving	390
Peanut Butter–Stuffed French Toast, page 87	1 serving	410
Penne with Mushrooms and Artichokes, page 163	1 serving	370
Pesto, page 122	2 tablespoons	71
Pesto Caesar Salad, page 121	1 serving	260
Pineapple and Pork Tacos with Avocado Crema, page 233	1 serving	420
Pistachio-Crusted Pork Scaloppine, page 238	1 serving	202
Poached Chicken Provençal, page 204	1 serving	316
Pomegranate Pepper Dip, page 260	1 serving	167

	AMOUNT	CALORIES

Flat Belly Diet Recipes—continued

	AMOUNT	CALORIES
Pork and Pine Nut Meatballs, page 230	1 serving	254
Pork Tenderloin with Olives and Rosemary, page 239	1 serving	219
Pumpkin Bisque, page 95	2 cups	210
Pumpkin Bisque, page 95, prepared without the pumpkin seeds	2 cups	170
Pumpkin Cream Roll, page 306	1 serving	229
Pumpkin Kugel, page 165	1 serving	372
Pumpkin-Raisin Muffins, page 90	1 serving	274
Red Fruit Crumble, page 301	1 serving	332
Rigatoni with Sardinian Sausage Sauce, page 224	1 serving	430
Roast Beef Panini with Avocado, Tomato, and Dijon, page 117	1 serving	270
Roasted Bell Pepper and Avocado Sandwich, page 115	1 serving	330
Roasted Bell Pepper and Avocado Sandwich, page 115, prepared without the avocado	1 sandwich	260
Roasted Monkfish with Olives, page 174	1 serving	300
Roasted Potatoes with Blue Cheese–Walnut "Butter," page 144	1 serving	242
Roasted Tomatoes with Garlic, page 274	1 serving	238
Rotini with Chicken and Broccoli, page 201	1 serving	421
Saffron Rice, page 148	1 serving	230
Saffron Rice, page 148, prepared without the pistachios	1 serving	140
Salmon Burger with Zesty Aioli, page 177	1 serving	313
Salmon Burger with Zesty Aioli, page 177, prepared without the aioli	1 burger	210
Scallops with Avocado-Kiwi Salsa, page 191	1 serving	290
Scallops with Lemon-Parsley Sauce, page 192	1 serving	282
Sesame Chicken with Snow Peas, page 212	1 serving	347
Sesame Crackers, page 255	1 serving	287
Sesame-Crusted Salmon, page 182	1 serving	400
Sesame-Oat Cookies, page 297	3 cookies	337
Sesame-Scallion Pancakes with Chutney, page 271	2 pancakes	302

	AMOUNT	CALORIES
Seville-Style Grilled Pork Chops, page 241	1 serving	230
Shrimp and Avocado Rolls, page 187	1 serving	374
Slow Cooker Moroccan Chicken with Olives, page 216	1 serving	388
Smoky Tomato Soup, page 98	1¼ cups	180
Smoky Tomato Soup, page 98, prepared without the avocado	1¼ cups	100
Southern-Style Dip, page 262	1 serving	281
Southwest Steak Salad, page 136	1 serving	306
Southwestern Fried Rice, page 146	1 serving	170
Southwestern Fried Rice, page 146, prepared without the pepitas	1 serving	130
Spaghetti with Roasted Cauliflower and Olives, page 164	1 serving	413
Spanish Shrimp with Garlic Sauce, page 184	1 serving	270
Spicy Baked Chicken with Squash and Walnuts, page 219	1 serving	375
Spicy Citrus-Spiked Olives, page 252	1 serving	107
Spicy Olive and Turkey Pita Sandwich, page 110	1 serving	242
Spinach Salad with Pears, Pecans, and Goat Cheese, page 132	1 serving	311
Spinach Salad with Pears, Pecans, and Goat Cheese, page 132, prepared without the pecans	1 serving	208
Spinach Steak Roulade, page 246	1 serving	320
Spinach Steak Roulade, page 246, prepared without the pine nuts	1 serving	206
Spring Rolls with Chili Sauce, page 186	1 serving	261
Spring Rolls with Chili Sauce, page 186, prepared without the peanuts	2 rolls	155
Squash Soup with Pecans and Greens, page 102	1½ cups	187
Squash Soup with Pecans and Greens, page 102, prepared without the pecans	1½ cups	80
Steamed Snapper with Pesto, page 172	1 serving	260
Steamed Snapper with Pesto, page 172, prepared without the pesto	1 serving	189
Stir-Fry Walnut Shrimp, page 183	1 serving	292
Strawberry Panna Cotta, page 320	1 serving	245

	AMOUNT	CALORIES

Flat Belly Diet Recipes—continued

	AMOUNT	CALORIES
Stuffed Dried Plums, page 268	1 serving	344
Stuffed Mushrooms, page 272	1 serving	242
Stuffed Mushrooms, page 272, prepared without the pecans	1 serving	180
Summer Salad with Green Goddess Dressing, page 120	1 serving	145
Summery Quinoa Pilaf, page 149	1 serving	300
Summery Quinoa Pilaf, page 149, prepared without the hazelnuts	½ cup	106
Super-Rich Chocolate Cake with Maple Frosting, page 308	1 serving	276
Sweet and Sour Blueberry Parfait, page 318	1 serving	248
Sweet Peanut Sauce, page 293	2 tablespoons	130
Sweet Potato–Tempeh Hash, page 157	1 serving	380
Tapenade, page 181	1 serving	60
Tapenade and Tomato Wrap, page 109	1 serving	189
Texas Caviar and Whole Grain Chips, page 263	1 serving	331
Tex-Mex Snack Mix, page 251	½ cup	371
Thai Corn and Crab Soup, page 105	1¾ cups	355
Thai Corn and Crab Soup, page 105, prepared with 1 tablespoon of oil	¾ cup	134
The-Best-for-Last Chocolate Mousse, page 323	1 serving	350
Thin Pizza Crust, page 279	1 serving	279
Tostones, page 270	1 serving	230
Tropical Fruit Dip, page 267	1 serving	380
Turkey Meat Loaf with Walnuts and Sage, page 225	1 serving	375
Turkey Sliders, page 221	1 serving	348
Turkey with Green Mole, page 223	1 serving	290
Tuscan Bean Soup with Bitter Greens, page 103	1 cup	290
Tuscan Bean Soup with Bitter Greens, page 103, prepared without the olive oil	1 cup	180
Vegetarian Picadillo, page 160	1 serving	290
Walnut "Pâté," page 259	1 serving	114

	AMOUNT	CALORIES
Walnut-Crusted Chicken Breasts with Pomegranate Syrup, page 203	1 serving	403
Walnut-Grain Burgers, page 155	1 serving	300
White Pita Pizza, page 276	½ pizza	129
White Pita Pizzas, page 276	1 serving	257
Whole Wheat Pizza Margherita, page 278	1 serving	393
Zucchini and Carrots with Walnuts, page 138	1 serving	154
Zucchini and Carrots with Walnuts, page 138, prepared without the walnuts	1 serving	60
Zucchini Cakes with Chutney, page 152	4 pancakes	380

{INDEX}

Underscored page references indicate sidebars.
Boldface references indicate photographs.

B

D

H

I

O

CONVERSION CHART

These equivalents have been slightly rounded to make measuring easier.

VOLUME MEASUREMENTS

U.S.	IMPERIAL	METRIC
¼ tsp	–	1 ml
½ tsp	–	2 ml
1 tsp	–	5 ml
1 Tbsp	–	15 ml
2 Tbsp (1 oz)	1 fl oz	30 ml
¼ cup (2 oz)	2 fl oz	60 ml
⅓ cup (3 oz)	3 fl oz	80 ml
½ cup (4 oz)	4 fl oz	120 ml
⅔ cup (5 oz)	5 fl oz	160 ml
¾ cup (6 oz)	6 fl oz	180 ml
1 cup (8 oz)	8 fl oz	240 ml

WEIGHT MEASUREMENTS

U.S.	METRIC
1 oz	30 g
2 oz	60 g
4 oz (¼ lb)	115 g
5 oz (⅓ lb)	145 g
6 oz	170 g
7 oz	200 g
8 oz (½ lb)	230 g
10 oz	285 g
12 oz (¾ lb)	340 g
14 oz	400 g
16 oz (1 lb)	455 g
2.2 lb	1 kg

LENGTH MEASUREMENTS

U.S.	METRIC
¼"	0.6 cm
½"	1.25 cm
1"	2.5 cm
2"	5 cm
4"	11 cm
6"	15 cm
8"	20 cm
10"	25 cm
12" (1')	30 cm

PAN SIZES

U.S.	METRIC
8" cake pan	20 × 4 cm sandwich or cake tin
9" cake pan	23 × 3.5 cm sandwich or cake tin
11" × 7" baking pan	28 × 18 cm baking tin
13" × 9" baking pan	32.5 × 23 cm baking tin
15" × 10" baking pan	38 × 25.5 cm baking tin (Swiss roll tin)
1½ qt baking dish	1.5 liter baking dish
2 qt baking dish	2 liter baking dish
2 qt rectangular baking dish	30 × 19 cm baking dish
9" pie plate	22 × 4 or 23 × 4 cm pie plate
7" or 8" springform pan	18 or 20 cm springform or loose-bottom cake tin
9" × 5" loaf pan	23 × 13 cm or 2 lb narrow loaf tin or pâté tin

TEMPERATURES

FAHRENHEIT	CENTIGRADE	GAS
140°	60°	–
160°	70°	–
180°	80°	–
225°	105°	¼
250°	120°	½
275°	135°	1
300°	150°	2
325°	160°	3
350°	180°	4
375°	190°	5
400°	200°	6
425°	220°	7
450°	230°	8
475°	245°	9

Lose up to 11 inches of body fat in 32 days!

INTRODUCING
flatbellydiet.com!

Finally, the editors of *Prevention* have developed a science-based diet that directly targets harmful belly fat! Lose up to 15 pounds while you slash your risk of heart disease, stroke, and type 2 diabetes. Here's just a sampling of what you'll get by signing up for the **FLAT BELLY DIET** online.

- **Easy-to-Use Food Logs and Meal Plans**
- **Access to Expert Help**
- **Daily Video Inspiration and Tips**
- **Community Support**

SIGN UP TODAY FOR YOUR 30-DAY RISK-FREE TRIAL AT:
flatbellydiet.com/freetrial